C000282496

S PATIAL
PRACTICES

S P A T I A L PRACTICES
Critical Explorations in Social/Spatial Theory

Edited by

Helen Liggett & David C. Perry

SAGE Publications
International Educational and Professional Publisher
Thousand Oaks London New Delhi

Copyright © 1995 by Sage Publications, Inc.

Cover art: *Converging Lines*, 1953, a painting by John Hultberg, The David Anderson Gallery, Buffalo, New York, is reproduced by kind permission.

All rights reserved. No part of this book may be reproduced or utilized in any form or by any means, electronic or mechanical, including photocopying, recording, or by any information storage and retrieval system, without permission in writing from the publisher.

For information address:

 SAGE Publications, Inc.
2455 Teller Road
Thousand Oaks, California 91320

SAGE Publications Ltd.
6 Bonhill Street
London EC2A 4PU
United Kingdom

SAGE Publications India Pvt. Ltd.
M-32 Market
Greater Kailash I
New Delhi 110 048 India

Printed in the United States of America

Library of Congress Cataloging-in-Publication Data

Main entry under title:

Spatial practices: critical explorations in social/spatial theory /
edited by Helen Liggett, David C. Perry.
    p.   cm.
    Includes bibliographical references and index.
    ISBN 0-8039-5114-0 (alk. paper).—ISBN 0-8039-5115-9 (pbk. alk. paper)
    1. Sociology, Urban. 2. Social sciences—Philosophy. 3. City
planning. 4. Space (Architecture) I. Liggett, Helen. II. Perry,
David C.
HT153.S68 1995
307.76—dc20   94-45180

This book is printed on acid-free paper.

95 96 97 98 99 10 9 8 7 6 5 4 3 2 1

Sage Production Editor: Diane S. Foster

Contents

Preface

The present collection of essays began with the 1990-1991 Albert A. Levin Lecture Series at Cleveland State University. The theme of the series, "Representing the City," was deliberately vague, meant to challenge speakers to be reflective about the ways in which the representations of urban life are components of that life. Michael Peter Smith and Helen Liggett presented a colloquium titled "New Theory." Robert A. Beauregard and Dennis R. Judd discussed "New Politics," and Claire Freeman and Phillip Clay spoke about "New Practice."

The colloquia raised questions about the politics embedded in familiar narratives of American city life and most particularly about the political, economic, and physical relations that constitute the city. Issues of the spatiality of these relations figured in each presentation. For example, urban space, in which the relations or operations of everyday life are embedded, and the broader geographies of political and economic power within which cities themselves are enmeshed, became core topics. It became clear to us that the overall subject of the "production of space"—one that had come to preoccupy scholars in other parts of the world—had become central for critical social analysts in the United States as well. We subsequently sought out additional essays by scholars of urban studies interested in issues of spatiality.

The chapters included here both critique and expand upon preexisting conventions and traditional approaches to the study of space. They challenge not only the traditional epistemologies but also structuralist tendencies in contemporary theory. Rather than approach the city, or society more generally, as a single coherent entity that is transformed over time, the scholars included here approach critical social theory in a way that forces reconsideration of the very idea of "(social) space" and the cities or societies identified in those terms. It is our hope that the collection as a whole will add to a growing literature exploring (urban) space as a mode of production rather than as a social product.

In addition to the aforementioned participants in the Levin Lecture Series, we would like to thank a host of others who deserve to be included as contributors to this enterprise. First, we would like to recognize the long-term financial and institutional support of the Maxine Goodman Levin College of Urban Affairs, the Albert A. Levin Chair of Public Urban Studies and Public Service at Cleveland State University, and the support of Maxine Goodman Levin in particular. David Sweet, the Dean of the Maxine Goodman Levin College of Urban Affairs, and the faculty and students of the college provided a fertile intellectual environment for the development of both the Lecture Series and the book. More specifically, we benefited from the support and advice of Norman Krumholz, Dennis Keating, Edward Hill, Masumi Hayashi, and Kathleen Mooney. In Buffalo this project has benefited greatly from the many contributions of Richard Guarino, Geoffrey Poremba, Margaret Wooster, Bradshaw Hovey, and especially Gilbert Chin. We are grateful for the wonderful aesthetic discussions we had with David Anderson and Luis Accorsi at the David Anderson Gallery, as we reviewed the paintings of John Hultberg—a true spatial essayist—whose work, "Converging Lines," appears on the cover of this book. Just as viewing the paintings of Hultberg has been an inspiration and critique, so conversations with certain outstanding colleagues have been important to this project. Here we would like to acknowledge the particular conversations we have had on topics related to this book with Niels Albertsen, Peter

Ambrose, M. Christine Boyer, Dennis Crow, Sten Gromark, Ibrahim Jammal, Jean LaMarche, Jacqueline Leavitt, Hans Mammen, Alfred Price, Robert Shibley, and Lynda Schneekloth.

We have been blessed with supportive and patient editors at SAGE headed by the redoubtable Carrie Mullen and her colleagues Myrna Reagons, Dale Grenfell, Tricia Bennett, Jacqueline Tasch, and Diane Foster.

Most important, as coeditors, we consider this book to be a project of mutual growth and understanding. A reading of any of the various articles or books we have published singularly or jointly in the past 5 years (and we certainly are not suggesting that one necessarily do this) would show how regularly we have benefited from each other's important intellectual counsel. This book is a product of many years of such supportive and shared learning—we have truly profited from working with each of the contributors to this project, but most important we have learned so much from working together as co-editors, authors, and friends. Finally, David Perry is especially grateful for the loving and patient support of Judith Kossy, Clayton, and Evan.

HELEN LIGGETT
DAVID C. PERRY

1

Spatial Practices

An Introduction

HELEN LIGGETT

DAVID C. PERRY

The form of social space is encounter, assembly, simultaneity. But what assembles, or what is assembled? The answer is: everything that there is in space, everything that is produced either by nature or by society, either through their cooperation or through their conflicts. Everything: living beings, things, objects, works, signs, and symbols. (Lefebvre, 1991, p. 101)

Practice is a set of relays from one theoretical point to another and theory is a relay from one practice to another. (Gilles Deleueze, in Foucault & Deleueze, 1990, p. 9)

THE TERMS OF THE DISCUSSION

In one of her more evocative images, Jeanette Winterson (1991, p. 11) presents the babble of voices rising like clouds above the city streets—the conversations of the day are floating off, entangled with each other, in the night air. So we might also imagine abstract discussions among theorists and policymakers. The Winterson image is a reminder that active economies of signs are at the core of social life, while also recalling the distance in time and space between ongoing practices and our representation of them. A murmur of an imagined cloud of theorizing about spatial practices might strike the reader similarly. We know there is a lot of action out there: revitalized rhetoric surrounding urban life, global restructuring, and the information superhighway; internecine quarrels over representation versus articulation; political debates over privatization and the racialization of social space. But given that most Americans are suburban dwellers with active home entertainment centers, what exactly is the point?

The point is to suggest that it is not useful to assume that the time and space of analysis exist as separate modes of operation or to treat them as distinct realms apart from everyday practices. As Deleueze presents it in the quotation reproduced above, theory and practice are relational, depending for their continued viability on mutual referral. Theory, then, does not flow above everyday life in a detached way: It comes from some place, and it is the responsibility of analysis to return it there.

The development of interdisciplinary research, the recognition of spatial and synchronic approaches, and the acknowledgment of the function of physical space in constituting, maintaining, and challenging social life are all major contributions enabling work in the in-between areas of a theoretical and practical world conditioned by deindustrialized urban markets and unsheltered homeless, by suburban shopping malls and global telecommunication networks. When Lefebvre (1991, p. 101) says that "everything" is assembled, this is not to collapse the analytic potential of space but rather to challenge research to consider new questions of action and representation, issues of *how?* How is social/physical space assembled? How do modes of construction in different human realms function in relation to each other? How are spatial conventionalities either taken for granted or disputed?

Space, Michel Foucault (1977) suggests, is no longer to be treated as "the dead, the fixed, the undialectical, the immobile" (p. 70). Rather to consider the spatializations of life is to fill out the context(s) of social formation—our daily and institutional practices, in all their "situatedness" (Said, 1984). This book studies contemporary American spatial practices as they are strategically, geographically, ideologically, and materially mobilized in the individual and collective conditions of society.

The chapters presented here are "spatial practices" as well. They represent different disciplinary approaches to the spatiality of social formation, and although they each offer substantially different perspectives on very different "objects" of spatial practice, they are also materially (between the covers here) and intellectually linked with each other, producing, as a collection, a discursive space on the constitution and conditionality of the spatial practices of the markets, politics, and communities of contemporary urban America. As such, the very notion of spatial practice is critically doubled, ideologically and representatively, by the authors in their chapters.

SPATIAL TEXTS/AMERICAN CONTEXTS

For many American geographers and social scientists, Edward Soja's (1989) work has functioned as an introduction to critical spatial theory. Soja's theoretical reach is broadly multidisciplinary. He identifies Lefebvre's (1991) work in *The Production of Space* with a revolutionary form of analysis based in space rather than time. Spatial analysis is opposed to an "enduring epistemological presence" of the "historical imagination," which persists in "defining the very nature of critical insight and interpretation. So unbudgeably hegemonic has been this historicism of theoretical consciousness that it has tended to exclude a comparable critical sensibility to the spatiality of social life" (Soja, 1989, pp. 10-11). Soja's analysis shows Los Angeles as a complex web of relations, not easily captured by notions of progression from industrial to postindustrial modes of production. For Soja, the notion of the city itself is inadequate to describe a fragmented world that is better understood using an approach that interrogates the role of both modes in spatial relation.

Although less willing to abandon time, given his commitment to historical materialism, David Harvey (1989) expands spatial theory as he links cultural and economic space in his analysis of postmodernity. This complexity is engendered by an approach to spatiality that goes beyond notions of literal geography to include realms, or domains, of social formation. For example, he ties urban design in the 1980s to the social meanings given to the urban riots of earlier decades. Where the riots were revolutionary in potential, constructed festivals such as the Baltimore City Fair co-opted this potential by linking it to urban redevelopment and more implicitly to keeping the peace. The institutionalization and proliferation of festive marketplaces, what Harvey calls an architecture of spectacle (pp. 89-91), is a clear example of the construction of cultural, economic, and architectural space that he identifies as *postmodern*.

Manuel Castells's (1992) recent work takes the notion of space even further away from geographic literalism, defining urbanism in terms of the "space of flows," which negates the unique identity of local places by a placeless logic that excludes all but functional relations of communication networks. M. Christine Boyer (1993) has pointed out the violence on the surface of what she calls the fixed systems of control in the space that computers operationalize: "their rhetorical error messages set up a series of paranoid fantasies—Abort? Retry? Ignore? Escape, Exit, Erase?—that relay a terminal terror of unspeakable violence" (p. 21).

There is a concern, not only in the design disciplines but also in culture politics and postcolonial studies, with the connection between space and violence. This connection comes from seeing spatial production as differentiation. The production of space thus implies division and hierarchy, cutting up, and also division from, not as avoidable evils, but as unavoidable conditions of the constitution of space (Wigley, 1993). This differentiation operates physically and socially. In respect to racialization in America, Nahum Chandler (1993) quotes DuBois:

> Between me and the other world there is ever an unasked question: unasked by some through feelings of delicacy: by others through the difficulty of

rightly framing it. . . . To the real question, How does it feel to be a problem? I answer seldom a word. (p. 26)

Rob Shields (1991), also writing from within a social theory perspective, uses spatial theory to analyze what he calls "marginal places" or communities and how they come to be split off from, but also remain connected to cultural centers. The combination of the sublime and the carnivalesque that shapes these marginal places at any one time is logically prior to those places in our cultural identity of them. An example of this, for Shields, is Niagara Falls. Each successive round of visitors brings to the Falls a set of expectations to which the Falls itself is merely an effect. Niagara Falls, as a place, therefore, is a product of these expectations—a marginal site totally different from the tourist's life "at home."

The application of spatial theory beyond absolute spaces to social/physical fields of cultural articulation has also proved fruitful when employed in the humanities and policy sciences. Philip Fisher (1991, p. 172), writing as a historian, identifies what he calls "democratic social space" with "Jefferson's Map" (The Land Ordinance of 1785). The ideology of Jefferson's map connects an abstract Cartesian scheme to the ideal citizen personified in the yeoman farmer (DeNeufville & Barton, 1987). The citizens of America, with their diverse immigrant and ethnic backgrounds, establish claims to national identity on the basis of being "like Americans." Fisher points out that this is a process of subtraction. Any distinguishing features, like the distinguishing features of physical space, are eliminated as obstructing the processes of actualizing democratic social space. DeNeufville and Barton's study of the myth of the yeoman farmer traces its transformations through policy debates, both foreign and domestic. The myth persists as a major component in shaping a national housing policy oriented around home ownership. What these examples show is how conventional categories of space, of symbolic meaning, and of practical use are not just the purview of academic speculation, nor are they discreet areas of inquiry; they are active components of ongoing political play and struggles to define and enforce social realities.

Space also appears both as an issue and as a tool in the visual arts. For example, the photographer Minor White gave the name *space analysis* to his explorations of psychic reality through photographic sequences. Among contemporary painters the work of John Hultberg is similarly identified with space as both issue and tool. What his work has in common with the other practitioners of space mentioned here is that it operates at several levels, redefining space in a way that challenges the conventions of his practice while also practicing spatial construction in ways that illuminate/reilluminate the subject and its function in cultural context(s). As "Converging Lines" (the painting that illustrates the cover of this book) suggests, Hultberg moves within but also beyond modernism's concern with the picture plane. In constructing the space of his paintings, he creates a place that simultaneously brings together the sublime and the destructive planes of both interior and exterior life (Campbell, 1993, p. 3). Harry Rand has said of Hultberg: "if his vision has been regularly unsettling, such reactions may not reflect the worth of his art as much as the dread with which we are entering the future" (Wescsler, 1993, cover).

To connect all the spatial theorists discussed above in their diverse modes of operation with this vision is not to slight others working in this area;[1] it is only to show how representative practitioners of spatial approaches take seriously the tasks of explicating and execut-ing the relationship between theory and practice and of illustrating the usefulness of spatial theory, in some of its changing configura-tions, for doing so.

SITUATING THIS COLLECTION

As the foregoing suggests, we mean spatial practice, broadly con-strued, as fields where space, ideology, and representation are joined in generative relations. The terminology of spatial theory is somewhat unstable, and so, in conjunction with describing the individual contributions to this volume, we would like to situate these chapters in relationship to forms of spatial theory that inform the broadest contours of our enterprise.

The works of Henri Lefebvre, Michel Foucault, and Michel de Certeau are foundational to spatial theory. Lefebvre's notion of space as process—as produced in inseparable, yet shifting physical and social contexts—is widely understood to have provoked a new area of study, not only for geographers, but also among humanities and social science scholars interested in urban life. Lefebvre (1991) focuses attention on the production of space by, among other things, constructing a model of various "processes of assembly" (pp. 31-33). These include "representations of space," "spatial practices," and "representational spaces." The model tends to distinguish professional practices such as planning (representations of space) from the spatial patterns of everyday life (spatial practices) from the symbolic meanings enacted in spatial form (representational space). Our usage of the term *spatial practices* is derived from Lefebvre's overall theory of space as a production but contains all three elements of his more detailed model.

What these mixtures are becomes a major topic for some of the authors in this collection. For example, in Chapter 4, M. Christine Boyer examines how patterns of the physical design of the city negate the existence of the city as a coherent unity; at the same time these patterns use traditional codes evoking the city as coherent. Boyer suggests that the notion of the city is itself becoming problematic, and she describes instead fragmented, hierarchical spaces in the form of well-designed nodes. Interstitial spaces are abandoned and the "disfigured space" of what were once the neighborhoods and work areas of the industrial city become increasingly undifferentiated. The figured space of the self-enclosed nodes take their functional reasons for being from their relative position in the global political economy, and they acquire their symbolic valence from highly marketed—and marketable—design features that identify them with an imaginary geography of the city as an icon of civilization. These spatial and aesthetic shifts bring into doubt the efficacy of culturally embedded stereotypes of the city as a coherent entity. They also threaten practices of democratic governance that are based on claims to equal citizenship. The yeoman farmer of myth was both confronted with spatial practices that demanded governance and was equal to the task; the urban forms Boyer describes work against both the development of self-governing subjects and the need for them.

In addition to using spatial practices as a synonym for the overall production of space, we differ with Soja's somewhat basic, albeit highly heuristic, call for the substitution of space-based analysis for time-based analysis. Rather, our position is to ask how the two are joined. Helen Liggett suggests in Chapter 9 that the constitutive relations among various modes of assembly can be seen as modes of articulation or ways of making sense. She relates the time/space of analysis to the time/space of social production through the creation of photographic images and narratives that re(enact) spatial patterns. This becomes a mode of exploring the spaces of everyday life that are often reduced or ignored by conventional modes of research. She argues that the work of Lefebvre can be enhanced by adopting a semiotic approach to analysis. If making space is viewed as ways of making meaning, as a poststructural semiotic approach would suggest, then we can think in terms of developing appropriate means for arresting these processes for the purposes of analysis. Liggett's argument for the photo/text is, in part, that it can be a means for articulating aspects of spatial processes that would otherwise be missed.

Michel de Certeau (1988) privileges "everyday operations" over abstract representations of space. He is not concerned with the psychological states of individuals who would author such everyday operations, or "schematas of action." He is also not concerned with space embodied in professional practice, the "optics of expert systems," as Derek Gregory (1994, p. 404) calls them. For de Certeau the space created through professional practices is both dominating and reductive. Here again our use of the notion of spatial practices is meant to use this issue as a tool for asking *how* abstract modes of representation are joined to everyday life. Chapter 8 by David C. Perry is illustrative, concentrating, as it does, on creating a definition of planning that honors its position as continual articulation of space both above and in the streets. He discusses the preoccupation in planning with "the plan" as taking on an abstract existence of its own. In contrast to planning construed as the fixed attainment of successful end states, he recommends an active theory of planning as the recursive "making of space." The breadth of planning activity then extends to various venues, or scales, where planners have participated in processes that make space, including housing projects, neighborhoods, and regional economies.

Richard A. Walker's analysis in Chapter 7 brings theory to bear on empirical evidence in a way that suggests current market practices are best understood through elements of Marxist theory that have tended to be deemphasized or forgotten in the race to have a handy explanation for the changes of the past two decades. Walker challenges both single variable explanations, represented by the flexible specialization school, and politically based interpretations, represented by the regulation school. After a review of the historical evidence, he shows how "logic of the capitalist mode of production," which is central to Marx, best explains the dynamics of industrial and postindustrial change. More specifically he looks at the inherent instability in the drive to accumulation, the intricacies of contemporary labor processes, and the abiding facts of uneven development. He suggests that the processes of industrialization produce space in a series of developmental moves that are not unpredictable but, as Marx would predict, "set some basic terms for the world [people] live in, mould to their ends, and cry over."

For Michel Foucault space is both a way of thinking synchronically rather than diachronically and a means for bringing together architectural or physical space and domains or realms of thought. Thus his notion of spatial practices is a complex constellation of the ideological and the material. Both Chapter 3 by Robert A. Beauregard and Chapter 5 by Stuart Alan Clarke are illustrative.

Beauregard looks at the staging of urban policy at both the national and local levels in a way that highlights the relationship between the representation of problems and formulation of policy to address them. In the first part of this chapter, he discusses the differences between characterizations of urban crisis, particularly those of urban poverty before the War on Poverty era and later during the Reagan/Bush era. He draws connections between the making of meaning and the formulation of policy by showing how the selective rhetoric of hopeless disorder in cities has been used by the policy community to both explain and legitimate inaction by the previous two administrations. In the second part of his chapter, he provides a short case study of neighborhood activism from the perspective of self-conscious participation in constructing issues of neighborhood renewal as public problems and in developing a strategy to address them.

In Chapter 5, Clarke examines a particular stage, the Apollo Theater stage, and shows it to be constitutive of a form of relating between performers and audience, which is, in turn, illuminating of the relations that characterize African American urban politics. The Apollo's Stage becomes a powerful metaphor for appeals based on gaining and holding political recognition on the larger stage of electoral politics. He discusses the cultural context in which the style of the Stage has currency and also analyzes the weakness of reductive stereotyping that follows. The separation of electoral politics and daily governance in American political culture facilitates the manipulation of radical black nationalism. The symbolic economy of the dichotomy between nationalistic and liberal politics explains how cultural heroes such as Martin Luther King Jr. and Malcolm X are transformed and used to promote provocative but politically limiting agendas. The complexities of urban life, in particular the force of the larger political economy in shaping urban space, are successfully masked by these single-minded identities.

One of Foucault's concerns in interrogating space as both materiality and ideology is as a means of understanding how *power* is constituted and operates. Chapters in this collection that follow this line of questioning include Chapter 2, Raphaël Fischler's close reading of the Roxbury, Massachussetts, plan as a mode of political representation and Dennis R. Judd's comparison in Chapter 6 of modern enclosed spaces, such as malls and CIDs (Common Interest Developments), to their predecessors, the medieval market and the democratic community.

Fischler's interpretation of the visual and rhetorical "instruments of persuasion" used in conventional forms of representing space within planning calls the profession to account. He details an intricate interweaving among tools of presentation within planning, the habit of defining development in terms of economic development, and expressions of legitimacy in planning discourse. From this point of view, the Boston Redevelopment Authority's "Roxbury Neighborhood Profile 1987" displays the elements of an implicit narrative requiring planning that compromises it. He makes the case that the "factual" presentation is highly political: Although purporting to merely report information, it also presents justification of a policy approach that is then seen as both rational and inevitable. If these habits permit planning practice to participate in the construction of "worlds that work," accepting them entails a notable cost for planning.

Judd looks at current spatial practices affecting the majority of Americans who are not poor and not urban dwellers. In "The Rise of the New Walled Cities," he analyzes current manifestations of the American "will to segregate." In central cities the "urban fortress" approach to designing hotel, convention, and retail sites creates minitotalities that mystify relational connections to the city beyond. Similar gestures in the suburbs create enclosed malls as controlled environments that celebrate and perfect consumership while devaluing other communal activities more likely to underwrite democracy. In parallel moves, CIDs intensify private solutions to public problems by expanding the notion of home ownership to include corporate control and continual monitoring of living and recreational space. As a kind of elite socialism these schemes trade off traditional freedoms for the promise of safety from a dangerous and unpredictable world outside. Judd's analysis leads to speculation about the future of privatized spaces that are joint reactions to crime in the streets and poison in the air. The "domed city of the hill" would be the material articulation in physical space of class distinction. As they become more rigid, these distinctions threaten community and the tools for actualizing democracy with an updated social Darwinism of place.

As should be clear from these brief summaries, the aim of this collection is not to nail anything down—fix either the theory or the practice of urban life. We seek not to be definite about American spatial practices but rather to explore the complexity of such matters. We choose the overall theme of spatial practices to describe a rich tapestry, sometimes even as it is being woven or coming unraveled, where space, ideology, and representation intertwine. This mode of inquiry is part of what we hope will continue to be fruitful analysis of the physical and social contexts in which we find ourselves.

NOTE

1. The following are key examples of additional critical analyses that draw on the spatial theory of Lefebvre: Castells (1977, 1983) and Gottdiener (1985). The long list of spatial theorists who discuss the complex notion of *time space* include: Immanuel Wallerstein (1991), Doreen Massy (1992), Derek Gregory (1994), and Scott Lash and John Urry (1994). Both Shields (1991) and Lash and Urry present extensive bibliographies.

REFERENCES

Boyer, M. C. (1993, April). Violent effacements in city spaces. *Assemblage, 20*, 20-21.

Campbell, L. (1993). Reminiscences. In E. Wescsler (Ed.), *John Hultberg: Visionary theater* (p. 3). New York: Denise Bibro Gallery.

Castells, M. (1977). *The urban question: A Marxist approach.* Cambridge: MIT Press.

Castells, M. (1983). *The city and the grassroots: A cross-cultural theory of urban social movements.* Berkeley: University of California Press.

Castells, M. (1989). *The information city.* Oxford, UK: Basil Blackwell.

Castells, M. (1992, October 17). *The space of flows: Elements for a theory of urbanism in the informational society.* Paper presented at the Conference on "New Urbanism," Princeton University, School of Architecture, New Jersey.

Chandler, N. D. (1993, April). Between. *Assemblage, 20,* 26-27.

de Certeau, M. (1988). *The practice of everyday life.* Berkeley: University of California Press.

DeNeufville, J. I., & Barton, S. (1987, September). Myth and the definition of policy problems. *Policy Sciences,* 1-25.

Fisher, P. (1991). Democratic social space: Whitman, Melville, and the promise of American transparency. In P. Fisher (Ed.), *The new American studies* (pp. 70 -110). Berkeley: University of California Press.

Foucault, M. (1977a). *Power/knowledge: Selected interviews and other writings.* New York: Pantheon.

Foucault, M. (1977b). *Discipline and punish.* New York: Pantheon.

Foucault, M. (1986, Spring). Texts/Contexts. *Diacritics, 16,* 22-27.

Foucault, M., & Deleueze, G. (1990). Intellectuals and power. In R. Ferguson, W. Olander, M. Tucker, & D. Fiss (Eds.), *Discourses: Conversations in postmodern art and culture* (pp. 9-16). Cambridge: MIT Press.

Gottdiener, M. (1985). *The social production of urban space.* Austin: University of Texas Press.

Gregory, D. (1994). *Geographical imaginations.* Oxford, UK: Basil Blackwell.

Harvey, D. (1989). *The condition of postmodernity: An enquiry into the origins of cultural change.* Oxford, UK: Basil Blackwell.

Lash, S., & Urry, J. (1994). *Economies of signs and space.* New York: Routledge.

Lefebvre, H. (1991). *The production of space.* Oxford, UK: Basil Blackwell.

Massy, D. (1992). Politics and space/time. *New Left Review, 196,* 65-79.

Said, E. (1984). *The world, the text, and the critic.* London: Faber & Faber.

Shields, R. (1991). *Places on the margins.* London: Routledge.

Soja, E. (1989). *Postmodern geographies: The reassertion of space in critical social theory.* London: Verso.

Wallerstein, E. (1991). *Unthinking social science: The limits of nineteenth-century paradigms.* London: Polity.

Wescsler, E. (Ed.). (1993). *John Hultberg: Visionary theater.* New York: Denise Bibro Gallery.

Wigley, M. (Ed.). (1993, April). *Violence and space* [Special issue]. *Assemblage, 20.*

Winterson, J. (1991). *Sexing the cherry.* New York: Vintage.

2

Strategy and History in Professional Practice

Planning as World Making

RAPHAËL FISCHLER

In her call for research that bridges the gap between theory and practice, Judith Innes deNeufville (1983) listed several "critical elements of planning that are poorly understood" and that "demand the attention of planning theorists" (p. 42). Among these are the issues of problem definition; of language, symbols, and indicators; of communication; and of the creation and provision of knowledge. One can say that Innes's call has been heeded or at least that she was giving voice to a growing movement in planning theory. The so-called "linguistic turn" in the social sciences certainly provided significant momentum for research on symbolization, communication, information, and related matters. Many planning theorists have turned to interpretive methods in order to understand what planners do, in order to see what collective decision making or the application of knowledge to action means in concrete terms.[1]

Much recent work in planning theory has consisted in research on the minutiae of daily practice. Careful studies of interaction between planners and other parties or among planners (Forester, 1989; Schön, 1983) have yielded very interesting insights into what goes on in the minds and lives of professional planners. "When we examine it," John Forester (1992) writes,

> ordinary action turns out to be extraordinarily rich. What passes for "ordinary work" in professional-bureaucratic settings is a thickly layered texture of political struggles concerning power and authority, cultural negotiations over identities, and social constructions of the "problems" at hand. (p. 47)

In this chapter, I will argue that it is not only what planners say that is valuable evidence for planning theory; *how* they communicate is also important. Not only the content of their discourse but also its form indicates how planners conceive of politics, society, and the problems of the city. That is, not only the words spoken or written by professionals but also the languages and styles they employ inform us about how they see the processes in which they are involved and the role they play in them. Analyzing the form of representations used in planning practice can reveal both the structural biases of planners' interventions and the strategic value of their statements in particular circumstances. As a complement to the study of speech acts, the study of how planners represent the city, their ideas, and themselves through speech, text, and image can help us bridge the gaps between planning theory and practice and between planning theory and history.[2]

Planning practice is the product of history. Neither in life in general nor in planning in particular is expression the direct product of arbitrary will. People are subject to explicit constraints, and they are limited in their deeds and words by all that is taken for granted as belonging to the order of things, by their culture and the "social construction of reality" (Berger & Luckmann, 1966). How planners choose to represent situations and processes and how they organize communication tells us about the intellectual and institutional tools of planning practice, tools that were designed and adapted to meet changing demands. The analysis of forms of representation in planning helps us ask and answer questions about the professional culture of planners, its historical origins, and its social and political meaning.

This chapter, then, is about representation in planning practice, about planning as a set of social functions performed with certain tools, and about planning theory and history as the study of these ends and means. The object of study is a particular aspect of planning practice, namely the creation and use of symbolic representations. At stake is how the urban realities that planners confront are constituted within the profession, how planners understand and address the world with which they deal. Also under scrutiny is the related issue of how we understand the exercise of power in planning processes.

The first part of the chapter presents a theoretical perspective, which emphasizes the relations among professional practice (in particular professional communication), professional identity, and power. The second part of the chapter presents the methodological framework for the case studies to follow. I explain in more detail why and how the study of planning documents and of the representations they contain is valuable to planning theory. I also introduce the terms and distinctions that will enable us to analyze maps, pictures, paragraphs, and other representations in a coherent way. The third part of the chapter contains the case-study material. Each case deals with a specific representation extracted from a traditional planning document. The analysis focuses on the specific way in which planners use a conventional form of representation. The fourth part of the chapter reconsiders the relationship between the technical, institutional, and political dimensions of planning practice and looks back to the historical origins of that practice. The conclusion presents recommendations for planning theory and planning education.

COMMUNICATION, PROFESSIONAL IDENTITY, AND POWER

Although the proximate object of this chapter is the representation of reality by planners, its ultimate object is their exercise of power.

Through a study of professional communication, the chapter aims at expanding our understanding of the relations between planning practices and processes of struggle and domination. The importance of symbolic representation in politics (Edelman, 1964) and the centrality of communication in planning (Forester, 1989) have been well-established. In both fields, as in life in general, the production and exchange of representations can be (and generally are) goal-oriented activities that aim at furthering particular interests. In fact, as Wildavsky (1973) notes, "power and planning are different ways of looking at the same events, namely attempts to influence behaviors for specific ends" (p. 132).

Yet the planning theory literature presents a multiplicity of voices, if not plain confusion, on the meaning of the term *power*, as does the literature in political science and social theory (Lukes, 1986; Wrong, 1988). In an article entitled "Pragmatism, Planning, and Power," Charles Hoch (1984) distinguishes three traditions of planning theory: the mainstream tradition (à la Schön), the Marxist tradition (à la Harvey), and the tradition of radical pragmatists (à la Friedmann and Forester). Each school of thought, he argues, rests on a different conception of "what counts as action" and offers a different understanding of the issue of power. The first emphasizes individual learning and communication; the second stresses structural inequality and social struggle; both consider power the ability to effect change in the environment. The third tradition tries to bring the first two views together by arguing about the meaning of action, rather than about its results; it speaks of power, as do Hannah Arendt and, after her, Jürgen Habermas: power is the capacity for (self-) realization that flows from agreement (Habermas, 1977).

Although Hoch (1984) provides a useful categorization of planning theories, he does not propose a definition of power that can be used to compare the various perspectives. He notes that "planning theorists with a Mainstream orientation treat power as the capacity individuals possess to learn from experience," whereas Marxist planning theorists view power as "the exercise of political domination based on the exploitation of the working class by the capitalist class" (p. 86). These two pictures are not representations of the same object; they deal with two different but related issues. One statement concerns the capacity of individuals to be effective; the other concerns actual domination of one group by another. The difference can be stated in terms of institutionalization: When a capacity to be effective is institutionalized, the result is domination. (And when domination is legitimate, it is called authority.) The difference can also be explained, in a parallel manner, in terms of the level of analysis that one uses: The attempts of particular actors to effect change here and now are framed by and contribute to social structures that transcend particular events. The distinction between strategic action, which is unavoidable and ubiquitous in social relations, and domination, which corresponds to institutionalized practices, is too often neglected in the planning literature.

The tension between these two perspectives can also be felt in the work of John Forester. On the one hand, the exercise of power is the work of structurally embedded "concentrations of economic power" (Forester, 1989, p. xi). On the other hand, planners and people need to be empowered in order to emancipate themselves from a situation of domination. By defining power in terms of communication, Forester, following Habermas (and Arendt), comes to see perfect communication both as the absence of strategic action—that is, the absence of power—and as empowerment of the people engaged in it. The acquisition of power coincides with its absence, a puzzle that requires, at the very least, a semantic solution: the distinction between *power to* and *power over.*

The work of Michel Foucault provides a way of integrating these two meanings of power.[3] He emphasizes the productive dimension of power and shows that constraint is a condition of action, much as effectiveness is a condition of domination. In addition, and more important for our purposes, Foucault's research sheds light on the ways in which planners exercise power and the ways in which they are themselves the objects of the exercise of power. Central to his work is the idea that fields of power are systems of practice through which actions as well as identities are shaped—not just the actions and identities of those on whom power is being exercised but also the actions and identities of those who exercise power. That perspective partially coincides with the study of "professional systems of cognition" (following Schön), the critique of the "ideology of planning" (following Harvey), and the analysis of the "systematic distortion of communication" (following Forester). But it forces us to pay greater attention to how the exercise of power is inscribed in the professional culture of planners through practices of representation, that is, through the selective organization of attention and the construction of meaning.

Power to, as well as power over, are at stake in professional uses of texts, images, charts, or tables. Indeed, argues Dennis Wrong (1988), relations of domination can be institutionalized through the unequal distribution of "means of persuasion" (p. 33). Although persuasion is not often considered a form of power, it must be classified as such precisely because it cannot remain unaffected by resources used in debate, such as articulateness, rhetorical skills, or psychological insight. More generally, persuasion is a form of power in that "it clearly represents a means by which an actor may achieve an intended effect on another's behavior" (Wrong, 1988, p. 32) and this, without resorting to misinformation. Although it is by no means a given that professionals can be more persuasive than lay people, it is most probable that, within a given area of special knowledge, they stand at a clear advantage, having benefited from a skewed distribution of intellectual resources (Hoffman, 1989).

The problem is not only that specialized language may not be comprehensible to lay people but that, in more general terms, professional planners are more adept at representing or discussing reality in precisely those terms that conceptually structure the intervention of which they are the agents. For example, they are better at visualizing the results of an urban design scheme, or they are more at ease with the calculations that shape an economic development plan. On the one hand, then, professionals are endowed with specific technical skills that are, if not specific to their profession, at least unequally distributed in their favor relative to most lay people. That physical planners have generally had training in drawing and can use graphic skills in discussion, whereas most residents cannot, does not really create a problem of comprehensibility as much as it raises the possibility of unequal persuasiveness: With the graphic tool in hand, the planner has a better chance of making a convincing point. On the other hand, planners have been educated to see the world in specific terms, under a particular light. The reference by physical planners to the city as a complex of "zones" is not only a means for systematizing plan making and control; it is also often constitutive of the public debates they lead. Likewise, the reference by social planners to people's strongly felt requirements as "needs" is not only a convenient way for them to categorize these demands and to structure the practical responses these get; it is also the way in which they format many of their discussions with service beneficiaries, making the latter speak in a "foreign language," an idiom they do not master well.

These inequalities, which are both consequences and sources of domination, do not fully account for the importance of persuasion in planning practice. Much of what planners do is motivated by the need to persuade the public of the merit of plans and policies, and much of what they write can be seen in that light (Milroy, 1989). But if, in their attempts to convince other parties, planners resort to a rhetoric of "urban systems" or to a rhetoric of "systems of needs," it is primarily because they operate professionally from within these perspectives. The lenses through which practitioners see the world are not so much distorting screens—no experience is immediate and pure—as they are filters that allow only certain aspects of reality to pass. Different (and competing) concepts of the city or of planning, although selective and partial, are not so many lies or illusions. They are different truths, perhaps not irreconcilable, but different and true nonetheless. Thus the relationship between representations of urban reality and the exercise of power in urban planning must also be understood within an epistemological framework, in terms of the production of valid knowledge. What constitutes (illegitimate) distortion and what constitutes truth are themselves, notwithstanding Habermas's pretensions to universal understanding, objects of struggle. What makes a statement acceptable as a true representation of reality is historically variable: The deference to past authorities in classical Greece does not square with the commitment to empirical observation in modern societies (Veyne, 1983). Today too, we fight about what is a legitimate representation of reality and about what enables us to evaluate the correctness and worthiness of this representation.

The striving for intellectual domination is a primary feature of the history of the professions. One of the greatest powers of professions is their ability to set norms by which situations are to be evaluated, their ability to set standards "that shape the constitution of the material and social world of modern society" (Freidson, 1986, p. 205). With a profession comes "a domain of objects about which it is possible to articulate true or false propositions" (Foucault, 1991, p. 79), a legitimate view of what that domain is like, as well as a particular way of defining problems—what Foucault would call a "regime of rationality." Planning is no exception: Planners are trained to understand and represent the world in certain ways, ways that are necessarily selective and partial but that help produce acceptable representations of reality. When different professional groups are involved in a decision-making process, they bring to the table varying conceptions of the situation, varying understandings of the problem at hand (Ellis, 1990). Clashes between these professionals are due primarily, one could say, to cultural differences. At issue are, to paraphrase Clifford Geertz (1983, p. 69), "the semiotic means by which [urban situations] are defined."[4]

Unlike the task of the cultural anthropologist, which is to make sense of the very variety of such semiotic means, the task of the planning theorist is to understand the dynamics that develop when different conceptions come to a head in a planning process. This cultural approach to planning does not remove the political dimension of the confrontation from the picture. Quite the contrary, it widens the domain of what is considered political and the scope of critical analysis. The struggle to determine the future of a given situation, to design the solution to a certain problem is first of all a struggle to impose one's view of the situation, to impose one's definition of the problem. Just as no situation or problem is simply given, no specification of the problem is socially neutral. "The struggle to define the situation, and thereby to determine the direction of public policy," Donald Schön (1983) writes, "is always both intellectual and political. Views of reality are both cognitive constructs, which make the situation understandable in a certain way, and instruments of political power" (p. 348).

In the struggle to have one's own view accepted as valid—that is, to have it accepted as the basis of action—rhetoric is a formidable weapon (Throgmorton, 1993). But rhetoric is not confined to the use of obvious metaphors; nor is it restricted to verbal expression. The analysis of representations in the following pages will show that forms of rhetoric are to be found in texts that are usually considered factual as well as in drawings. Rhetoric helps to persuade in part by making people see things under a specific light, from a particular perspective. That perspective is a direct function of people's background, in particular of their professional culture. One's professional culture gives one a predisposition to frame situations and problems in particular ways, that is, to analyze them according to specific categories, to synthesize them into specific structures, and to represent them in specific verbal, graphic, or numerical ways. But professional culture does not follow solely from formal education, with its methods and ideas. Professional culture is also the product of a confrontation with conditions of practice, with a field of strategic action. This is why planners' representations reveal not only their image of the city but also their image of their position in the planning process and in the process of urban development.

Acts of representing are attempts to create views that are internally coherent, proper to the teachings of the profession, effective in eliciting in others a desired response, and capable of solving personal dilemmas. When planners justify their proposal by referring to the common good, for example, they may be repeating an expression learned in school, they may be fostering consensus, and/or they may be trying to legitimate their own authority in front of a recalcitrant neighborhood organization. When they write memoranda defining the crisis of homelessness in the country as a housing problem, they may be applying a framework shared by colleagues, they may be appealing for public action on the part of superiors at the U.S. Department of Housing and Urban Development, and/or they may be attempting to resolve a conflict between their professional commitment and their feeling of helplessness in the face of misery. When they present their plan by means of a colorful bird's-eye view of the future city, they may be showing off the skills acquired in studio after studio, they may be hoping to impress their audience, and/or they may be putting the best possible face on a process of uneven development. In these three cases, and in general, professional culture, in its institutional and individual dimensions, helps to construct a coherent (but not comprehensive) representation and thereby turn a complex reality into a more or less manageable situation.

The issue of representation in planning is not just a matter of concepts and models; more important, it is a question of professional practices, of techniques and tactics. In Foucault's (1991) work on the rise of modern government and the professions, "the target of analysis wasn't 'institutions,' 'theories' or 'ideology,' but practices" (p. 75). The target of analysis, in fact, was "regimes of practices." These are "programmes of conduct which have both prescriptive effects regarding what is to be done (effects of 'jurisdiction'), and codifying effects regarding what is to be known ('effects of veridiction')" (p. 75). Therefore it is insufficient to approach representation within the framework of the sociology of knowledge; it must be seen within the larger framework of the sociology and history of practices, both discursive and nondiscursive. The example of zoning comes readily to mind. Created and sustained under the political pressure of property owners and developers fighting to maintain or increase their assets, systematized and institutionalized under the influence of scientific and legal developments, and nurtured by popular myths of home ownership and ideologies of social distinction, zoning is an intellectual as well as an instrumental construct (deNeufville & Barton, 1987; Haar & Kayden, 1990; Makielski, 1966; Perin, 1977; Toll, 1969; Weiss, 1987). It exists in specific practices of symbolic representation (e.g., the city as a set of zones on a map, the zone as realm defined by specific standards) and in specific practices of social action (e.g., the creation and application of standards, the permitting process) that are interdependent. It is a complex web of theory and practice, of knowledge and power. To use zoning as a cure for the problems of a poor neighborhood (as did the planners whose representations we will study below) is to impose a certain logic of understanding and of intervention on the situation, to select particular practices of action and cognition.

In the study of contemporary planning, ethnographic studies of planning practice can help establish the relationship between techniques, discourses, and institutions. The purpose of this chapter is to show that one possible avenue for such a project is the analysis of planning documents. The formal characteristics of these documents and of the representations they contain offer insights into the professional culture of planners—the culture of design, of economics, of social action—and into their professional practices: mapping and illustrating, tabulating and calculating, mediating and policy making. The substantive contents of these documents, the arguments and ideas they present, tell us how planners see the city, the models and theories they bring to bear on the city's problems. The production and use of documents, their distribution and adoption give us clues about the organization of the planning process and the urban development process. In all these features, finally, in form, content, and use, we can see planners in action, their habits and strategies, their professional identity.

That identity is the result of historical processes, the crystallization of new understandings and political regimes, the effect of new laws and statutes. It is also the product of the material context of practice, of international economic conditions and local struggles, of personality and inner conflict. Planners' representations reveal the various tensions they experience: between visionary design and technical standards, citizen participation and political demagoguery, formal status and lack of authority; between the city as abstract geometric space and as living community, low-income neighborhoods as blight and as strongholds of civic traditions, economic growth as act of God and as fruit of our labor; between planners as politicians and as bureaucrats; between plans as steps toward a better future and as cover for domination.

THE STUDY OF REPRESENTATION IN PLANNING

Planners devote much of their time to the production of written and graphic material. Broadening the field of inquiry to include these documents means that we become sensitive at the same time to two related issues: the symbolic structures that frame what is being said, written, and shown during planning processes; and the political structures that frame interaction during those processes. This represents a shift from *communication* to *representation* as the key concept of analysis—a shift made by Lisa Peattie (1987) in her book *Planning Ciudad Guayana*.[5]

The interdependence of symbolic (or cognitive) and political issues is contained in the very term representation:

All forms of representation are abstractions from reality which bring some aspects forward to the attention and leave some in the background or eliminate them completely. At one end of the continuum (formed by the different meanings of the word) the descriptive meaning of . . . "representation" is emphasized; at the other, the political meaning. But a description, because it selects and emphasizes, because it makes a statement about the world, to the degree that people attend to it or are influenced by it has political effects. And at the other end of the continuum, the institutions that we call "representative" stand as, and are intended to be . . . descriptions of the societies they represent. (Peattie, 1987, p. 112)

A focus on representation, then, makes us question the way in which urban realities are being represented, as well as the way in which interested individuals, groups, institutions, and constituencies are being represented in the planning process. The purpose here is to focus on mechanisms of symbolic representation rather than on mechanisms of political representation, even though both are inextricably linked. This approach is important because, as discussed above, the means of symbolization available to planners and other actors are not neutral tools. They partake of specific modes of knowing the world and, more important, specific modes of acting on it: Representing is "world making" (Goodman, 1976b).

Modes of representation—verbal or visual—cannot be considered merely as benign systems of reproduction; they stand in relation to different ways of construing the relationship between objects, between subject and object, and between subjects. In effect, they follow from different "conceptions of social, cultural, and political value" (Mitchell, 1986, p. 2). Representing the city through either text or drawing clearly means more than opting for a specific aesthetic effect or following a bureaucratic requirement. The choice of word over image or image over word constitutes a strategy and responds to specific desires and interests.[6] The respective characteristics of types of representation—pictures, diagrams, paragraphs, or charts—also make them particularly suitable and, hence, desirable for specific purposes, from technical ones to political ones. The same is true for means of representation—printed documents, formal presentations, or direct dialogue—as practitioners and students of citizen participation know well. How the representation of things and people is organized, how the encounter of people with their environment and with others is mediated, is indeed a matter of strategic importance.[7]

The central question when following the present line of inquiry is therefore: How do planners (consciously or unconsciously) use the specific potentials and limitations of various forms of representation in their tasks?[8] The question is not how the use of a form of symbolization affects the contents of a message, but how particular forms lend themselves to specific uses (and abuses) in planning processes. The emphasis lies on the ways in which professionals choose and use forms to fit their purposes; on the ways in which forms of symbolization in themselves represent conceptions of the city, of its process of development, and of the role planners play in this process; on the ways in which forms of planning and forms of symbolization coincide.

In the vignettes that will be presented below, three different types of representation are used: a drawing, a metaphor, and a paragraph. The meaning of each will be analyzed in terms of symbolic representation and in terms of political representation. The analysis will move back and forth between a consideration of the nature of the type of representation (i.e., its structural characteristics) and a consideration of the specific use that is being made of it (i.e., the way in which these characteristics were used to create a certain effect). Despite a stated emphasis on form, this movement will correspond to a dialectic between form and content. For example, a perspective drawing requires a focal point, sometimes two; we can therefore ask: What object has been selected as focal point in this particular drawing and what does that tell us about the ideas and values of the planners who are responsible for this representation?

THE VIGNETTES

The representations that will be analyzed are drawn from a document used in Boston in the early stage of a neighborhood planning process that has attracted national attention. *The Dudley Square Plan: A Strategy for Revitalization*, in its "Briefing Book" version of December 1984, presented a preliminary plan of the Boston Redevelopment Authority (BRA) for the Dudley Square area (Boston Redevelopment Authority, 1984). Dudley Square is the historic center of the district of Roxbury, a part of Boston characterized by much poverty and physical decay. In another document, the BRA explained the context of its planning effort as follows:

Over the last decade Boston's economy as a whole has begun to expand into new vista's of post-industrial America—professional, business, medical, and educational services, finance, real-estate, insurance, communication, and high-technology industries. The Roxbury community, however, has not yet shared in this new economic future, to any extent. The challenge that presents itself now is how to bring the prosperity of Boston's economy to Roxbury. (Perkins, 1987, p. 8)

In fact, in 1984, private market forces had already started making Roxbury part of Boston's postindustrial arena: The combination of proximity to downtown, availability of land, and low real-estate values made it an ideal place for office expansion. The problem was how to use these market forces in a way that benefited the local residents. In order to address this problem, the BRA developed a strategy for intervention that essentially called for a new zoning code and an urban design plan. The Briefing Book from which this case study draws its material was issued by the BRA as a means to publicize its proposal for the area and to demand public feedback on that plan.[9]

A Drawing

The picture (Figure 2.1) under consideration occupies the first page of the Dudley Plan, behind the cover (title page) and before the page with the table of contents. The picture is a drawing. That is, it is not a photograph: The choice of elements to be shown does not occur merely by framing and orientation, but it is a conscious selection of significant elements. Some of them are means to create the context: natural features, such as rivers, coastlines, and roadways. Some represent specific items within this structure: places, buildings, parks. The image is a picture indeed: Its elements resemble the real things they represent and spatial configurations are recognizable.

In Figure 2.1, several items have been numbered, and a small list in the lower righthand corner spells out what each number stands for. These items have been singled out as landmarks in the area and as means to situate Dudley (and Roxbury, of which Franklin Park is the most salient feature): Prudential/Hancock, Downtown, Logan, Harvard/MIT, and JFK/UMass. The drawing shows us the planners' view of the city of Boston, what they see as its most significant elements. Its use by the planners means that they assume that the

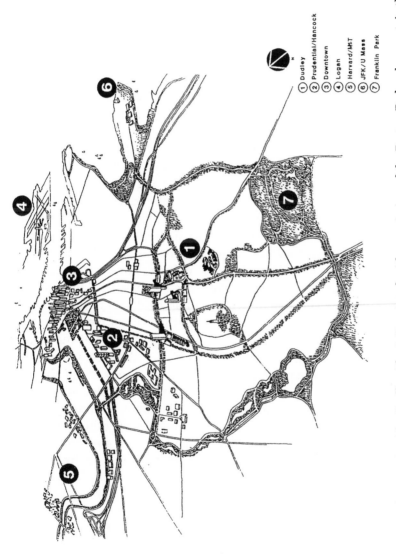

Figure 2.1. The Drawing (the Dudley Plan). Reprinted with permission of the Boston Redevelopment Authority.

① Dudley
② Prudential/Hancock
③ Downtown
④ Logan
⑤ Harvard/MIT
⑥ JFK/U Mass
⑦ Franklin Park

readers of the document are able to understand this map and, more important, that they can identify with it, that they can take this map as a fair representation of the city and of the position of their neighborhood in it. The drawing serves the purpose, albeit unconscious, of influencing the way in which the viewers (the residents in particular) "frame the picture"; in effect, it propagates the BRA perspective.

Using a drawing enables one to select representative elements in the situation and leave out others. It does so even more than a photograph, which has its own strengths (essentially resulting from its realism) but allows for less selectivity.[10] Note how much has been left out of the drawing that would have been included in a photograph: a multitude of spaces and buildings, cars and people, trees and light poles—all the elements that constitute the daily urban environment. Selection in drawing does not only proceed by means of inclusion and exclusion but also by means of a choice of focus. Some pictorial elements will form the context, the background for central objects; some elements are primary and others are secondary. This difference in status can be indicated in a drawing in various ways: by the elements' position in the composition, by their technical treatment (level of detail), by their color, and so on. In a drawing like this one, which uses features of perspective composition (although it is not really a perspective drawing), hierarchy depends very much on position. It is primarily the product of the logic of perspective: The composition sets as central objects the ones that lie at the convergence of its lines of perspective. This kind of drawing supposes the choice of a definite point of view. It says to the viewer: "Reality is to be seen from here and from nowhere else." The choice of a point of view is crucial in the organization of the depiction because it disposes things in a specific spatial relationship to each other and to the viewer. The organization reveals some objects and hides others behind the first ones, and it puts certain items in a central position while leaving others in a peripheral position. In this way a hierarchy is created: the more central an element, or the more it "faces" the viewer, the more prominent and, hence, important it is.

In the aerial view under our eyes, the focus of the perspective is downtown Boston. The drawing emphasizes its centrality by revealing the convergence of the pattern of streets and coastlines. All roads lead to downtown, so to speak, and it is therefore not Dudley that is at the center of the composition but the financial and administrative heart of the city. On the other hand, Roxbury is closer to the viewer. But the greater distance to downtown is compensated for by adjustments in the density of depiction and in the level of detail, which are not too different from those of the middle ground, if not from those of the foreground. A quick look at the height of the buildings in different places will make this clear. The rules of perspective drawing are being violated in order to make the center of the city and of the composition more important than normally warranted in such a representation. Downtown is thus being highlighted and emphasized in two ways: by its location in the focal point of the composition and by a manipulation of pictorial features contrary to the standard requirements of this type of drawing. In addition, the possibility of filling in some of the details of Roxbury, a possibility afforded by the amount of space the area occupies on the page, has not been exploited, and Roxbury appears as rather empty and devoid of intrinsic interest.

The drawing shows how the ability to choose a point of view and orientation and the ability to manipulate graphic expression make this type of representation suitable for conveying a specific, value-laden view of an area. To the extent this tinkering with graphics is in contradiction with the formal requirements of perspective drawing, it can be seen as a distortion. On the other hand, not adapting size and detail for downtown would have made it nearly invisible. One should be even more cautious about applying the label "distortion" to the structure of the picture as a whole, that is, to the choice of downtown as focus of the composition. The choice of focus conveys a particular message. And because the image shows all it has to show, all it is, the viewer is left with no alternative: this is the way to look at this view (Meunier, 1980, pp. 47-48). No amount of movement of either the picture or the viewer will give the latter another perspective, another experience of Dudley's position and context. The picture imposes, if only for a brief moment, a particular view of the situation, heavy with implications for the definitions and solutions of problems. One could argue that the choice of downtown as focus is malign. On the other hand, this view does give Roxbury a large presence on the page. Had Dudley been chosen as focal point instead of downtown, downtown would have filled a larger part of the drawing and planners could have been faulted for displaying an insensitive view of the neighborhood, in effect saying: "This is how we see you from our office window." In addition, a different perspective would probably have been graphically much less interesting, given the local topography (i.e., downtown Boston is located at the head of a land mass surrounded by water). Aesthetic concerns cannot be dismissed lightly, not if we take the professional culture of planners and urban designers seriously.

There is more to this representation. As if to compensate for the hierarchy arising from the perspective composition, seven landmarks of the urban landscape have been numbered, with No. 1 being Dudley. The message, here, is: "Yes, Dudley comes first in the list of our concerns." Also, the status of landmark has been bestowed on very different things. Dudley is made as significant as downtown or Harvard University, Franklin Park as important as Logan Airport or the Hancock/Prudential complex. The text is a means to clarify the picture, to stabilize its meaning (Barthes, 1978). But the way in which the text is being used—the specific items included in the list and their numerical ordering—is in itself a statement: "We are dealing here with Dudley and we approach its problems in a citywide perspective."

This drawing, then, is the sum of two vectors: the need to create a coherent and intelligible representation and the will to deliver a specific message. On the one hand, we have the need for a focus, for representative elements, and for the unambiguous identification of these elements; on the other hand, we have the choice of downtown as focus, the selection of seven specific landmarks, and their numerical ordering. The picture is the product of a dialectic between the nature and the use of aerial views, a game of technical requirements and strategic choices, a play of structure and agency. The resulting message is ambiguous: Downtown is the center of all things Bostonian, but Dudley is No. 1.

We can interpret the ambiguity of the drawing as a sign of the double meaning of representations in planning in general. Representations are both instruments of persuasion (public-oriented) and instruments of city building (aimed at implementation). Could we say that the composition itself corresponds to the planners' own view on the matter, as shaped by their political-economic context, whereas the numbered list represents the message the officials want to convey? Could it be that the planners did not manage to free themselves from their conventional view on the city, in which downtown is the source and background of all intervention? Could it be that they let themselves be guided above all by an aesthetic sense, according to which the convergence of river and harbor shorelines and of roadways at the downtown hub is an asset for a strong perspective drawing? To the extent that these questions can receive positive answers, we may infer that political tradition (the centrality of downtown) and professional tradition (the aesthetic value of a representation) have helped shape the message. In this case, we may ask ourselves whether planners should not have been able to reframe their view from a City Hall-centered one to a neighborhood-centered one—to see the problem from another angle, both literally and figuratively—and whether or not they should have been able to resist the temptation to let aesthetic concerns override social ones. We may wonder, more generally, about the difficulty of the profession to let go of traditional views and to adopt new perspectives.

As preliminary and circumscribed as it is, this analysis does illustrate how the formal features of a representation participate in the creation of specific perceptions of reality. In this drawing, Dudley exists in relation to downtown, in part because planners work (for) downtown and have chosen their professional home as focal point of the perspective, and in part because such an orientation makes for a nicer drawing. The influence of formal features onto perception and understanding is all the more meaningful if we realize that a representation, once made, acquires its own validity and autonomy, shapes people's approach to the problem, and thereby influences decision making. Residents who "buy" this drawing may get more than what they bargained for, more than a nice impression, namely the idea that Dudley does not amount to much without the intervention of public and private downtown forces.

A Metaphor

The Dudley Square Plan contains descriptions of the history and present condition of Roxbury, as well as the BRA's ideas about the future of the area. One particular figure of speech, that of the tide (italicized in the following passages), is used in various places to characterize this past, present, and possible future:

The tide can turn. Public policy and planning leadership, combined with bold private sector initiatives and community participation, can help achieve the important goal of revitalizing the Dudley Square area as a place to work and live. (Boston Redevelopment Authority, 1984, p. 3)

Inability of Public Investment to stem the tide.
    In the face of *this ebb tide of economic, demographic and fiscal streams,* . . . substantial public investment . . . could not succeed in stemming decline, and stimulating private development investment. (p. 5)

Roxbury's era of throw-away housing and cast-away land is over. Values of residential and nonresidential property are rising. Tax-foreclosed structures are being redeemed. Most structures in Dudley Square are in productive use. *Private market forces are moving with the new tide.* (p. 7)

Public policy and planning, working with the tide, can help achieve important advances for the Roxbury community. Though City public investment dollars will be scarce, the City has a major challenge in marshaling and monitoring the potential for private development investment, and the state and federal investment role, in a new planning effort with the Roxbury community. (p. 8)

In order to analyze these four passages, some preliminary discussion is needed of the specific form of representation at stake in this vignette: the metaphor. Essentially, a metaphor describes something through something else, a "something else" that belongs to another category of things. Indeed, "a metaphor might be regarded as a calculated category-mistake" (Goodman, 1976a, p. 73). Metaphorical description operates by relating the object of discussion (say, a city) to an analogue whose features are well-known, relevant, and important (say, a human body). This allows for a transfer of these features onto the object and its consequent illumination. The object can now be perceived in the light of the analogue (in our example, the transportation system as the blood circulation system). In addition, research by cognitive scientists suggests that the metaphor "requires a joint consideration of the mediational function of both verbal and imaginal symbolic processes" (Paivio, 1971, p. 475). This is due to the fact that "concrete sentences (are) high-imagery material" (p. 453). That is, their meaning

is not tied to the specific words but to the world of objects and events to which the words refer; such meaning, according to the present theory, is mentally represented in the form of nonverbal imagery. Comprehension of that meaning therefore depends upon the arousal of such imagery, and it is the imagery that is retained—that is, the nonverbal referential meaning of the sentence. (Paivio, 1971, pp. 459-460)

By referring to a concrete object or person, as it most often does, a metaphor stimulates the imagination. Yet the word and the image that the word evokes belong to different realms. The former is explicit and common to all; the latter is implicit and idiosyncratic. This difference in status allows for a certain openness. People need only agree on the structural similarities between the object and its analogue in order to share the metaphor, but they remain free in their personal interpretation and elaboration of the figure. Another source of openness is the fact that the object and its analogue are similar yet different, conceptually related yet categorically separated. This creates the possibility of giving meaning in a transitive way: If objects A and B are both similar to analogue C, then A and B are similar, too. This capacity of metaphorical representation for establishing transitive relations, as well as its openness to idiosyncratic involvement, will be important in the following analysis of the quotes excerpted from the BRA document.

Another important feature of the metaphorical mode is that the strong imaginary and/or emotional response elicited by words is not limited to the time of immediate perception. The response influences the perception of the whole sentence, perhaps the whole passage in which the metaphor itself is located.[11] Understanding a metaphor is a creative act, which puts things in a certain perspective. These "things" are not just the one object to which the metaphor refers literally, but indeed other, related objects. Understanding the metaphor is not only accepting it, it is also entering a community of thought with the speaker, by following him or her in the departure from normal (literal) language, in a side step into the realm of the imagination. Having accepted the metaphor, one is made particularly sensitive to its later occurrences; one's "imaginal investment" is available for subsequent use, a few sentences or pages later. One is thereby exposed to the use and abuse of rhetorical persuasion, but one has also entered a covenant that can provide the grounds for collective action.[12]

The possibility of using the same metaphor in relation to two or more different phenomena finds application in this vignette. The verbal figure of the tide is used, in the first two quotes, to describe the past and present dynamics of the area—that is, decline—whereas it is used in the third and fourth quote to describe a force going in the very opposite direction—that is, renewal. There is "the tide" and "the new tide." In both cases, what matters, what constitutes the basis of the metaphor, is the reference to a gigantic mass, a sweeping momentum, as an analogy for the forces that shape the area. This allows the writer(s) to capture the importance and scale of a past phenomenon— a phenomenon that may very well be experienced by most local residents as a tide against that no one can stand—and to endow the new (hypothetical) phenomenon with the same features. But immensity, mass, energy, and force are not the only relevant features; another one is the impossibility for people to control the course of things, to steer the process.

The BRA seems to suggest that the old tide is making space for a new one, that the momentum of the tide has been redirected from one direction to another. This shift has certainly happened with the imaginal power of the metaphor, but in terms of the real processes to which these metaphors refer, things are definitely much more complicated. This is so, first, because the forces of decline and of renewal are not similar, in that they do not operate through the same channels or according to the same mechanisms; nor are they necessarily of the same magnitude. There is also, despite these differences, no reason to believe a priori that the BRA will be able to control the new tide when it has not been able to control the old one. Economic tides are of a different nature than aquatic ones and cannot be controlled by means of engineering works (and we know how poorly human efforts fare in their attempts to tame nature). In short, the analogy between a societal and a natural tide and the equation of different economic tides have limited empirical validity. Yet this limitation is exactly what the metaphor does not convey and in fact obfuscates. Bridging reality gaps, it establishes equivalencies between economic and physical phenomena and between the old tide and the new one.

The role of the metaphor is to mobilize attention, energy, and commitment and to cast a new light on the problem. But an important question arises: Are the planners only trying to persuade their audience of the likelihood and benefits of the new tide, or are they also trying to convince themselves of their own ability to use this tide to bring about positive changes in the area? Perhaps they are trying to defuse opposition, but perhaps they are also trying to persuade all participants, themselves included, that things are under control and that planning can make a difference. The tensions that this representation reveals are those of the profession as a whole. The multiple use of the metaphor of the tide suggests more than the ambivalence of specific individuals in the face of a difficult situation; it speaks to the continued search of a professional group for a role in the city's politics and history. At stake here is not just the validity and effectiveness of a representation but the legitimacy and efficacy of planning as a mode of public intervention.

A Paragraph

In an attempt to explain to local residents why Roxbury is in trouble and why intervention by the BRA can help, the planners describe the economic situation as follows:

BOSTON'S ECONOMY
- Boston has a leading role in the nation's change to a service economy.
- This leading role means that Boston's economy should continue to grow faster than the national average.
- Downtown growth means more jobs and more opportunities for neighborhood improvement.
- Boston's economy serves and creates growth in the regional economy. Suburban growth is slowing as outlying cities and towns reach their development capacity. The lack of suburban development sites will make Dudley a very attractive area for investment.
- Because of its location, the Dudley area can become the region's best secondary office market.
- To become a strong Business Park, the Dudley area must have two things—a price advantage and an adequate labor supply.
- Price advantage can be obtained through lower land cost and higher allowable building heights. An adequate labor supply exists in Dudley, and it can be expanded through education and training. (Boston Redevelopment Authority, 1984, p. 11)

This paragraph will help us understand how the nature of text, as a particular type of representation, allows for specific uses of language in social interaction. We will concentrate on two essential features of language: its capacity to express chains of logical statements and, especially, its capacity to relate chains of events. The paragraph at hand presents a special form of text. Rather than being a continuous flow of clauses telling a story, it is made of a set of points, each containing a separate argument. This specific form, the text as set of bullets, is critical. First, it means that reality has been chopped into pieces, into separate sentences. Articulation is proper to language in general, but in this case, interrelationships between elements have been left more or less open. Second, the reduction to bullets not only sets things apart but also follows from a conscious selection of material: Some things are presented, others have been rejected. Each point of the text carries an argument. Taken separately, some of these arguments are mere expressions of "facts"—about Boston's role, about the meaning of growth, and so on. Other arguments provide simple deductions and implications: given X we have Y, in order to have X we need Y, and so on. Each can be attacked on its own terms, but each can also be defended on its own terms. In fact, most of these arguments are not just right, they are truisms.

What is the purpose of the paragraph? It is, most likely, to provide support to the BRA's proposal to turn Dudley Square and some of the surrounding area into a business park. Taken together, the points being made suggest that such an evolution is possible, even desirable; that it will require that certain conditions be met; and that the conditions can indeed be met readily. Yet the whole functions like one of those verbal puzzles, in which each sentence is true but in which the end doesn't agree with the beginning. The mistake then generally lies at the point of passage between two sentences, in the unarticulated zone between two arguments. Let us see what the text would become if we filled in the gaps, if we turned it into a story (italics indicate added passages):

Boston has a leading role in the nation's change to a service economy. This leading role means that Boston's economy should continue to grow faster than the national average. *We can therefore expect a significant amount of growth in the coming years, especially proceeding from the existing downtown service industry.* Downtown growth means more jobs and more opportunities for neighborhood improvements *thanks to these jobs, but also thanks to additional public revenues, such as taxes and linkage payments.* Boston's economy serves and creates growth in the national economy. Suburban growth is slowing as outlying cities and towns reach their development capacity. The lack of suburban development sites will make Dudley a very attractive area for investment, *especially given its location next to downtown Boston.* Because of its location, the Dudley area can become the region's best secondary office market, *to accommodate the expansion of service and R&D companies. This expansion requires the constitution of business centers, or business parks, which provide a comfortable and efficient environment for their activities.* To become a strong Business Park, the Dudley area must *be attractive to investors. It therefore must* have two things—a price advantage and an adequate labor supply. Price advantage *for prospective developers* can be obtained through lower land cost and higher allowable building heights *than in competing locations.* An adequate labor supply exists in Dudley, *given the high unemployment rate and the amount of young people,* and it can be expanded through education and training.

The new text reveals a contradiction between, on the one hand, the fact that Dudley is attractive to developers thanks to its location and to the economic climate and, on the other hand, the fact that it needs to be made attractive to developers if it wants to become a strong business park. More important, at no point in the text is the will of the local residents being mentioned. Nowhere does one read something like: "If the community welcomes the business park idea."

What the edited text reveals, by its shift from a discontinuous to a continuous discursive form, is the presence of time and of actors. That is precisely what the story form is all about: the presentation of events in time, of sequences of actions, and of causal links between them. Behind the actions are actors, in this case companies, developers, the government. These are the people behind the "new tide" mentioned above. With actors, the text introduces interests and motivations, as well as the potential threats they represent to some readers. This is what the bullet form, the style of separate points, makes it possible to leave out. As a set of static descriptions, it gives the impression of being merely factual and thereby endows arguments with an air of neutrality. As Lisa Peattie (1987) points out, the more selective the representation—that is, the more it reduces the amount of representative elements and takes them out of their context—the less capable it is of conveying the "reality" of life: the struggle, the fight, the clash of interests, or the cooperation, the mutual support.

The fact that a flowing, discursive form was not used here cannot be explained by the general format of the document. True, as an early draft, it contains much text that is written in bullets; but some text is continuous. What, then, made the planners choose this simpler form of representation? One possible reason is practical: facts are much more controllable than events and processes. In the same way that language fragments the continuum of phenomena into separate pieces (words) in order to make it manageable, so do lists of facts. Lists enable one to have a stabilized representation of the situation, a representation in which discrete elements offer ease of understanding and ease of intervention, through the identification of a limited number of points where things can go wrong and about which one can do something.

But another possible reason is more strategic: The planners may have an interest in "forgetting" about the presence of actors and motivations. Both they and the residents are in a way threatened by the freedom of private commercial initiative. While residents may lose their rental units because of private development, planners may lose professional autonomy and the ability to make a difference in the future of the city. The job of planners is precisely to guide development, and they must therefore be able to initiate, anticipate, and respond to development initiatives. A retreat into the neutral world of facts would be a self-defeating escape from the political and economic reality of planning. The point for planners is precisely to understand and make use of forces and interests in order to satisfy the common good, to cater to needs, or otherwise to ensure beneficial results from urban development. The specific form of this representation, this disjointed text, reflects a search by a team of planners for the security of facts over the messiness of interests and motivations. It illustrates the uneasiness of the profession as a whole in the face of conflict and uncertainty.

REPRESENTATION IN SOCIOLOGICAL AND HISTORICAL PERSPECTIVE

The vignettes illustrate how the form of a representation can tell us about the content of a planning process. They show how each form requires choice and selection and offers potential and opportunity. The vignettes involve choices of focus and perspective, the selection of visual elements or conceptual points; they provide the possibility to influence views and frame problems and the opportunity to stimulate emotional involvement and obfuscate conflict. The first vignette, a perspectivistic drawing, shows how the choice of a point of view allowed planners to set Dudley Square literally in a downtown perspective. Through this choice, the message of the representation is that the right way to look at Dudley is as an area adjacent to if not dependent on downtown. Its development must be considered in a citywide perspective; it follows lines of force emanating from downtown. But at the same time, Dudley is number one on the BRA's list of concerns.

The second vignette, the metaphor of the tide, was used to show how metaphorical language too is pregnant with potential for strategic action. This form of verbal representation involves not only words but also mental images, and it carries an "emotional appeal under the guise of defining issues" (Edelman, 1964, p. 137). The ensuing personal involvement can be tapped and used for arguments made later in the text or speech. In this case, the character of irresistibility, which local residents most probably experience when confronted with the tide of decline, has been transferred to the hypothetical tide of renewal and improvement. The implicit meaning of this representation—a meaning that arises from the specific use of the metaphor—is that the sweeping forces shaping the urban environment can be redirected and that their momentum will be as great in their positive effects as in their negative impact.

The third vignette, a particular form of text, the list of bullets, shows how the specific characteristics of verbal representation can lend themselves to the creation of specific perceptions and attitudes. In this case, the potential of text to represent human will and interest has been disregarded, leaving the paragraph as a mere addition of facts. Rather than using the potential for argumentation creatively, in a dialogue on the social and political dimension of urban development and change, the planners have tamed the text so as to neutralize it, in effect doing away with interest and conflict. The specific form of symbolic representation corresponds to a specific form of political representation in the planning process, one in which residents are set as passive spectators and "recipients" of development. The Habermasian goal of perfect communication, of open dialogue, was not on the planners' agenda.

In all three vignettes, representation is abstraction: it simplifies the complex and continuous stream of perception into discrete symbols and removes chosen elements from their context. Representation is formalization: It recasts reality into a new reality; it formalizes communication, structures it according to accepted forms. Representation is codification: It transforms reality into signs and organizes these into systems. These symbolic systems shape the ways in which we perceive reality, argue about it, and plan for its evolution. They (sometimes literally) frame our view and understanding, our problems and their solutions. And although they can serve the goal of domination, the point is not to brand all symbolic systems and structures as inherently repressive (Baudrillard, 1981). Structure, of course, is both constraining and enabling (Giddens, 1984). As the present case study suggests, systems of representation are structures in which agency lives.

The document from which the representations were extracted was meant to persuade people from Roxbury (and others) of the value of the BRA's view. Specific formal features of the representations were used in order to convey and "sell" that view. It is tempting to characterize these representations as manipulative and the planners' attitude as cynical. We have reasons to believe, however, that the planners were as much trying to persuade themselves as they were trying to persuade their readers, that they were producing these specific images of the situation in good faith and with good intentions. Aha, chuckles the "critical" reader, isn't that precisely what ideology is about, this good faith in wrong ideas, this false consciousness? Isn't that a condition for the perpetuation of the inequality, if not the repression, from which the residents of Roxbury suffer? True enough, but there is more to planners' statements than false consciousness, and that is precisely what the vignettes illustrate.

First, what the analysis shows is that the ideological definitions of situations and problems that planners may present are much more than the fruit of some kind of indoctrination. Such representations are also responses to the context in which planners work, to the constraints that they experience in their daily practice. The drawing focusing on downtown Boston, the double use of the metaphor of the tide, and the juxtaposition of economic facts tell us about how BRA planners communicate with local residents; they also tell us how these professionals experience and negotiate their position in the games of planning and urban development. The analysis suggests that the planners are unsure of the importance of their action and ill at ease vis-à-vis the political, economic, and social systems through which they can exercise power. This raises further questions about how planners relate to downtown and City Hall, to economic tides, to grassroots mobilization. The drawing, the metaphor, and the paragraph of bullets provide further reasons to believe that planning has an ambivalent, confused relation to the larger forces of society.

The analysis suggests, second, that the idea of a social, political, and economic order constraining the work of planners must be specified. The actual practical constraints that planners experience are not so much those of society at large as they are those of intermediary systems. Systems of representation give planners a claim to professional knowledge and give planning public legitimacy. These systems are media between planners and the city as an object of understanding. They enable planners to answer the questions, "What is out there and what is wrong with it?" Similarly, activity systems stand between planners and the city as object of action; it helps them answer the questions, "What needs to be done and how can we do it?" To the extent that action in planning is collective action in the public domain, the last question can be translated into, "How do we organize interaction?" Here again are the issues of symbolic and political representation, the selection of objects to represent the city in word and image and the selection of people to represent urban society in person.

It has been my argument that the symbolic and political aspects of representation are complementary. I would like to argue now that recognizing this complementarity is an important step on the way to bridging the gap between theory and practice. The link between theory and practice must be more than a set of contacts between theorists and practitioners; it must reside in the methodological framework of planning theory itself. It must be built, first, on the idea that theory is a product of practice (Liggett, 1990). It must rest, second, on the idea that the categories that form the basis of theories are at the same time instruments of understanding and of action. To bridge the gap between theory and practice, planning theorists can therefore do more than analyze *what* planners think and say. They can also study *how* planners think and speak and, more generally, how they do what they do or, more precisely, how they give meaning to their action. The starting point of this inquiry can be the discursive and nondiscursive practices that those involved in the planning process (official planners and others alike) follow to perform the activities that make up the planning process. Following Friedmann's (1987) view of that process, standard practices, which are at once intellectual and strategic, include the following:

1. Defining the problem to be addressed in ways that will make it amenable to action or policy intervention.
2. Modeling and analyzing the situation for the purpose of intervention with specific policy instruments, institutional innovations, or methods of social mobilization.
3. Designing one or more potential solutions in the form of policies, substantive plans of action, institutional innovations, and so on.
4. Carrying out a detailed evaluation of the proposed alternative solutions in terms of their technical feasibility, cost effectiveness, probable effects on different population groups, political acceptability, and so on. (pp. 37-38)

Defining the problem, modeling the situation, designing plans of action, and evaluating probable effects—all these activities are being conducted in mentally and socially structured ways. All are informed by "regimes of rationality" and "regimes of practices" that are specific to a time and place (Foucault, 1991). Regimes of rationality are not overarching worldviews or *zeitgeists* but specific ways of defining both the ends and the means of practical action, specific ways of making reality amenable to action. Regimes of practices are not disciplinary constraints but the set of practices that follow from the definitions of what counts and what works.

As Paul Rabinow (1989) makes clear in his genealogy of French planning, modern city planning emerged from the convergence of new models of urban space and society, strategies of state intervention, assessments of well-being, tools of analysis, techniques of administration, and other innovations that together constituted an apparatus for the regulation of the city. This perspective on planning, with its focus on specific strategies and practices rather than on absolute goals and theories, can help us bridge the gap between knowledge and action because it can also help us close other divides: between structure and agency, between the production of knowledge and the exercise of power, and between the constitution of objects of analysis and the constitution of subjects of action.

Rabinow's (1989) book shows how the work of Foucault can serve the work of planning historians and theorists. Foucault's research can be useful not for his substantive views on modern society—views that have been misapplied, I would argue[13]—but for his methodological contributions, in particular for his approach to the issues of knowledge, power, and subjectivity. His perspective implies that our traditional distinctions between structure and agency, knowledge and power, objectivity and subjectivity, need to be overcome: There is no agency without structure; knowledge and power are mutually dependent; subjectivity is the product of objective practices. This is not the place to explain these arguments at length and to redo, much more poorly, the work that others have done. Yet a couple of points that have a direct bearing on the issue of representation and on the study of planning practice deserve further discussion.

The relationship between knowledge and power has traditionally been studied in planning in terms of the unequal distribution of information and the contribution of ideology to domination. Instead, focusing on practices of representation entails analyzing the ongoing constitution of knowledge, and not only its static distribution, as well as analyzing strategies of action, and not only of the ideologies that legitimate behavior. If "the traditional epistemology of (professional) practice holds a potential for coercion" (Schön, 1983, p. 345), it is not merely because planners have been corrupted by an "ideology of planning" that helps them justify their contribution to the reproduction of capitalist order (Harvey, 1978). It is also because the practical means by which planners gather data and transform it into meaningful and useful information—say, surveys and statistical analysis—give voice to some more than to others and privilege certain interests and wants over others. That the American planners mentioned by Lisa Peattie (1987) in her book on Ciudad Guayana designed a city to the greater benefit of the dominant groups of Venezuela cannot simply be explained by their own class origins or the origin of their monthly checks. That fact must be explained in terms of "the organization of the planning enterprise and the techniques used for planning" (Peattie, 1987, p. 163), for instance the ways in which local residents were represented (or not represented) in decision making or the ways in which the conditions of the site were analyzed.

Planning theorists who belong to Hoch's category of "new pragmatists" have clearly moved beyond issues of ideology and the distribution of information. Using the language of collective empowerment, they have also moved beyond a purely negative definition of power, a definition based on what Foucault (1980a) calls the "repressive hypothesis" and that ascribes to power only the capacity to reduce and limit. However, one more step needs to be taken. We need to move away from the idea that power is a capacity one has or doesn't have, as well as from the idea that relations of power are direct lines between a group of oppressors and a group of oppressed (Foucault, 1980b). We should look for power in its exercise, in the practices by which people constrain what others and they themselves can do. We should see relations of power as complex fields in which all actors form and transform themselves according to the requirements of the strategic relations in which they are involved. This means that the exercise of power is an action on subjects of interaction as well as on objects of action; it shapes who we are at the same time as it manipulates things and people. It does more than constrain: It makes us know and understand. But it does so in specific ways, in ways that create the world we take as given and shape the identities we see as natural, our own included.[14] "Power," Dreyfus and Rabinow (1983) explain, "is exercised upon the dominant as well as on the dominated; there is a process of self-formation or autocolonization involved." They add an illustration: "In order for the bourgeoisie to establish its class domination during the nineteenth century, it had to form itself as a class. . . . there was first a dynamic exercising of strict controls primarily on its own members" (p. 186).

The idea that power has an influence on identity is, of course, not unique to the work of Foucault. It is part and parcel of Steven Lukes's (1974) theory of power, and it has found expression in planning theory as well. Forester (1989), as we have seen earlier, agrees that "exercise of power exists in the ability of major actors to shape the self-conceptions, the sense of legitimate expectations, and finally the needs of citizens" (p. 44). However, the distinction between major actors and citizens should not make us lose sight of the fact that some effects of power shape all actors, major and minor.[15] More important, the distinction should not make us forget that between major actors and citizens we generally find a set of intermediaries who help the major actors plan and implement. These intermediaries are members of the professions, people who have internalized particular cognitive and behavioral systems and who would love to see others internalize them as well. The exercise of power shapes the reality we take for granted when thinking and acting; it creates our sense of "what . . . counts as being self-evident, universal and necessary" (Foucault, 1991, p. 76). Planning is one of the professions (albeit a minor one) that, in modern society, have played a key role in shaping reality.

Students of planning (and policy analysis) have recognized the importance of systems of meaning. One scholar writes of the profession's "paradigms of inquiry and analysis" (Anderson, 1985, p. 197), another of its "mental blinders" (Smith, 1979, p. 248), and a third of its modes of representation that rest on the "inherent violence" of abstraction (Lefebvre, 1991, p. 289). The last idea forces us to ask ourselves whether the effects of objectification and abstraction, of formalization and codification, are purely negative, or if a mode of representation that is "inherently violent" has redeeming values. Take the simple and innocuous street plan, for example, that planners (and others) so often use as underlay for their maps. The street plan reveals a highly abstracted representation of urban space. Of urban space indeed: place does not exist, only space does, that is, a homogeneous medium in which activities, in particular the planner's activities, can unfold without influence or hindrance from subjective thought or old practices. Rational planning demands the objective identification of elements in space and, therefore, the objectivation of space itself. This abstraction of space does violence to the people who are attached to a place and even to the planners who try to understand that place and its inhabitants.

To remedy the self-imposed limitations of planning, two avenues can be taken. We can foster a more phenomenological understanding of urban space and society in the profession. At the same time, as we affirm that professional city planners are necessary to control, rationalize, and guide urban development, we can subject professional practices of knowing and doing to constructive criticism. We can scrutinize forms of knowledge and action for their social effects and, in part to further that goal, we can analyze the historical conditions under which these forms have been molded. The media through which planners perceive the world, the theories that help them understand it, the normative schemes they apply to evaluate it, and the role frames on which they rely to make sense of their own action in it (Schön, 1983)—these cognitive systems are the products of historical processes, as are the systems of activity in which planners are engaged on a daily basis. Much can be learned by studying the structures within which planners must act, the historical and institutional "stage" on which "complexly structured social action" takes place (Forester, 1990, pp. 43-44).

I would like to insist in particular on the value of historical research for the study of planning, on its value in helping us bridge the gap between theory and practice. It can help, in particular, by highlighting the unity of understanding and action in professional practices. Paul Rabinow (1989), for instance, explains what made the emergence of modern planning in France both intellectually and socially possible, namely a new way of conceiving of the city and of its problems, a conception that made urban society into an object of public intervention. The unity of knowledge and action is most apparent in the role that key concepts have played in the emergence and evolution of planning. We should remember, for instance, that the first national planning conferences were called "National Conference on City Planning and the Problems of Congestion." The concept of congestion was fundamental to the development of modern city planning. It helped define the problem of the city and organize public intervention at the turn of the century (Scott, 1971). The French planning and housing historian Christian Topalov (1988) emphasizes the dual role of the category of congestion in structuring discourse as well as practice in the reform era. "This category," he writes,

> is at the center of an ensemble that inextricably links knowledge and evaluation, objectives and techniques of action. It is simultaneously cognitive and practical, and thereby gives reformist action the legitimacy and the instruments of science, at the same time as it organizes scientific thought in function of a project of social transformation. (p. 12; author's translation)

Topalov also notes that the term *congestion*, as used in planning, is a metaphor. Echoing remarks made about the metaphor of the tide from the BRA document, he writes that being a figure of speech endows the notion with great "imaginary efficacy." He adds:

> The use of the term (congestion) makes it possible to affirm the unity of heterogeneous phenomena, the classification and respective causes of which will afterwards be learnedly discussed. At the same time, it supplies the strategic orientation around which all the tactical and technical apparatuses [*dispositifs*] will be ordered. (pp. 12-13)

Recent work on the history of zoning and subdivision controls is another source of inspiration. Marc Weiss (1987), for example, explains what made the use of certain techniques of regulation by American planners practically and politically valuable. By describing the participation of the real estate industry in the creation of our city planning apparatus, Weiss contributes to our understanding of the political processes that led to the institutionalization of planning as a public function and to the adoption of specific planning techniques as tools for the exercise of that function. Then as now, the professional identity and culture of planners has been shaped in accordance with particular perceptions of social problems and in response to pressures from specific social interests. Thus community builders (builders of large-scale residential developments) put the need for public planning on the political agenda and pushed for planning to be accepted as a legitimate function of government. Most important, perhaps, they helped develop specific procedures of land-use planning: "Technological and institutional changes, government and industry policies, were consciously created and shaped with the purpose of achieving the goal of community building" (Weiss, 1987, p. 160). The result was an integrated set of planning institutions and a coherent set of planning techniques and instruments. This "planning system, including deed restrictions, zoning and subdivision regulations, master plans, and agency review, all represented a newly designed system of administrative coordination" (Weiss, 1987, p. 161)—a system designed for specific purposes (e.g., the orderly creation of large residential developments) and with specific interests in mind (e.g., profit making).

But not only did the new planners provide support for a specific form of private enterprise; not only did they sustain a specific form of urban development; not only did they develop the necessary ideology to justify their activities in the face of structural inequality. They also adopted and transmitted to later generations of planners the particular modes of representation that served the purposes of the time. Not only did they acquire and diffuse certain theories of the city, certain political values, and certain conceptions of their own role. They also learned and taught to others how to use specific types of maps, styles of language, and techniques of evaluation.

The modern planning apparatus was shaped under political and economic pressure, under the influence of a variety of actors pursuing diverse ends. From them came a set of institutions, discourses, and practices that still haunt us and help us today. The growing presence of real estate financing in planners' education and practice provides a contemporary illustration of this process. The point is not that these techniques are inherently bad. Mastery of the ins and outs of real estate financing is surely beneficial to planners and to local communities in negotiations with developers or in the creation of low-cost housing. The point, rather, is that planners must be able to use such techniques critically. That is, they need to understand fully their social and political implications and should learn to apply these techniques in ways that benefit people who are at a disadvantage. Likewise, the development of geographic information systems is likely to have a profound impact on planning practice. With the new tools come specific ways of representing and modeling reality. It is imperative for planning educators to sensitize (prospective) planners to the particularity and limited validity of these forms of symbolization and analysis.

IMPLICATIONS FOR RESEARCH AND EDUCATION

Based on the preceding analysis, I would like to make five observations. The first two concern planning theory and research, the other three concern planning education. First, it is important that planning theory and planning history not be treated as separate endeavors. Because planning practice is historically staged, planning history can give us a deeper understanding of the structures within which planners work today.[16] Historical research can help explain what planners do by shedding light on the conditions of their practice. By the conditions of practice can be understood, on the one hand, the historically produced institutions within which planners work and, on the other hand, the historical developments that made possible the emergence of their practices. A useful point of departure is the idea that planning has evolved because people have used different means of making crises and problems of urban society amenable to public action. Therefore we have to study the concepts and models that planners have brought to bear on reality to analyze and evaluate it, and we need to study the techniques and institutions that they have developed in order to structure and coordinate their efforts. A return to the period in which new ideas emerged will inform us about what made them possible and valuable; a look back at the years in which new procedures were developed and adopted will tell us about their preconditions and their purposes. These insights, in turn, will help us understand the contemporary effects of modes of thinking and doing, the constraints and dilemmas that they generate for planners (Fischler, 1993).

A second conclusion is that the "communicative turn in planning theory" is a welcome development (Healey, 1993).[17] With three vignettes, I have tried to show that the practical meaning of communication can be better understood if one takes into account, on the one hand, the formal characteristics of representation and, on the other hand, the relationship between symbolic and political representation. By analyzing a representation in the light of the constraints imposed and the opportunities offered by a specific instrument of symbolization, we are able to grasp more fully the meaning of the discursive action taking place, in particular its political meaning. Seeing a statement (verbal or graphic) not only as a description but also as a strategic move in a struggle to define the problem (and shape its solution) makes us more sensitive to the dilemmas that planners face. In addition, we will be in a better position to sensitize planners to issues of power in planning if we study communication from the wider perspective of representation. Communication has a material and organizational support that structures interaction and gives different people and groups access to arenas of problem framing, agenda setting, and decision making.

The emphasis on communication found in much critical planning theory is justified insofar as most of what planners do is indeed to communicate. Yet a theory of planning-as-communication-only could be seen as a concession to those who argue that planners exercise no control over the implementation of (their) plans, that they deal solely with process and not with product. For those who believe that the mandate of the planning profession is, like that of any profession, not just to talk and argue but to make things happen, and for those who believe that planning theory must also take results into account, the issue of power has a very different meaning than it has sometimes been assigned. Gone is the purely negative view of power, the view of power as repression, the view of power as something inherently destructive, as something "dirty." Instead, there is an understanding of power as a necessity of political action, as a natural component of interaction between people with diverging interests. According to this view, planners too exercise power; they cannot avoid doing so. But historically they have been primarily a means by which others have exercised power. In addition, planners have too often failed to recognize this state of affairs and have too rarely been able to justify receiving greater latitude and freedom in their exercise of power.

To help planners exercise power in a more independent way, educators can sensitize prospective planners to the institutional context of planning; they can enable them to deal more productively with the social structures and organizations within which they will work. In particular, they can help planners assert with greater effectiveness the validity of their views and objectives. A critical and empowering planning education teaches students that "urban politics is not a simple marketplace of ideas where truth is bound to prevail in the long run" (Smith, 1979, p. 263). Planners cannot simply claim to have Truth and Rationality on their side. And although Reason is their guide, it can only lead them to where they want to go, where their own interests and values take them. Professionals should therefore be able to argue convincingly for their particular ethical and political positions, to articulate and legitimate their own interests and principles. They should learn "to construct, assess, and present normative arguments because planning practice will demand these abilities—not incidentally but fundamentally" (Forester, 1989, p. 201). Both practitioners and theorists need to confront issues of ethics and political philosophy because the legitimation of progressive planning, indeed the empowerment of progressive planners, depends on a clear sense of value and on its articulation in the public sphere.

To help planners work effectively within their institutional context, educators should inform their students about their future social positions and duties. This second recommendation echoes Emile Durkheim's (1956) call for a critical education in his course on pedagogy. Teaching their jobs to teachers, he claimed, means not just to communicate to practitioners-to-be a certain number of procedures and recipes but to give them a full consciousness of their function. One need not accept Durkheim's functionalism to see the virtue of his idea. The goal is to make future professionals aware of their position in the political-economic system that produces urban space and to make them conscious of the models, theories, and ideologies that inform and legitimate their work. This should not be taken in a purely negative way, even if the terms used have radical connotations. One need not follow David Harvey all the way in his indictment of planning as the coordination and legitimation of the urbanization of capital. Planning is there to rationalize urban development indeed. Its purpose is to rationalize, first, by applying knowledge to action and by making that action and its outcomes efficient. Its purpose is to rationalize, second, by submitting planning to moral reasoning. The traditional justification for governmental intervention, of which planning is one type, does hold up in the face of critique: to provide public goods and to promote social equity. But planning students should know the historical and institutional stage on which they will try to perform these tasks.

A third and final conclusion for planning education comes from the analysis of forms of representation. Both the forms themselves and the uses to which they are being put are important. As rules of a game, all forms impose certain constraints and grant certain opportunities. The procedures that planners use to apply knowledge to action have particular potentials and limitations with respect to the creation of knowledge and the conduct of action. Every form of representation and of planning is better able to account for some phenomena and aspects of reality than for others; it is more open to one group of interests than to a different one; it is more capable of solving one type of problem than another. In terms of professional culture, the modes of representation that planners tend to master are those that the earliest planning professionals used: the architectural drawing, the technical diagram, the statistical table. Written and oral expression, the prime weapons of political reformers, somehow did not gain the institutional status that the other modes acquired. The history of planning being what it is, planners are better equipped intellectually to process abstract information on a plan area than to use personal testimonies of life in the neighborhood, and more at ease performing a benefit-cost analysis than they are in directing a process of consensus building. Likewise they are better equipped institutionally to design an urban design plan for a neighborhood than to implement that plan or to foster economic revitalization in that same neighborhood.

Instruments of thought and action have all been developed in response to the needs and demands of historically situated actors. But it is within the capacity of every generation to adapt and alter what its members have inherited, to modify the application of techniques and to invent new ones, to adapt rules to new circumstances and to use existing ones for new strategic purposes. This capacity cannot be taught, perhaps, but planners will be in a better position to overcome the limitations of the tools at their disposal if they understand the ends for which these means were created, on the one hand, and the inherent limitations and potential of these means, on the other.

There is no lack of important research projects for planning theorists, historians, and educators to undertake. Whatever their choice of focus, a critical perspective will be de rigueur, a perspective that directs our attention to the ways in which power is exercised in the creation of plans and in the creation of tools of planning. According to this perspective, planners are not only victims of or relays for the exercise of power by dominant parties; they also exercise power themselves. And they not only affect others by their exercise of power, they are themselves affected as subjects who exercise power. The education of critical planners is also the education of self-critical planners, of practitioners who challenge "the institutions and power arrangements that support [their] practice" (Innes, 1990, p. 41). To use a rather ugly word, it problematizes planning as it teaches it.

Surely, the point is not to condemn all institutionalized systems of cognition and action, to condemn rationalization or abstraction as such, or to condemn professionalism and specialization per se. The point is to try and improve their applications and, first of all, to know what price we are paying for them. "People," Foucault once said, "know what they do; they frequently know why they do what they do; but what they don't know is what what they do does" (Dreyfus & Rabinow, 1983, p. 187).

NOTES

1. See, for example, the work of Innes (1992) herself on "Group Processes and the Social Construction of Growth Management."

2. I use the term *planners* to refer to urban planners working for the government and the term *planning* to refer to public intervention in urban processes.

3. Having mentioned the names of Foucault and Habermas, I must clarify that this chapter is not an exercise in postmodern thinking at the expense of modernism. I take a pragmatic road: Social theory is an intellectual toolbox for planning theory. If a theory can in any way help us make sense of planning practice, then that theory's label as pre-something or post-whatever should be disregarded without any feeling of guilt. If only specific parts of a scholar's work open up new vistas on planning, then the rest of that work can be put aside without scruples. Without worrying too much about the philosophical differences between schools of thought that heavy-handed and jargon-filled writings describe, we should search for concepts and models that can help us make sense of things in a constructive way.

4. The original sentence is: "What do we claim when we claim that we understand the semiotic means by which, in this case, persons are defined to one another?"

5. In terms of approaches to language and communication, the shift is one from Habermas to Bourdieu and Foucault, from an emphasis on the universal truth conditions of utterances to an emphasis on the historical and social conditions under which they are produced and received (Bourdieu, 1991; Foucault, 1972; Habermas, 1979, 1984). This shift is also implicit in John Forester's (1989, p. 43) argument that there is a distinction between legitimate and illegitimate, necessary and needless, unavoidable and avoidable, involuntary and deliberate distortions of communication. The issue is not distortion as such but the fact that certain instances of distortions—that is, illegitimate, needless ones—are bad (my term). The problem is to distinguish these bad instances from the good ones and, more important, to recognize that one also exercises power when legitimately distorting communication. The problem, in other words, is purely ethical and thoroughly political. In this perspective, "good" communication is not true to reality as much as it is true to a good cause.

6. For a historical perspective on the tension between the verbal and the visual in city planning, see Françoise Choay's (1980) study of the seminal works of urbanism. The various forms that the General Plan has taken over the last decades attests to the actuality of the issue: Proponents of visionary plans (i.e., graphic designs of the future city) are pitted against believers in policy plans (verbal statements of problems, goals, and opportunities). The difference between plans made by municipal "subarea planners" and those produced by neighborhood organizations, as discussed by Barry

Checkoway (1984), is also noteworthy. The latter, he writes, are "not a series of colored designs describing an ideal future but a statement of practical problems and community-based strategy searching for resources" (p. 106).

7. In the case studied in this chapter, the planners resorted to the distribution of brochures and the presentation of slides, as well as the organization of hearings for feedback on what they had written and shown. These choices indicate not only that the planners had the authority to publish documents and to shape the form of public input but also that they preferred to interact in ways that maintained their distinct professional status and allowed them not to face the local population in a dialogue of equals.

8. It is true that representations are not always being made (written, drawn) by planners. Yet insofar as representations carry their proposals and insofar as people receive and perceive representations as products of a planning effort, one may consider them as the expression of the planners' ideas and values. Whether or not they use technical assistance, planners are responsible for what they present in their interaction with others.

9. It must be noted that the strategy did not bear its expected fruit and that the Dudley Square area has become the site of a very interesting grassroots planning effort. The Dudley Street Neighborhood Initiative (DSNI), a local organization that was opposed to the BRA intervention when the document under analysis was issued, has since been recognized as a semi-official planning and development agency for the area. DSNI organized a truly participatory planning process, the validity of which was acknowledged by the BRA. DSNI managed to create a development corporation, Dudley Neighbors, Inc., endowed with the power of eminent domain. Long-term organizing, technical skills, and political support (from Mayor Flynn, among others) have contributed to its success (Institute for Community Economics, 1990). As this chapter went to press, notice arrived of a new book devoted to the DSNI experience (Medoff & Sklar, 1994).

10. On the specificity of photography, see the analyses of Barthes (1978) and Sontag (1977). However, the distinction between drawing and photograph is put into question by computer applications that allow for the extensive manipulation of photographic images.

11. This may be due to the fact that in language, meaning arises from synthesis rather than from addition (as is the case in pictorial representation), from the space between and around the words, as it were, rather than from the words themselves (Merleau-Ponty, 1960, chap. 1 and 2).

12. For a study on the role of metaphors in organization building, see Yanow's (1992) work on the Israel Corporation of Community Centers.

13. Although it is not fair to single out one piece of work for criticism, I believe that M. Christine Boyer's (1983) history of American city planning illustrates the problem. Boyer depicts planning as a disciplinary enterprise and society at large as a disciplinary system. I believe that modern planning can be more accurately characterized as a regulatory activity relying on sociological normalization (rather than disciplinary normalization) and that disciplinary institutions must be seen as very specific parts, inherited from the 19th century, of 20th-century society (Burchell, Gordon, & Miller, 1991; Ewald, 1986). Thus, in Christian Topalov's (1988) history of U.S. planning, the part of the monograph that deals with the first phase of modern city planning is entitled "L'âge des réformes: du corps à corps disciplinaire à la norme scientifique (1900-1920)." This title, which can be (loosely) translated as "The age of reforms: From bodily

discipline to scientific norms (1900-1920)," makes clear that the primary object of disciplinary techniques is the human body itself (Foucault, 1979). It also makes clear that regulation of development and construction practices rather than personal surveillance of individual activities is what rationalized the city. This does not make the ongoing practices of disciplinary control in modern institutions any less important or deserving of critique.

14. Foucault did not disregard political and economic domination but focused his attention on the origins of what we take for granted, on the historical constitution of subjects and objects that form the supposedly stable basis of our identity and understanding. In a way, Foucault and Habermas can be seen as working from the same point, but in different directions. Habermas (1979) starts his analysis of social life from the idea that speakers and hearers "demarcate" themselves from four "domains of reality": external nature, lifeworld, internal nature, and the medium of language itself. External nature refers to "the objectivated segment of reality that the adult subject is able (even if only mediately) to perceive and manipulate"; lifeworld stands for "that symbolically prestructured segment of reality that the adult subject can understand . . . (as a participant in a system of communication)"; internal nature means "all wishes, feelings, intentions, etc., to which an 'I' has privileged access and can express as its own experience before a public"; language, finally, includes all symbol systems, propositional and nonpropositional, which present themselves "to the speaker and the actor (preconsciously) as a segment of reality sui generis" (pp. 66-67). Foucault (1983), on the other hand, takes as his object of analysis the practices of objectivation and subjectivation that produce "objectivated" and "symbolically prestructured" segments of reality as well as the access that an "I" has to itself, to use Habermas's terms. He zeroes in on what Habermas puts in parenthesis: even if mediately (i.e., systems of mediation), "as a participant in a system of communication" (i.e., fields of power), and "preconsciously" (i.e., the *doxa*, the taken-for-granted). Taking one step further the demarcation from domains of reality that Habermas sees as implicit in the act of speech, Foucault looks at these domains historically, to show that they are changing constructs and to explain their origins. Neither the subject who speaks nor the objects to which he refers in his speech are given a priori; they are constructed historically.

15. This does not mean, of course, that all people are subjected to the effects of power in the same way, or that all are able to exercise power to the same extent, far from it. If Foucault calls disciplinary techniques "techniques of domination," that is for a good reason indeed. That power affects all actors rests on the simple ideas that there is interdependence between major and minor actors in a given field and that the exercise of power has its price, material and especially nonmaterial.

16. As the earlier reference to the work of Rabinow suggests, the genealogical method will be valuable for this project. Introduced in contemporary scholarship by Foucault, this method comes to us from Nietzsche, via Foucault's mentor, Georges Canguilhem. The idea of a "history of the present" can also be found in the work of other theorists, among them Durkheim (1977). "What is history," he writes, "if not an analysis of the present?" (p. 14).

17. For Healey (1993) the "communicative turn" has made research more sensitive to the ongoing processes through which participatns and the city are being fashioned: "knowledge for action, principles of action, and ways of acting are actively constituted by the members of an intercommunicating community situated in the particularities of time and place" (p. 238).

REFERENCES

Anderson, C. W. (1985). The place of principles in policy analysis. In M. Wachs (Ed.), *Ethics in planning* (pp. 193-215). New Brunswick, NJ: Center For Urban Policy Research, Rutgers University.

Barthes, R. (1978). *Image music text.* New York: Farrar, Strauss & Giroux.

Baudrillard, J. (1981). *For a critique of the political economy of the sign.* St. Louis, MO: Telos.

Berger, P. L., & Luckmann, T. (1966). *The social construction of reality.* Garden City, NY: Doubleday.

Boston Redevelopment Authority. (1984). *The Dudley Square plan: A strategy for revitalization.* Boston: Author.

Bourdieu, P. (1991). *Language and symbolic power.* Cambridge, MA: Harvard University Press.

Boyer, M. C. (1983). *Dreaming the rational city: The myth of American city planning.* Cambridge: MIT Press.

Burchell, G., Gordon, C., & Miller, P. (Eds.). (1991). *The Foucault effect: Studies in governmentality.* Chicago: University of Chicago Press.

Checkoway, B. (1984). Two types of planning in neighborhoods. *Journal of Planning Education and Research, 3*(2), 102-109.

Choay, F. (1980). *La règle et le modèle.* Paris: Éditions du Seuil.

deNeufville, J. I. (1983). Planning theory and practice: Bridging the gap. *Journal of Planning Education and Research, 3*(1), 35-45.

deNeufville, J. I., & Barton, S. (1987). Myths and the definition of policy problems: An exploration of homeownership and public-private partnerships. *Policy Sciences, 20,* 181-206.

Dreyfus, H. L., & Rabinow, P. (1983). *Michel Foucault: Beyond structuralism and hermeneutics* (2nd ed.). Chicago: University of Chicago Press.

Durkheim, E. (1956). *Education and sociology.* New York: Free Press.

Durkheim, E. (1977). *The evolution of educational thought.* London: Routledge & Kegan Paul.

Edelman, M. (1964). *The symbolic uses of politics.* Urbana: University of Illinois Press.

Ellis, C. D. (1990). *Visions of urban freeways, 1930-1970.* Unpublished doctoral dissertation, University of California at Berkeley.

Ewald, F. (1986). *L'état Providence.* Paris: Bernard Grasset.

Fischler, R. (1993). *Standards of development.* Unpublished doctoral dissertation, University of California at Berkeley, Department of City and Regional Planning.

Forester, J. (1989). *Planning in the face of power.* Berkeley: University of California Press.

Forester, J. (1990). Reply to my critics. *Planning Theory Newsletter, 4,* 43-60.

Forester, J. (1992). Critical ethnography: On fieldwork in a Habermasian way. In M. Alvesson & H. Wilmott (Eds.), *Critical management studies* (pp. 46-65). Newbury Park, CA: Sage.

Foucault, M. (1972). The discourse on language. In *The archeology of knowledge* (pp. 46-65). New York: Pantheon.

Foucault, M. (1979). *Discipline and punish: The birth of the prison.* New York: Vintage.

Foucault, M. (1980a). *History of sexuality: Vol. 1. An introduction.* New York: Vintage.

Foucault, M. (1980b). *Power/knowledge: Selected interviews and other writings, 1972-1977* (C. Gordon, Ed.). New York: Pantheon.

Foucault, M. (1983). The subject and power. In H. L. Dreyfus & P. Rabinow (Eds.), *Michel Foucault: Beyond structuralism and hermeneutics* (2nd ed., pp. 208-226). Chicago: University of Chicago Press.

Foucault, M. (1991). Questions of method. In G. Burchell, C. Gordon, & P. Miller (Eds.), *The Foucault effect: Studies in governmentality* (pp. 73-86). Chicago: University of Chicago Press.

Freidson, E. (1986). *Professional powers: A study of the institutionalization of formal knowledge.* Chicago: The University of Chicago Press.

Friedmann, J. (1987). *Planning in the public domain: From knowledge to action.* Princeton, NJ: Princeton University Press.

Geertz, C. (1983). *Local knowledge: Further essays in interpretive anthropology* (pp. 55-70). New York: Basic Books.

Giddens, A. (1984). *The constitution of society.* Berkeley: University of California Press.

Goodman, N. (1976a). *Languages of art.* Indianapolis, IN: Hackett.

Goodman, N. (1976b). *Ways of worldmaking.* Indianapolis, IN: Hackett.

Haar, C. M., & Kayden, J. S. (Eds.). (1990). *Zoning and the American dream: Promises still to keep.* Chicago: APA Planners Press.

Habermas, J. (1977). Hannah Arendt's communications concept of power. *Social Research, 44*(1), 3-24.

Habermas, J. (1979). *Communication and the evolution of society.* Boston: Beacon Press.

Habermas, J. (1984). *The theory of communicative action: Vol. 1. Reason and the rationalization of society.* Boston: Beacon Press.

Harvey, D. (1978). On planning the ideology of planning. In R. W. Burchell & G. Sternlieb (Eds.), *Planning theory in the 1980s: A search for future directions.* New Brunswick, NJ: The Center for Urban Policy Research, Rutgers University.

Healey, P. (1993). Planning through debate: The communicative turn in planning theory. In F. Fischer & J. Forester (Eds.), *The argumentative turn in policy analysis and planning* (pp. 233-253). Durham, NC: Duke University Press.

Hoch, C. J. (1984). Pragmatism, planning, and power. *Journal of Planning Education and Research, 4*(2), 86-95.

Hoffman, L. M. (1989). *The politics of knowledge: Activist movements in medicine and planning.* New York: State University of New York Press.

Innes, J. (1990). *Knowledge and public policy: The search for meaningful indicators* (2nd ed.). New Brunswick, NJ: Transaction.

Innes, J. (1992). Group processes and the social construction of growth management. *Journal of the American Planning Association, 58*(4), 440-453.

Institute for Community Economics. (1990). The Dudley Street neighborhood initiative. *Community Economics, 19,* 8-11.

Lefebvre, H. (1991). *The production of space.* Cambridge, MA: Blackwell.

Liggett, H. (1990). The function of crisis: The theory/practice split in planning. In D. Crow (Ed.), *Philosophical streets: New approaches to urbanism* (pp. 52-69). Washington, DC: Maisonneuve Press.

Lukes, S. (1974). *Power: A radical view.* London: Macmillan.

Lukes, S. (Ed.). (1986). *Power.* New York: New York University Press.

Makielski, S. J., Jr. (1966). *The politics of zoning: The New York experience.* New York: Columbia University Press.

Medoff, P., & Sklar, H. (1994). *Streets of hope: The fall and rise of an urban neighborhood.* Boston: South End Press.

Merleau-Ponty, M. (1960). *Signes.* Paris: Gallimard.

Meunier, J.-P. (1980). *Essai sur l'image et la communication.* Louvain-la-Neuve, Belgium: Cabay.

Milroy, B. M. (1989). Constructing and deconstructing plausibility. *Environment and Planning D: Society and Space, 7,* 313-326.

Mitchell, W. J. T. (1986). *Iconology: Image, text, ideology.* Chicago: University of Chicago Press.

Paivio, A. (1971). *Imagery and verbal processes.* New York: Holt, Reinhart & Winston.

Peattie, L. (1987). *Planning Ciudad Guayana.* Ann Arbor: University of Michigan Press.

Perin, C. (1977). *Everything in its place: Social order and land use in America.* Princeton, NJ : Princeton University Press.

Perkins, G. (1987). *Roxbury neighborhood profile 1987.* Boston: Boston Redevelopment Authority.

Rabinow, P. (1989). *French modern: Norms and forms of the social environment.* Cambridge: The MIT Press.

Schön, D. A. (1983). *The reflective practitioner: How professionals think in action.* New York: Basic Books.

Scott, M. (1971). *American city planning since 1890.* Berkeley: University of California Press.

Smith, M. P. (1979). *The city and social theory.* New York: St. Martin's.

Sontag, S. (1977). *On photography.* New York: Dell.

Throgmorton, J. A. (1993). Planning as a rhetorical activity: Survey research as a trope in arguments about electric power planning in Chicago. *Journal of the American Planning Association, 59*(3), 334-346.

Toll, S. (1969). *Zoned American.* New York: Grossman.

Topalov, C. (1988). *Naissance de l'urbanisme moderne et réforme de l'habitat populaire aux États Unis, 1900-1940.* Paris: Centre de Sociologie Urbaine.

Veyne, P. (1983). *Les Grecs ont-ils cru à leur mythes?* Paris: Éditions du Seuil, Collection "Points."

Weiss, M. A. (1987). *The rise of the community builders: The American real estate industry and urban land planning.* New York: Columbia University Press.

Wildavsky, A. (1973). If planning is everything, maybe it's nothing. *Policy Sciences, 4,* 127-153.

Wrong, D. H. (1988). *Power: Its forms, bases, and uses.* Chicago: University of Chicago Press.

Yanow, D. (1992). Supermarkets and culture clash: The epistemological role of metaphors in administrative practice. *American Review of Public Administration, 22*(2), 89-109.

3

If Only the City Could Speak

The Politics of Representation

ROBERT A. BEAUREGARD

If the city could speak, what would it say to us? Would it tell of its moral angst over racial inequalities and ethnic discrimination? Would it talk of crumbling infrastructure and fiscal strains? Would we hear of vibrant neighborhoods, myriad cultural activities, dedicated school teachers, and dynamic industrial districts? Would a rich public life be claimed, one characterized by widespread democratic debate? What would we be told?

AUTHOR'S NOTE: This chapter is based on a talk given at the Colloquium on Urban Politics, Albert A. Levin Lecture Series, Cleveland State University, February 20, 1991, and has benefited greatly from the critical comments of Helen Liggett, David Perry, and Iris Young.

The city, of course, cannot tell us of its problems or its prospects, its successes or its failures. The city is not a speaking subject. Rather, it is the object of our discourse. We speak for the city; it is spoken about. We say what is good and what is bad, what should be done, when, and by whom. The city is represented; it does not represent itself.[1]

In the March 1959 issue of *The Nation*, Joseph S. Clark—a former mayor of Philadelphia, a hero in the mythology of Philadelphia's postwar economic rebirth and salvation from the clutches of political corruption, and at that time the senior senator from Pennsylvania— spoke for the city. He wrote: "Our schools are deteriorating, traffic is strangling our cities, slums are spreading quicker than we can eradicate them, and in the midst of affluence there is poverty." The problems of the cities were obvious and familiar:

> The decay of the older areas . . . ; blight and slums; the flight of the middle class to suburbia; the vicious cycle created as talented people desert the central city, leaving a leadership vacuum filled by those less skilled culturally, economically, and politically. (Clark, 1959, p. 199)

His grim diagnosis led him not to detachment or despair but to commitment.

For Senator Clark to connect his dismal assessment to proposals for policy reform, he had to represent the city in a different way, one that opened up avenues for public action. He did this by equating cities with civilization. The city, he noted, "is more than form; it is substance, life, spirit." For this reason, "the desire to live in cities, the desire for urban culture—these will continue as long as civilization lasts" (p. 121).

Clark (1959) argued further that the United States was no longer a rural nation. He called upon the federal government to recognize this new reality and create a national Department of Urban Affairs, allocate more money for cities, encourage the metropolitan integration of governments, and reduce the gap between planning capabilities and political action.

Representing the city as in dire need, essential to civilization, and indicative of the character of the nation—all rhetorical devices typical of 20th-century commentary on urban decay—Clark established compelling reasons for governmental intervention.[2] He shaped the possibilities for action and simultaneously evoked the price of inaction, thereby casting the city as an object of public policy. Through these representations, Senator Clark hoped to influence members of Congress and subsequent legislation.

As Senator Clark well understood, people will not undertake collective political action in the absence of persuasive representations of public issues and convincing reasons to act. Yet he surely realized that adoption of his proposal would require more than a convincing argument from him. The necessary and sufficient political conditions for the establishment of a cabinet-level Department of Urban Affairs were not in place during the Eisenhower Administration. Clark's compelling presentation had equally compelling rebuttals, and the sum of political interests did not then favor an institutionalized federal urban policy (Gelfand, 1975).

Neither the formulation nor implementation of urban policy can proceed without significant political support, but that support is also contingent upon the meaning that urban policy has for political actors. Murray Edelman (1988) has written that the critical element in political maneuvering is the creation of meaning: "political language *is* political reality" (pp. 103-104).[3] People take positions and act when strong arguments persuade them that these actions are needed and that the consequences will be favorable. To quote the planning theorist John Forester (1989): "What gets done depends heavily on what gets said, and how it is said, to whom" (p. 23).

The purpose of this chapter is to explore the ways in which the city is represented as an object and a site for collective action. My central argument is that discourse shapes our sense of the future through the public negotiation of imagined futures. Expectations are subject to argumentation, and on the basis of those constantly contested meanings we decide whether or not to act. Unable to imagine a better future, we become debilitated. Able to envision improvement and success, we undertake new endeavors.[4]

Those who speak for the city constitute the city as a meaningful object of public debate, even if they ultimately advise benign neglect or abandonment. In fact, much of what has been said about U.S. cities in the postwar period has tended to separate citizens from the city. Americans are encouraged to be concerned but also to be detached, and the resultant combination undermines collective reform. We become empathic but precariously so, such that resolve remains elusive. We are discouraged from imagining ourselves as urban and cities as different. This popular discourse, expressed mainly in the mass media and often by conservative critics, is cynical; it fosters disbelief in effective intervention and engenders political resignation. Discourse "in the streets" is often quite the opposite. There, people committed to their place in the city search for solutions to the irritants and abuses of urban life. Cynicism, for them, is a luxury.[5]

This argument highlights the central theme of the chapter: the relationship between modes of representation and political action. The performative force of familiar ways of representing urban conditions is explored below, using two extended and quite different perspectives for linking politics and the city. The first is a newspaper series depicting the current state of the cities and addressing the need for the national government to respond. The second is the mobilization of a Philadelphia neighborhood in response to a threat to its tranquility.

CITIES, THE MEDIA, AND PUBLIC POLICY

In January 1991, *The New York Times* presented a three-part series on the current condition of U.S. cities that essentially reproduced the dominant rhetoric of postwar urban commentary.[6] Readers were taken to a familiar intersection of public discourse and political action, one that left them ambivalent about the plight of cities, confused about what might be done, and thus indifferent to government intervention.

The series was likely motivated by the then-recent release of the decennial U.S. Census population counts. Those data failed to validate the sense of urban renascence that permeated the mid-1980s. Many of the older industrial cities that had been under the spell of urban decline and, in the 1980s, had been the targets of significant capital investment in office construction, waterfront marketplaces, and gentrified neighborhoods continued to lose residents.[7] Such news reinforced the ultimately debilitating assessment that was offered.

The New York Times articles proclaim poverty the most pressing problem of the cities and seem to imply that government intervention is a distinct possibility. Specifically the political context is one that includes presidential decisions concerning the war with Iraq and a deepening domestic recession. Urban poverty is an "internal enemy," and the title of the first installment—"Suffering in the Cities Persists As U.S. Fights Other Battles" (DeParle, 1991)—suggests that a military-type excursion is needed, a renewed War on Poverty. President Bush is accused of neglecting the cities, and H. Ross Perot, the Texas entrepreneur, is quoted as saying, "we have stopped trying to solve domestic problems" (DeParle 1991, p. 15). Although negative in tone, the criticisms do not preclude, and even imply, a rationale for an aggressive urban policy.

However, before we attempt a solution, we must first understand the problem.[8] Urban poverty is not only an "entrenched force in American life" but also "increasingly destructive" and a prime contributor to "urban disintegration" through its complicity with AIDS, homelessness, and drugs; its inseparability from race; its contribution to the underclass, a "new and hardened population of poor people" that "rubs raw the notion of equal opportunity;" and its laceration of the "larger civil fabric." One cannot speak of present-day cities in the United States without speaking simultaneously of poverty's many consequences and correlates. We are faced with a "second, separate America, a nation within a nation" that evokes images of Calcutta (DeParle, 1991, p. 15).

Such understandings are cast as widespread. Different types of evidence are layered to produce an undeniably dismal portrait. For example, public opinion, as represented by a *New York Times* poll, overwhelmingly favors the belief that poverty is worse today than it was 10 years ago and more difficult to overcome. Problems of homelessness, drugs, and crime are widely perceived to impinge on blacks and whites, cities, suburbs, and rural areas, and people of different incomes. This public perception is reinforced by "seas of available statistics." The percentage of individuals below the poverty line is no longer falling, federal income assistance is shrinking, and, compared to 25% of whites, "72 percent of the blacks born in 1967 spent at least a year on welfare before their 18th birthday" (DeParle 1991, p. 15).

Expert knowledge is used to reinforce these conclusions. Senator Daniel Patrick Moynihan, Nicholas Lemann (author of a book on black ghettos), Theda Skocpol and Christopher Jencks (sociologists),

Sheldon Danzinger (professor of public policy), Mickey Kaus (editor of
The New Republic), and Eleanor Holmes Norton (the U.S. congressional
representative from the District of Columbia) offer their observations.
Each elaborates, but does not contradict, the negative picture portrayed
by public opinion data and the findings of statistical analyses.

Individual experiences, presented in the second article (Applebome,
1991, p. 12), further strengthen the diagnosis. We read of Rose Bailey
of New Orleans struggling to raise her children in a "patchwork of
decay" known as the St. Thomas housing project. Chink Ogden, a
34-year-old lawyer from the same city, moved his family to the
suburbs to escape the threat of crime, although he also noted somewhat nostalgically that "this city was the greatest city in the world to
live in." Irene Choi Stern of Manhattan is planning to leave the Upper
West Side and the "turmoil of the city streets." She has tired of "being
a victim of a series of violent or abusive incidents."[9] This assault of
evidence removes any doubt that urban disintegration has taken hold.
Our gaze is fixed on overwhelming decay and destitution, and this
view of urban life seemingly pervades the consciousness of the
nation.

The discourse suggests one obvious response: avoid urban decay
by living beyond the cities where such problems are not entrenched.
The second article of the series (Applebome, 1991) turns away from
urban areas, not to proclaim the wonders of suburbia and the coun-
tryside but to point out, as the title states, how "Although Urban
Blight Worsens, Most People Don't Feel Its Impact."

The "dreadful toll of inner-city decay" (Applebome, 1991, p. 1) is
confined to central cities. As a result, many people are able to isolate
themselves from the problems of the poor. More affluent households
migrate from the city to the suburbs, jobs precede or follow them,
metropolitan racial residential segregation becomes more rigid, and
political power becomes increasingly concentrated outside of distressed urban areas (Schneider, 1992). Money enables people to
realize a geographical solution—residential decentralization—to the
threatening consequences of urban poverty.

Although suburbanites are aware of urban disintegration, few are
immediately affected. Michael Rosenzweig, a lawyer in Atlanta, is
quoted (in Applebome, 1991, p. 12) as saying "I find I simply am not
forced to confront those problems physically or visibly in any real

way. I read that stuff in the papers and see it on the news, but I don't ever really experience it." Charles Lockwood, who writes on urban and architectural issues, comments that "in New York, you're forced into dealing with people on the street or on the subway; here [in Los Angeles] so much of life is lived behind the windshield of your car, you're insulated." The immediate impact of city problems is "distant and elusive" for most Americans.

The policy dilemma is clarified by this line of thought. If the people who suffer urban poverty and live amid urban disintegration are increasingly powerless, and those with economic and political power are increasingly detached and insulated, what discursive space exists for imagining a solution? Under these conditions, what *deus ex machina* can possibly reveal avenues for effective political action?

The New York Times reporters use a common rhetorical tactic for negotiating the terrain of urban decay, one used by Senator Joseph S. Clark: the equating of cities with civilization. Kevin Starr, a professor of urban and regional planning, is quoted as saying that "in the decline of cities comes the decline of everything." Obviously, sensing that this threat might not be sufficient, another rhetorical device is called forth, the well-known organismic analogy. Starr proposes that cities are "organs whose health is essential to the survival of the social body" (Applebome, 1991, p. 12). We must remove the blight within the cities. If we fail to eradicate the cancer, civilization will wither and the nation will die.

Civilization and national pride thus demand that we commit ourselves to remedial action. A powerful rationale is thus mobilized for supporting governmental policy that attacks the manifold problems of the cities. That policy can draw upon the "many new proposals" devised by social science researchers. Numerous ideas exist for attacking the causes of urban poverty and eliminating the underclass.

In the third article (DeParle & Applebome, 1991), we are told that four schools of thought vie for political attention and support. The first argues that existing governmental programs targeted on schools, housing, health care, and job training have had successes in breaking the cycle of poverty and should be expanded. Advocates of this approach, one reminiscent of the liberal agenda of the War on Poverty, believe that money can be made available and that a sufficient commitment will have significant results.

A second school, building on the ideas of the sociologist William Julius Wilson, emphasizes economic policies to generate a greater number of high-wage jobs. By expanding employment opportunities, training and relocating displaced workers, and increasing educational opportunities, many social problems could be made to disappear.

A third argues for welfare reform as the centerpiece of an antipoverty strategy. Such reform would combine income maintenance with employment and training programs, increases in the minimum wage, tax credits to low-wage workers, child care assistance, health insurance, and government jobs.

The fourth school, represented by Jack F. Kemp, then Secretary of the U.S. Department of Housing and Urban Development, takes a much different approach. It calls for the merging of entrepreneurial capitalism and political empowerment. Kemp favors tax policies and enterprise zones that attract businesses to the inner city and create new jobs. Moreover, he wants the government to develop programs that turn public housing over to its inhabitants and open the educational system to competition.

Expert disagreement abounds, and no mechanisms seem to exist for selecting among competing perspectives. Each has its advocates and detractors, and each lacks the political consensus and commitments that would make it the clear choice. Once again, we seem to be locked into a discursive space in which awareness fails to become empathy and alarm stops short of public action. Approaching the problems of the cities through this perspective thwarts the formulation and implementation of an effective and compassionate policy response.

How is it that what seems to be a balanced and objective presentation of urban problems leaves us indecisive and passive, unable to imagine effective policy or how we might engage politically? Reading this series of articles does not encourage us to imagine ourselves as a nation overcoming our urban problems. Why?

Notice first the emotional sequence. The series begins by positioning us on the brink of despair, using different types of evidence to reinforce the impression that cities are unlivable. Urban problems seem insurmountable, even wicked in their ability to defy solutions. Many people have fled the city, and the social and moral ties between them and those left behind have been severed. Pessimism is firmly established. Then it is revealed that experts have solutions and are optimistic. Good reasons exist for considering governmental intervention worthwhile. However, disagreement among experts quickly dispels the possibility of ameliorating urban poverty, and the resultant confusion leads to resignation and despair.

This emotional sequence is paralleled by a political one. It begins with a deficit of presidential attention—foreign policy obligations and domestic problems preclude directing resources to the cities—and without any discussion of existing policy initiatives. Rather, current policy is implicitly portrayed as insufficient, ineffective, and bankrupt. Yet numerous policy options exist; there is no dearth of ideas on how to solve the urban poverty problem.[10] Political necessity also seems to compel action. Nonetheless, political support is lacking, for reasons never made fully clear. Inaction seems inevitable, and thus reasonable rather than a result of partisan political choice.

Like our emotional journey, the political journey never achieves a satisfactory destination. Political action is always receding in the distance, consensus is lacking, and a host of material conditions— economic recession, the costs of war, presidential inattention, middle-class indifference, geographic isolation, widespread alienation, and the political powerlessness of the poor—prevent us from overcoming the disintegration of cities. The discourse is debilitating.[11]

One of the reasons that this particular urban discourse stifles political action is that it is essentially about detachment and separation. It is a discourse of exclusion that heightens differences of fortune and accomplishment and casts them in a stark spatial distinction of city and suburb.

Poverty and its attendant problems are situated in a social space that few of us occupy, thus reinforcing the geographical and class distances that separate city dwellers from suburbanites. This urban discourse detaches its readers from the subject of its analysis. The readers of the series are assumed to share the opinions and perspectives of experts and former residents. On the other hand, poverty, drugs, and dysfunction are assumed to be alien to the readers. The isolation of geographical distance thus reinforces an imaginative distance that undermines a practical empathic response.

Political response is further deflected by an urban discourse replete with dilemmas. Clarity exists on the definition of problems, but the obstacles to developing solutions and taking political action are incapacitating. Political will is nonexistent, and experts disagree. Even if we had the resources, we cannot decide how to use them effectively. Yet not to act is to watch as urban disintegration spreads into the suburbs.

Political dilemmas operate at an even deeper level. Think back on the various choices presented to the reader. Each is cast dichotomously as an either-or proposition that leaves little room for accommodation and compromise and thereby truncates a collective negotiation and imagination of solutions: economic recession or the eradication of poverty, despair or hope, familiar incompetence or novel failure, foreign influence or domestic tranquility, isolated cities or polluted suburbs, civilization or nothingness.[12]

Static choices exacerbate the pessimism of will that pervades such writings: continue with bankrupt policies or undertake new and untested initiatives that might well be even more counterproductive. Other choices are seriously undefined and a bit perplexing—what does it mean to say that cities are the essence of civilization? Could it be that the elimination of urban disintegration would weaken that civilization whose fate is being lamented?

On the one hand, an urban discourse about choices is also a discourse about political possibilities. On the other hand, the oppositional form in which it is presented is paralyzing. We are directed toward choices that require pure responses. Not to be wholly successful, not to solve urban poverty in one swift attack, is unacceptable and a defeat. Intermediate positions, partial solutions, and contradictory actions are implicitly rejected. The combination of journalistic equivocation and the totalizing tendencies of oppositional thinking result in a debilitating discourse. The overwhelming sense is of dilemmas from which we cannot possibly escape.

Such discourses create new quandaries while deepening and distorting existing ones. For example, not all policy is ineffectual; governments are not simply incompetent, and they are staffed by numerous dedicated and committed individuals. Moreover, neither solutions nor failures are possible in the absence of action. The possibility of failure should not be a reason for inaction. Or consider the choice between isolating the cities and opening the suburbs to socially different and economically precarious urban households. In reality, the geographical distribution of poverty and affluence is more fine-grained than implied, particularly by statistical aggregations that lump together all urban places, consistently juxtapose poverty with being black, and generally make invisible middle-class black households and lower-class white households. Cities contain many affluent households and suburbs many poor ones. Although often racially segregated, African American, Hispanic, and Asian suburbanites are not uncommon. Thus the options for political action are not as limited as the discursive perspective used in *The New York Times* series implies.

This is not to say that there are no political obstacles. For example, any serious solution to urban poverty will engender significant opposition from the historically entrenched racism of American political culture. Furthermore, policies that are supported politically by the nonpoor are likely to be much less efficiently and effectively targeted on those truly in need.[13]

Still, an even more fundamental dilemma pervades these writings. It involves the problematic interplay of negotiated perceptions and shared realities. Within these three articles, this interplay unfolds quite uniquely as we move from problem to solution. On the point of urban disintegration, impressions, opinions, and reality coincide. Public opinion, statistical evidence, expert pronouncements, and individual experiences are all in agreement. On the point of political action, representation and action diverge. We can perceive solutions, and we can imagine the allocation of governmental resources in support of them, but political actors are presented as lacking consensus and will. The paths for negotiating a common understanding and governmental commitment are uncharted, and we are once again left politically adrift.

In a departure from many earlier discussions of urban decay, the reporters for the series explicitly refer to this interplay of negotiated perceptions and shared realities (DeParle, 1991, p. 15). At present, they argue, political engagement is stifled by a lack of compelling images: "The civil rights movement had provided a barrage of sympathetic images: young men in ties sitting at segregated lunch counters, children willing to face fire hoses." These scenes have been replaced by ones that suggest idleness: "young men standing around empty oil barrels, welfare mothers whiling away their days in front of televisions."[14] In addition, we lack a language "that is frank while also being empathetic." Liberals are afraid to sound like racists, and conservatives seem to be devoid of compassion. Imagery and language prevent deep-rooted problems from becoming public issues and receiving the attention they deserve.

In speaking for the city, *The New York Times* highlighted the social and material conditions that threaten us.[15] Not unexpectedly, the series explored neither the structures of oppression that support and perpetuate urban poverty nor the structures of opportunity that need to be expanded.

The possibility of mobilizing affected groups—the poor, the homeless, people with AIDS, inner-city residents more broadly—in order to address the undesirable conditions under which they are forced to live is wholly absent. The politics of these articles is confined to the level of public policy. Notions of citizenship or, more broadly, of a politically robust civil society are missing and hence people are not assumed to be empowered. Rather we (and they) are told to look toward the government (and to social science researchers) for solutions. However, across this avenue, numerous barricades curtail travel. This makes the lack of any attention to collective political action even more frustrating.[16]

Also notably absent from these articles, and urban discourse generally, is any discussion of the necessary and sufficient conditions for a viable urban existence for all people. The "good life" of suburbia is offered as the ideal, with little reflection on what type of society might produce cities of limited inequalities, social and economic justice, a tolerance for cultural differences, and political empowerment. Because our culture lacks a coherent sense of how to negotiate its contradictions and imagine collective commitments, a moral perspective on urban life has yet to form (Bellah, Madsen, Sullivan, Swidler, & Tipton, 1986). Like most postwar writings on urban decline, the discourse's pessimism precludes an imaginative realm for the liberation of politics and thus for a politics that liberates.

The potential for solving urban problems with effective public policies is thereby constrained by discursive understandings based on exclusionary representations of the material realities that shape language, open and close political opportunities, uncover dilemmas, and segregate political resources from social need. Policy cannot be made without first speaking to the problems and talking about solutions. Nonetheless we do so always as prisoners of discursive representations whose weight anchors the status quo.

Is it possible, then, to represent the city more optimistically? If we cannot make the city an object that compels governmental action, can we at least make it a discursive object of collective imagination? For people engaged with the city, unable or unwilling to live elsewhere and faced with the unrelenting frictions of urban life, negotiating the city often compels joint activities. In these instances, success or failure depends in part on effective representation. It is to one such story that we now turn.

AN URBAN TALE

One summer night in 1989, residents of Northern Liberties, a Philadelphia neighborhood just north of Center City, were jolted from their sleep by a continuous stream of raucous music that lasted into the early morning hours. A block from the northwest corner of the neighborhood, a local entrepreneur had established a club on the second story of a large building that had previously been used as a social hall. It came to be known as Club Pizazz, although that was only one of the many names under which it operated. On an irregular basis, but mainly on weekend nights, including Sundays, large crowds of young adults gathered from well beyond the neighborhood, and loud music pulsated throughout the adjacent residential blocks.[17]

Residents closest to the club found sleep difficult on those nights, particularly in the summer when windows were open both in their houses and in the club itself, which lacked adequate ventilation. The music reverberated against the hard surfaces of this brick rowhouse, inner-city neighborhood. The large number of patrons attracted drug dealers, led to frequent fights outside the club that often spilled onto residential streets, and left the edges of the neighborhood littered with beer and wine bottles after each event. The squeal of tires, as boisterous celebrators took to their automobiles, and a few gunshots added to the concern. During and after each event, residents called the local police district office to complain, and every Monday calls went to the city's licensing agency, but to no avail.

A number of residents who were already involved in forming a "neighborhood watch" in response to a small crime wave began to talk among themselves and to others about taking action to have the club closed. With the help of the neighborhood association, a little research turned up an interesting fact: Club Pizazz did not have a license to operate as a nightclub (that is, on a continuous basis), although the hall could be used for single events. The owner of the hall, who ran a "supply" store on the street level of the building and lived outside the neighborhood, was leasing it to the entrepreneur. In addition, the city's Department of Licenses and Inspections (L & I) had already rejected the entrepreneur's application for a license under another club name. Although the entrepreneur was allowed to stay in business because he ostensibly staged "events," he ran many events, had built an elaborate sound system and dance floor, and advertised as a nightclub. Thus he functioned as a nightclub. From the standpoint of the residents, this was an intrusion that had to be eliminated.

Residents talked among themselves about what was going on and what to do. They told some interesting stories. One was that Club Pizazz was connected physically to the bar next door and owned by the same people. Because that bar had recently been raided by drug agents, many viewed Club Pizazz as a place where drugs were sold but, more important, as an outlet for drug money. Another story was that the club's entrepreneur had the backing of a politically wired businessman who had operated a bar a few blocks away and within the neighborhood. That bar had a reputation as a place to buy drugs. Neighbors had complained and, at the time, it was "closed for renovations." The neighborhood gossip was that the owner wanted to run for city office and was cleaning up his act.

The point here was that the well-connected entrepreneur and the budding politician could not be defeated. Representations of their alleged power precluded effective action. In the first case, to protest was to tempt danger. In the second, once the democratic facade of the city government was pierced, the residents would simply encounter a highly politicized and unyielding bureaucracy more responsive to a nascent city councilman than to a handful of mere voters.

A number of residents believed that the entrepreneur was paying off the licensing inspectors. How else could an illegal club continue to operate? The licensing agency argued that inspectors had visited the club, but when they arrived upstairs the dance floor was empty, and no violations could be found. The police captain could not close the club for a lack of license; that was the job of the Department of Licenses and Inspections. (Parenthetically, the club owner was incredulous that the police harassed him even though he had contributed to various police benefits. He told this directly to the police captain, who then repeated it at one of the licensing hearings, as did the club owner.) These stories represent the situation in a very cynical way and close off the imagining of effective political action.

Other residents saw the possibility of working through the licensing agency. The owner wanted a nightclub license and could no longer act (albeit illegally) like a nightclub now that the district police captain and L & I (the licensing agency) were aware of his operation. Moreover, the police district captain was very supportive of the residents and a major help; problems at the club were straining his resources at a time when the police budget was being cut.

Someone suggested contacting the local councilman, a traditional politician whose strength was built upon service to his constituents and not a little patronage. For this and other reasons, he was always suspect. In fact, certain residents claimed that he was being paid off by the club owner. Still he never missed an opportunity to rush to the front of a large group of his constituents. At one meeting, he told residents that the way to get the licensing board to deny the license was to go to the hearing, make a lot of noise, and scare the board into action.

The possibility of blocking the license increasingly became the focus of resident activity. With the help of the police captain, the councilman, an energetic and outraged local priest, and the neighborhood organization, residents devised a strategy of complaint and public protest. The date of the license hearing was determined, people were assigned the task of bringing out residents, others prepared testimony and coordinated speakers, and still others circulated a petition. Northern Liberties' residents packed the hearing room and were prepared to make their case. The petition was accepted, but the entrepreneur came wholly unprepared, the hearing was postponed, and a second hearing scheduled.

To make their opposition even more apparent, a few weeks after the first hearing, residents blocked traffic on the major street adjacent to the club. The police allowed the demonstration to go on for hours, TV stations and the newspapers provided coverage, and the owner of the hall closed his store early that day, intimidated by the crowd. The license for a nightclub was eventually denied.

These residents of Northern Liberties were able to tell themselves stories in which political action, and thus opposition to a very unpopular activity, became possible. They discussed failure, impossibilities, and dilemmas, but they also talked about opportunities for resolving the issue in their favor and linked those opportunities with actions that could be successful.

Nonetheless, their more hopeful lines of inquiry might well have remained just talk if it had not been for the presence of certain realities that made effective action feasible. The support of the police captain and the local councilman, the assistance of the neighborhood association, the persistence of the priest, the presence of legal requirements governing nightclubs, police opposition to the nighttime antics surrounding Club Pizazz, and the lack of organized support for the club were important elements. They only became sufficient conditions because residents were willing to take the time to attend hearings and engage in protest; because discussion was open to all, and people listened to each other; because cynicism was suspended; because people were willing to take responsibility for tasks and to work with others. Early successes, no matter how small, gave them momentum and eventually the residents achieved their goal.

REFLECTIONS

The three ways of representing urban life presented above emphasize different aspects of the city and talk about it in quite distinct ways. Senator Clark treats the city as a single entity with many problems and argues that these problems can and should be addressed through a single governmental policy. As an elected representative of the people of Pennsylvania, he speaks for the city in a legitimate fashion and offers a plausible and implicitly democratic solution. Senator Clark is optimistic, undaunted by the present, and his voice is that of a leader urging us forward to a resolution. Through him, we can act effectively.

The reporters from *The New York Times* are not elected representatives but write from within an organization that prides itself on presenting undistorted news of current events. Their voice is objective, detached, and cautious. The various manifestations of urban poverty are fused into a single and formidable problem and even though numerous solutions are available, neither popular opinion nor political will are sufficiently strong to overcome the divide between urban suffering and suburban indifference or to resolve conflicting expert analyses. The quest for journalistic balance becomes equivocation. Cynicism reigns, and what results is pessimism and resignation.

My description of the mobilization of (some of) Northern Liberties' residents to oppose a neighborhood nuisance casts me as a credible reporter of events but as neither a legitimate representative of the city nor a conduit for the views of others.[18] The story I tell is about people talking among themselves and negotiating a possible future within a socially heterogeneous and spatially fragmented city. Residents searched for security within their community and, when threatened, verbalized to each other the ways of the city as they impinged on their neighborhood. In doing so, they forged new solidarities, drew new boundaries, and (re)created their sense of place. They were able to act together and effectively.[19] The voice that speaks is political and celebrates democracy from below.

Despite having the city as a common object, then, these are quite distinct discursive strategies. Different people are representing the city and doing so in ways that characterize it as more or less susceptible to public action. Clearly, for people to act together politically they must understand public issues in ways that suggest action and reveal the efficacy of citizenship, not just be appalled by prevailing conditions.

If we are to act collectively, rather than only speak for the city, we must negotiate a path through these intersecting discourses. On our journey, we must avoid the cynicism of elected officials (Senator Clark is an exception) and the mass media. Moreover, we must respect two important elements in the politics of representation: the ways in which imagination links meaning to action and the ways in which language mediates the material bases of action.

Through representation we give meaning to our experiences and to the world of which they are a part. We are able to act because we are able to assign moral weight to everyday life and to decide whether we want conditions to continue as they are. As we act, the consequences of our actions change our representations and we reassess earlier meanings.[20] "Unless understanding leads to actions and new experiences," Peter Marris (1987) has written, "nothing more can be learned from it; and unless it can assimilate these experiences within its interpretive structures, the process of learning becomes traumatic" (p. 7). Meaning, and the language that carries it, are central to our ability to control our lives. Without them, we are incapable of learning and thus incapable of challenging what oppresses us or protecting what nurtures us.

Essential to collective political action is the ability to conceive of the world as different; we have to develop and exploit the "capacities to imagine critically empowering alternative political practices—to open up discursive spaces for calculation, assessment, and strategy" (Clark, 1990). Although understanding allows us to assess the strengths and limitations of our capabilities, action additionally requires that we assimilate into our consciousness a sense of how the world might be changed. This requires a critical imagination that frees us from the structures of the present and the past. George Orwell (1961) captured this with a famous aphorism from *1984*: "Who controls the past controls the future: who controls the present controls the past" (p. 32). Through language and historical discourse, the Ministry of Truth convinced residents of Oceania that organized action would be futile and conditions could not be other than what they were.

Joan Scott has offered a more inclusive thought: "There is no social experience apart from people's perception of it" (quoted in Palmer, 1990, p. 180). This aphorism serves as a useful point for reflection on the limits of any analysis that is confined to the interplay of representations. Meanings are socially constructed and those constructions are not only directed by the constitutive properties of language but also by a "material life [that] sets the boundaries within which language and politics develop" (Palmer, 1990, p. 133).[21] Although language and imagination allow us to construct a range of fantasies about the world, even fantasies must be made up of imaginative materials that are themselves historically specific and materially constructed (Williams, 1983, pp. 259-268). Thus, as we imagine discursive spaces for political action, we do so influenced by, but not wholly servile to, the material conditions that compose our existence.

To the extent that language opens up and closes off possibilities for action, constricts or expands our imagination and expectations, reminds us of past successes or hides present opportunities, it contributes to the prevailing structures of oppression or to a politics of empowerment and liberation. This position neither adheres to the extremities of dualistic choices nor poses language as the essential incentive for action. Rather it posits language as mediating but constantly being negotiated and transformed and casts discourse as a form of action. An imaginative discourse of empowerment is both an essential element in effective political action and an imperfect guide. The interplay of discourse, material reality, and practice is forever unstable and unknowable.

Talk about the city, then, particularly as it dwells on decay and disintegration, is also about whether and how we should act. Embedded in these representations are implications concerning the identity of legitimate spokespersons and assumptions about where we should live, how we should live, what governmental policies to support, whether to take to the streets or sit in front of the television, why one should or should not flee to the suburbs, and where one should invest.

Discourses that speak for and against the city, then, like all discourses, are strategic incursions into our imaginations. Reading them, hearing what they say, and being influenced also by their silences, we learn about possibilities and imagine ourselves voting for increased police protection, more low-income housing, or against annexation.

To contemplate public policy for our cities or to consider acting collectively requires not merely an analysis of the conditions available for success but also a reflective understanding of the language with which we represent those conditions. This is not, by any means, a cynical call for symbolic action, "sound-bite" politics, or propaganda, but a plea to direct our attention to the simultaneity of discourse and history, the importance of negotiated imaginations, and the power of material conditions. It is also a warning: When we talk about, listen to, or read about the city, we must understand these discussions as inherently political. To think clearly and act effectively, we must neither ignore nor underestimate the politics of representation.

NOTES

1. Making urban representations problematic is the social heterogeneity and spatial disarticulation of the contemporary city, a point not addressed here but considered in Sayer (1984).

2. On the equating of cities and civilization, see Beauregard (1993b, pp. 9-17 and 286-289), Mumford (1961), Sharpe and Wallock (1987), and White and White (1962).

3. George Orwell (1946) warned us of the political use of language.

4. Fred Weinstein (1990, pp. 93-111) discusses the importance of imagination (he labels it fantasy). My argument does not address the social maldistributions of resources, power, and authority that influence imagination.

5. For a general discussion of cynicism in American political discourse, see Goldfarb (1991).

6. The three articles, in chronological sequence, are DeParle, 1991; Applebome, 1991; and DeParle and Applebome, 1991. Each began on the front page of the national edition.

7. Six of the 20 largest cities by population size in 1980 were sites for major reinvestment and could be considered older industrial cities. Two gained population between 1980 and 1990: New York (3.5%) and Boston (2.0%). Four lost population: Chicago (7.4%), Philadelphia (6.1%), Baltimore (6.4%), and Washington, D.C. (4.9%) (U.S. Department of Commerce, 1991). On urban revitalization, see Teaford, 1990.

8. That problem analysis should precede policy formulation is a central assumption of most policy discourse. See Friedmann (1987).

9. This is an interesting phrase; it allows for all violent or only abusive incidents, a range that suggests quite different experiences. To this extent, the phrase is cynical.

10. Edelman (1988, p. 19) notes how opposing texts support each other and thus make the discourse more impenetrable.

11. Hirschman (1990) comments on the "action-arousing gloomy vision."

12. On the use of dualisms in urban theory see Beauregard (1993a).

13. For a discussion of this policy approach see Wilson (1987).

14. That images are historically conditioned should not go unmentioned. Compare the meanings conveyed by a 1990s image of homeless men standing in an empty lot and warming themselves around a fire with the meanings attached to a similar Depression-era image.

15. On the meaning of social problems, see Gusfield (1989).

16. Popular urban discourse oscillates between finding solutions in government and in civil society more generally, for example, in neighborhood mobilization. On civil society and political action, see Friedman (1991).

17. The story is based on my observations while living in the neighborhood and my participation in this event.

18. On the use of "presence" to legitimate narratives, see Geertz (1988).

19. On the importance of a public sphere where citizens can deliberate shared concerns, see Fraser (1990) and Young (1990). For an extended consideration of how "personalization" of the public sphere diminishes civility, see Sennett (1976).

20. Without reflection on the consequences of one's action, effective action is wholly a matter of chance. However, even reflection cannot assure the intended results.

21. On the constitutive nature of language, see Williams (1977, pp. 21-44).

REFERENCES

Applebome, P. (1991, January 28). Although urban blight worsens, most people don't feel its impact. *The New York Times* (national edition), pp. 1, 12.

Beauregard, R. A. (1993a). The descendants of ascendant cities and other urban dualities. *Journal of Urban Affairs, 15*(3), 217-229.

Beauregard, R. A. (1993b). *Voices of decline.* Cambridge, MA: Blackwell.

Bellah, R. N., Madsen, R., Sullivan, W. M., Swidler, A., & Tipton, S. M. (1986). *Habits of the heart.* New York: Harper & Row.

Clark, J. S. (1959). A voice for the cities. *The Nation, 188*(10), 199-201.

Clarke, S. A. (1990). *Black politics on the Apollo's stage: The return of the handkerchief heads.* Paper presented at the Annual Meetings of the American Political Science Association, San Francisco.

DeParle, J. (1991, January 27). Suffering in the cities persists as U.S. fights other battles. *The New York Times* (national edition), pp. 1, 15.

DeParle, J., & Applebome, P. (1991, January 29). Ideas to aid poor abound, but consensus is wanting. *The New York Times* (national edition), pp. 1, 12.

Edelman, M. (1988). *Constructing the political spectacle.* Chicago: University of Chicago Press.

Forester, J. (1989). *Planning in the face of power.* Berkeley: University of California Press.

Fraser, N. (1990). Recreating the public sphere: A contribution to the critique of actually existing democracy. *Social Text, 8*(3) and *9*(1), 56-80.

Friedman, S. (1991). An unlikely utopia: State and civil society in South Africa. *Politikon, 19*(1), 5-19.

Friedmann, J. (1987). *Planning in the public domain.* Princeton, NJ: Princeton University Press.

Geertz, C. (1988). *Works and lives.* Stanford, CA: Stanford University Press.

Gelfand, M. (1975). *A nation of cities.* New York: Oxford University Press.

Goldfarb, J. C. (1991). *The cynical society.* Chicago: University of Chicago Press.

Gusfield, J. R. (1989). Constructing the ownership of social problems. *Social Problems, 36*(5), 431-441.

Hirschman, A. O. (1990, October 11). Good news is not bad news. *The New York Review of Books, 37*(15), 20.

Marris, P. (1987). *Meaning and action.* London: Routledge & Kegan Paul.

Mumford, L. (1961). *The city in history.* New York: Harcourt, Brace & World.

Orwell, G. (1946). Politics and the English language. In *A collection of essays by George Orwell* (pp. 156-171). New York: Harcourt, Brace & World.

Orwell, G. (1961). *1984.* New York: New American Library.

Palmer, B. D. (1990). *Descent into discourse.* Philadelphia: Temple University Press.

Sayer, A. (1984). Defining the urban. *GeoJournal, 9*, 277-285.

Schneider, W. (1992, July). The suburban century begins. *Atlantic Monthly, 270*, 33-44.

Sennett, R. (1976). *The fall of public man.* New York: W. W. Norton.

Sharpe, W., & Wallock, L. (Eds.). (1987). *Visions of the modern city.* Baltimore, MD: The Johns Hopkins University Press.

Teaford, J. C. (1990). *The rough road to renaissance.* Baltimore, MD: The Johns Hopkins University Press.

U.S. Department of Commerce. (1991, January 25). *195 cities have population over 100,000, New York first; Los Angeles, second; San Antonio joins top ten; Mesa, Arizona, fastest growing city* [press release]. Washington, DC: Author.

Weinstein, F. (1990). *History and theory after the fall.* Chicago: University of Chicago Press.

White, M., & White, L. (1962). *The intellectual versus the city.* Cambridge, MA: Harvard University Press.

Williams, R. (1977). *Marxism and literature.* New York: Oxford University Press.

Williams, R. (1983). The tenses of the imagination. *Writing in society* (pp. 259-268). London: Verso.

Wilson, W. J. (1987). *The truly disadvantaged.* Chicago: University of Chicago Press.

Young, I. M. (1990). Impartiality and the civic public. In T. Young (Ed.), *Throwing like a girl and other essays in feminist philosophy and social theory* (pp. 92-113). Bloomington: Indiana University Press.

4

◉

The Great Frame-Up

Fantastic Appearances in Contemporary Spatial Politics

◉

M. CHRISTINE BOYER

INTRODUCTION TO IMAGISTIC PUBLIC SPACE

Over the past several years, I have been concerned with articulating a theory of urbanization based on the notion of the city composed as a series of carefully developed nodes generated from a set of design rules or patterns. Fragmented and hierarchized, this abstract city space is like a grid of well-designed and self-enclosed places in which the interstitial spaces are abandoned or neglected. Grids generate horizontal, vertical, and diagonal linkages that suppress any sequential ordering of reality. Consequently, these isolated segments of

development—or nodes—represent a choice of architectural styles
and a variety of arrangements that I refer to as *figured*. This figured
city is *imageable* and remembered, because its parts are easily recognized and structured to form a mental image (Lynch, 1960). Whether
these are well-designed spaces of strong visual identity; special
districts controlled by contextual zoning or design guidelines; historic districts whose spatial forms are regulated or frozen by ordinances; shopping malls, festival marketplaces, and theme parks whose
visual decor and ambience are cleverly managed and maintained; or
cluster developments of luxury housing, vacation retreats, or retirement communities: their sense of place rests on clearly articulated
and comfortingly familiar themes. Although seldom related physically, these spaces are linked imaginatively to each other, to other
cities, and to a common history of cultural interpretations.

I have also been haunted by the *disfigured city;* that is, by the
invisible city covered over by this figured city. To alter one's perspective is to see the figured city surrounded by abandoned segments. But
usually the disfigured city remains unimageable and forgotten and
therefore invisible and excluded. Being detached from the well-
designed nodes, the disfigured city actually has no form or easily
discernable functions. Thus the connecting in-between spaces are
forgotten easily, allowing instead a rational and imaginary order of
things that glorifies the figured city to dominate our vision and
imagination. In addition, contemporary notions of the city and practices of the production of urban space reject the notion of the city as
a total entity (or totality): either as an object of study, as a design
issue, or as the focus of development. Instead ornamental fragments
of the city are being planned or redeveloped as autonomous elements
with little relationship to the metropolitan whole and with direct
concern only for adjacent elements within each node.

Embedded in the detached perspective that is cultivated by these
ritual celebrations of urban revival is the viewer's complicity in
denying the concomitant distortions of the ideal of a city as a special
place: the center of democratic exchange and a place where every
person can do well and even expect certain basic social services. Thus
these so-called public places that are making an appearance across
the surface of many Western cities have implications not only for the
meaning of urban life but also for the practices of democratic govern-

ance. Understanding these places in the context of the political economy that produces them and then interpreting the discursive economy that sustains them and makes them convincing stand-ins for the notion of the city as a totality is to begin to explore the political implications of the nodal, privatized public space of the figured/disfigured city.

Postmodernism did not invent urban hierarchy and uneven development or even the spatial separation of wealth from poverty, but the mechanisms by which these are maintained in the current era have not been fully explicated. We might expect, as capitalism shifts its form and mode of operations, that so its spatial and aesthetic politics would be transformed. Thus interpreting the dynamics of the imaginary geography of contemporary urbanization is inseparable from examining the economic restructuring and new iterations of cultural meaning that have appeared in the past 2 decades. Explaining the cultural efficacy and political implications of these emerging forms is one way to catch theory up with practice.

THE POLITICAL ECONOMY OF IMAGEABILITY

During the last 2 decades new forms of urbanization emerged and became prominent. On the one hand, a new network of global cities or command and control centers arose, taking charge of coordinating the worldwide circulation of capital, goods, labor, and corporations. These "first-tier cities," such as London, Los Angeles, New York, and Tokyo, are partly the creation of an integrated worldwide economy, which has blended into one large global market not only the exchange and distribution of goods, but also financial transactions, advertising, insurance, fashion and design, art, music, and film. The downtowns of first-tier cities were transformed during this period into globally oriented financial and business service centers. This transformation was accompanied by pressure for new office spaces, luxury residential spaces for financial and service workers, new entertainment spaces, and new upscale market spaces. At the same time, manufacturing declined in these cities, pushed out by bonfires created in the more lucrative financial, insurance, real estate, and service sectors (FIRES), or lured away to regions where labor is cheaper, raw materials available, and the cost of living less expensive (Soja, 1989). Economic development and revitalization in these first-tier cities came to be defined as attracting and retaining the headquarters of multinational corporations and the business services that these corporations demanded, including international banks, advertising agencies, and legal, accounting, and communication support. In consequence, during the 1970s and 1980s, the first-tier cities were increasingly transformed into work, home, and play spaces for highly paid white-collar workers in the expanding sectors of FIRES.

At the same time, many midsize American cities grew and were transformed into "second-tier cities" by the increasing flexibility of capital. In part because of computerized technology and in part because of the economies of scale of multinational corporations, it became easier for capital to seek out and move according to perceived locational advantages (Harvey, 1989). Given the ease and likelihood with which larger corporations under unified command shift around various segments of their operations, many cities both inside and outside the United States found themselves in competition for new capital investment, often to replace an eroding manufacturing or resource extraction base. In some cases foreign corporations were lured to invest in America, where higher production and operating costs can sometimes be offset by the benefits of having direct access to the world's largest retail market, the latest technological and scientific innovations, and the opportunity to earn superdollars (Ryans & Shanklin, 1986). Several states established investment and trade promotion offices in Brussels and in Tokyo. These and other forms of industrial recruitment competed by emphasizing the labor advantages of their regions, the resurgence of the Sun Belt, and their states' advantageous location for targeting the American market (Duchacek, 1986).

As cities and regions began to compete more intensely for employment and revenue-generating investment, the public sector became increasingly involved in offering support. Underwriting from the public took many forms, from incentives for industrial start-up and retention, enterprise zones, and job training programs to research and development parks, corporate income tax and local property tax shelters, and a series of infrastructure and development incentives such as bonus zoning allotments and site enhancement.

In the process of the race for investment advantages, the American art of city boosterism as an economic development tool was honed and transformed into an obsession, with imageability as a battleground and necessary aspect of marketing places. It is as if marketing the ideal destination of tourism were shifted into advertising the ideal destination for you and your company. In both first- and second-tier cities, the dynamics of imageability involve a complex mix of claims to distinction and assurances of comfort based on homogeneity. Both the urge to differentiate among spaces and to create instant recognition of desirable places developed in a manner both continuous with and discontinuous from earlier forms of boosterism in the service of economic development.

In the early 20th century, city boostering was organized around planning for the entire city, which involved the city government and the profession of architecture. The "City Beautiful" movement at the turn of the century was created in part because city elites knew they had to bolster their cities' image if they were to attract and capture both industries that were relocating from the center of the city to the suburbs and also newly centralized corporations developing center-city office buildings and administrative headquarters. The photographs from any promotional city book of the late 19th and early 20th centuries, the illustrations from a myriad of city plans, or the civic improvement guidelines that Charles Mulford Robinson and other flourishing city planners presented to numerous mercantile clubs and Chambers of Commerce are exemplary. The image of cities was a commodity that could be packaged and sold, and incidentally this activity helped shape the new profession of planners as city beauticians and marketers.

For example, the "Better Binghamton" movement of 1911, which Robinson helped to encourage, noted that in the competition for industries, Binghamton, New York, had special advantages: It was located in the heart of America's manufacturing belt; its water power had untapped potential; it lay close to coal fields and to the largest retail markets; it had excellent rail transportation and freight-handling facilities. The Better Binghamton movement also called for a city plan for the whole city, to enhance its image. The plan was supposed to erase the negative threat of labor and ethnic conflicts by developing educational opportunities for a skilled labor force. It would beautify neglected streets and shabby public places. It would regulate congested housing conditions while also developing zoning that would provide room for commercial and office uses to expand. Furthermore, the plan contained provisions for the water, sewer, power, and transportation services that a manufacturing base requires (Robinson, 1911). In short, the image of the city as an ideal site for capital formation was based on claims to a reorganized and efficient government able to respond rationally to and support the technical operations of company headquarters and factories that the city wished to attract. Developing a city plan and capturing the image of the city in promotional city books, which were sold as souvenirs, were essential ingredients in boostering the early 20th-century city's image as a good place for industry and corporations to invest and locate. Imageability of the early industrial city assumed the metaphor of the city as an efficient machine: like a well-run factory each part was needed and was kept in the best condition to contribute to the success of the whole. This city as a mechanical entity was to be shaped by the needs of the roving capital suitor. Thus imageability was also a way of legitimating exploitative labor practices, Americanization programs, and laissez-faire allocations of basic social welfare services such as housing, health, education, and unemployment insurance.

If an image of an efficiently working city is part of the cultural underpinning that justified the practices of the industrial city and made it possible, we have to ask about the shift in cultural logic that accompanies the imageability of postindustrial urbanization. Two of the central themes were suggested above: differentiation between places and spatial homogeneity. Differentiation, or distinctiveness, is important to both first- and second-tier cities in order to draw on their competitive advantages. Homogeneity is related to expectations of livability and is packaged as a form of urbanity that increases the cultural capital of both first- and second-tier cities yet tends to make them interchangeable and thus comforting and reassuring in their sameness. On one level there is continuity here with the City Beautiful model, but a commitment to a machine or systems notion of the city as a totality no longer appears. The political economy of imageability that we are increasingly familiar with in the figured/disfigured city does not include commitment to the city as a working system. Instead it advertises well-developed spaces as places of distinction, and it promotes their qualities as indicators of a desirable urban lifestyle. The physical infrastructure of industrialization required a city as a totality. This vision lingers with us as our notion of a normal city, but when capital no longer requires the whole city, the dynamics of imageability shift. The postindustrial city requires linkages and dependable well-appointed duty stations, somewhat like the starship platforms of science fiction literature. The fault with the rationally planned industrial city from the perspective of advanced capital is that this mode of imageability advocates the production of static space. It promotes the building of an industrial infrastructure, including the regulation of congested housing and the ordering of public and commercial space through zoning, and it conditions the planning and design professions to administer this vision. But static space is an impediment to modes of capitalist production that require mobility and that rely increasingly on the symbolic world of information rather than on the concrete world of industrial plants. An imagistic dialectic compels the shift insofar as the very core of the vision emanating from early 20th century boosterism is a mode of spatial production advanced capitalism seeks to transcend. Thus we can begin to understand the shift to a new cultural logic based on aesthetics and fragmentation rather than on professional expertise and a rational ordering of the city.

Architectural associations are aware that cities must improve their image if they are to play in the relocation game, but they are less prescient about the mode of imagistic presentation required. So, for example, the American Institute of Architects and the Royal Institute of British Architects convened a Remaking Cities Conference in Pittsburgh during the spring of 1988. Their brochure advertising the conference claimed that

after more than 100 years, the industrial revolution is dying. Smokestacks are coming down; a global economy is emerging. Information networks, instant communications, and fast, efficient transportation allow things to be made where and when they are needed. People and businesses are no longer tied to places. . . . Cities, the basic building blocks of industrial nations, are challenged by dramatic and rapid change. . . .

Businesses and individuals—increasingly free to locate where and when they want—select cities with the finest features and benefits. They look for history, culture, safe neighborhoods, good housing, shops and education, and progressive local government. Cities are competing, and their edge is livability. . . .

Livability is the new measure of cities. It is the qualitative scale on which they must compete for emerging opportunities. . . . New coalitions of public-private investment, especially in neighborhoods, are top priority. . . .

Every city must become a rewarding place to visit and live—a city must be a good host. . . .

Our vision of the emerging city is full of promise. There is potential for spectacular achievement, but we have a long way to go. ("Remaking Cities," 1988)

In the competitive war now being waged among cities, style of life or "livability," visualized and represented in spaces of conspicuous consumption, becomes an important asset that cities proudly display. But as the quotation above reveals, architects do not reflect on the partiality of the images of this new city. Space already fragmented, hierarchized, and homogenized now takes on minute differentiations within well-articulated patterns and nodes, but not outside of them. And in these nodes, design interventions of architects and commercial artists are focused on the discriminating and distinctive tastes of white-collar spectators and/or consumers. Their target is not the mass leisure audiences and suburbanite popular tastes of the 1950s and 1960s. A whole series of marketing narratives have developed that place the new city consumer inside an imaginary representational order that multinational capital now determines and provisionally tunes with the specific distinctions of regional and local taste (Smith, 1989).

EXERCISES IN PARTIALITY AND
DIFFERENTIATION: SELLING THE CITY

Creating both city images and commodity images were innovative ideas of the fledgling improvement and advertising industries in the early decades of the 20th century. The history of how advertising works is a template for understanding how representations of the city, with a sleight of hand, are moved from a total system to the elevation of a partial vision that promises complete security, including a set of distinctions and differentiation from one's neighbor. Advertising's concern is only partly with the referent, that is, claims about what this product will do for you are mixed in varying degrees with the product itself. Advertising is also concerned, and to an increasing degree, with identifying the product as signifier for a desirable life or way of life, which takes its meaning from broad-based cultural codes.

To begin with a historical example, in the mid-1870s Enoch Morgan's Sons, a New York soap-making firm, began to produce a small grey cake of scouring soap with the Latin-sounding name of Sapolio. Sales of the product peaked during the spring and fall house-cleaning seasons. In 1900 a brilliant advertising campaign was developed that turned Sapolio within a few brief years into the most recognized trade name in America. Advertising jingles began to appear in serial additions on streetcar placards, and they quickly caught the eye and imagination of travelers, who eagerly awaited new installments. Sapolio was a mythical spotless Dutch town, and the jingles sounded something like this:

This is the maid of fair renown
Who scrubs the floors of Spotless Town
To find a speck when she is through
Would take a pair of specs or two,
And her employ isn't slow
For she employs SAPOLIO. (Presbrey, 1968)

By 1904 real estate boosters, city beautifiers, and government efficiency experts helped to pass town resolutions to become as spotlessly clean and as efficiently managed as Sapolio advertisements claimed any household could and should be. The manufacturer even printed a play with musical accompaniment for some of the soap jingles, with full instructions for Spotless Town Performances (Presbrey, 1968).

In this early example the referent and the contextual fantasy are both present even, or especially, when the spectator knows that the jingle is just in fun. Enhancing a product's unique qualities, but also providing it with an image that sells, is to instill meaning where none may dwell previously. Today consumers, whether of products or of a city's particular locational advantages, are increasingly urged to buy because they identify with the style of life or the people who use the product or place. The referent is presented in a reductive way, organized more by the codes of urban desirability than the routines of urban life. Under the reign of this cultural logic an actual appearance by a city can get in the way.

A recent report has claimed that advertising gives a greater return on investment than any other kind of sales promotion ("Study to Cheer," 1989). In a not so surprising gesture that links the promotion of businesses with that of cities, 40 large companies, including IBM, American Express, and New York Telephone, formed the Alliance for New York City Business in the 1980s and sponsored a pro bono advertising campaign in print and on television that extolled New York City as a dynamic business center and an excellent place to live ("Pro Bono," 1989).

In the competitive wars now being waged for consumer alliance, marketers of multinational consumer products are less interested in an advertising agency's "unique selling propositions," which give products a specific theme and distinct identity, and are instead more concerned with the ability of an agency to place a product globally and to develop special themes for different markets ("Global Reach," 1987). These markets are defined around consumption abilities and styles of life. Thus the specifics of place, the distinctions of regional taste, the minute differentiations of style become fundamental marketing ploys in the selling of both goods and urban images. As information is the nervous system that allows flexible capital to shift locations, the production of this information from and about cities, regions, and nations selling their locational advantages becomes an important element that successful players in the global economy require. Ironically, style-of-life marketing devices, such as regional and city magazines, place globally manufactured products in consumer lives in part by crossing over and selling affinity or bonding for particular regions and places. In terms of modes and particular campaigns, there is no clear distinction that holds between the selling of goods and the selling of cities.

Advertising is about the selling of goods and cities, but that does not imply that the identity of these goods or cities is presupposed or even necessarily a part of the process. In the grammar of advertising, goods and cities have symbolic claims because advertising structures a context in terms of which they take on meaning. By juxtaposing the image of a commodity against architectural settings, natural landscapes, or exotic territories, an advertisement operates in such a way that it actually encourages viewers to imagine that they also exist in the space of this image and thus through association to transfer the meaning of one set of images to another. For example, one current advertising strategy often presents a given product with a set of goods or images arranged in a theatrical stage set that depicts a particular style of life. Thus there is a blending of entertainment, tourism, and leisure time—all pleasurable experiences that are identified with special commodities and places (Angus, 1989).

Image sets and atmospheric milieus have become the normal background for our modern mode of consumption for goods from around the world. These same image sets are also used to advertise cities and to legitimate public agendas in ways that circumvent, by rendering irrelevant, channels of public debate and traditional concerns such as the public interest. Here again there is a conflation between the logic of city images and the logic of commodity images. In the upmarket, upscale, contemporary city where businesses and corporations want to relocate, the public is offered a series of entertainment sites where a city's culture and history become fused with consuming goods and posing narrations. There is a difference in advertising between the older arguments about the quality of the product and the newer arguments that make the product stand as a necessary *part* of a totality (or style of life). Every consumer's identification, pleasure, and education become linked to a particular kind of subjectivity whose sources are the lifestyles showcased and staged in advertisements and well-designed fragments of the city.

In addition, postproduction artists apply a series of editing techniques that redefine the meanings and narrate new ideological themes for recently designed urban nodes. After the architectural and real estate production of these atmospheric places has taken place, a series of so-called editors rearrange these images for special narrative effect. The duality between the real and the image is transformed into cleverly manipulated complexes that recontextualize the look of a place in television commercials, advertisements, and the outpourings of media graphics, in public celebrations of place, and in architectural commentaries that extol the virtues of spatial restructuring and

triumphant economic recovery. The *part*—the well-designed node—
in other words, is intended to stand for the whole.

For example, the official opening in October 1988 of the World
Financial Center located in Battery Park City, New York, was accompanied by 5 days of celebrations, including boats, carnival floats,
dance and musical performances, and the appropriate circuslike
posters, buttons, banners, and shopping bags (Vagnoni, 1988). A
series of photographic essays entitled "City Tales" was a fundamental
part of the selling campaign. *Vogue* magazine claimed that

> one of the best pieces of writing of late in *The New Yorker* was a sketch by
> humorist Mark O'Donnell, which turned out not to be a piece, per se, but
> an ad! . . . part of a campaign developed for the World Financial Center by
> Drenttel Doyle Partners—a series of two color ads featuring original photo-
> graphs and essays about the city. (Young, 1989)[1]

This advertising campaign wanted to create an image for Battery Park
City and in addition to attract business for the more than 20 shops,
restaurants, and cafes that lined the lobby corridors of the World
Financial Center. This ad joined others by poet Dana Gioia and the
writers Guy Martin and Jamaica Kincaid, all extolling the virtues of
New York City's emblematic spaces. The writers were given a free
hand to describe their favorite public spaces of New York, the kind
of place they encounter every day living and working in the city.

Two city tales were particularly exemplary in displaying the grammar of the imagistic figured city.

Poet Dana Gioia used arrivals and departures as her theme and
elected to talk about Grand Central Station. Claiming that most
contemporary travel feels more like commuting, she noted that one
experience, that of Grand Central Station, still actually feels like
travel as one enters or departs New York's greatest indoor public
space. In this "democratic precinct," really a theater stage, one can
meet people from all walks of life, each with his or her own compelling story. Grand Central's architectural triumph, moreover, lies in
its ability to blend functional and impressive forms that "not only are
unintimidating but inviting. This is a place that recognizes the
importance of each arrival." Yet there is no recognition in this essay
that Grand Central Station is simultaneously a magnificent landmark

structure from New York's historic heritage and a shelter for hundreds of homeless, that every arriving person is greeted not only with a view of its cavernous lobby but also with the outstretched hand of panhandlers and the wretched face of poverty, and that a war over public space has its seamiest sites in the station.

David Rieff's "Feeding Patterns: All Night Fruit" (1993) is another city tale in which New York is represented as a special place, but again in terms of an image that is partial and that ignores any connection to or responsibility for the rest of the city. In this case the photo essay ignores the pressures on city life brought about by, and the conditions of life endured by, its new immigrants. "Feeding Patterns" notes that New York is a special space for single people, who by some magical law all become hungry around midnight. Thank heavens for the Korean fruit stands, which began to appear all over town about 15 years ago, set up by a group of newcomers who made New York into an all-night city the way it used to be.

> It was the greatest event in the lives of single people since the invention of the VCR. . . . The paradox is that it was the arrival of a new group of foreigners that allowed the city to remain not as it is but as it was. (Crilley, 1993, p. 245)

No matter that the essay misrepresents the fact that services supporting figured urban spaces and their associated styles of life depend on the bifurcated occupation structure of advanced capitalism, where contact between well-employed New Yorkers and the foreign immigrant service providers comes down to the privilege of being able, in the small hours of the morning, to "buy a nectarine, a bag of designer taco chips, or a box of blueberries" from a Korean all-night fruit stand.

The cultural logic of urbanism allows the creation of a text that displaces both the end and the contextual conditions of representation. It becomes clear that the differentiation that matters is not among places but among types of places or the emergence of an imaginary geography that sorts as it celebrates. So inside the advertised city, as a place of distinction among other cities, is an opposing sorting system that divides space (not alternative cities) into class-specific sites. Lefebvre's abstract space hits the ground in the nodal figured city, but not because it is a particular *place*; rather because it stands for or represents a particular *kind* of place. Figured urban spaces require and have framed themselves within the partial spectacle of the nodal city. The viewers' complicity in the construction of well-formed images of the city, as well as their motivation in denying its figural distortions, are part of the cultural mechanisms that make it work. In the end we have to ask whether it is possible to retain a critical evaluative position while being entertained with(in) the well-designed nodes of the city.

VIRTUAL URBANISM: THE PLAY'S THE THING IN THE STRUGGLE FOR DISTINCTION

The series of well-designed spatial nodes in cities around the world being produced within the context of global capitalism can also be thought of as theatrical stage sets. A shifting occupational structure in a perpetual state of flux is something that the postindustrial city has in common with mercantile and industrial cities. All three cities operated in ways that radically transformed the means of acquiring the cultural and political capital used to define social hierarchy. Urban spectacles both past and present are part of the vanity fairs through which city fathers fearful and fearfully ambitious make, break, and maintain the grounds of social identities in times of cultural transition. As with advertising there are continuities and discontinuities between the solutions proposed and communication technologies deployed in the mercantile and industrial eras and those now being devised and operating within the figured city. So once again we can interrogate earlier textual sources on theatrical urban forms for insight into the uses to which contemporary communications media are being put in their attempt to manage cultural transition.

Tableaux vivants were popular 18th- and 19th-century theatrical amusements in which live performers recreated static scenes drawn from famous paintings or sculpture. Viewed through elaborate picture frames these "living pictures" in three-dimensional depth were close enough to the original that spectators were supposedly struck with wonder. Diderot in the late 18th century referred to the tableau as a "fetishistic snapshot" in which the transitoriness of the world comes to an ideal fixity (Caplan, 1985, p. 18). The tableau becomes a monument, or a commemorative ritual, to the perfected world that should have been, an entombment of an idealized present in the future, reconciling the mobility and transitoriness of life with a desire for the static, fixed, and immobile (Caplan, 1985, pp. 26, 34, 89-90).

Centered tableaux, "by circumscribing, disciplining, and subjecting disruptive energy," particularly in times of crisis and dispersion, are mechanisms of sociopolitical control (Spanos, 1993, pp. 104-105). If we look for architectural and urban design examples, what better tableau for absolute power, perfected harmony, beauty, and utopian hierarchized order can we find than the centered circular cities and buildings that so many Enlightenment architects dreamed of: whether it be the circular city of Chaux by Ledoux or Boullee's Cenotaph for Newton? These circular tableaux of beauty/power hark back to Greek and Roman antiquity, when spatial oppositions were first set up between the center and the periphery, or the metropolis and the provinces (Spanos, 1993, pp. 33-34).

Eric Hobsbawm (1983) notes that traditions have been invented, constructed or formally instituted when there is desire among those then in power to inculcate a set of values and behaviors through repetition and commemoration. The very fact of repetition, either real or imagined, implies continuity with the past. In most cases invented traditions, like the tableau vivant, arise because the present is turbulent or in flux, and the invented tradition or tableau seeks to establish stability and order through continuity with a past.

In the 19th century these aspects of the tableaux vivants were combined with and altered to accommodate the problems of distinction and uncertainty of position that accompanied the rise of the bourgeoisie. Walter Benjamin (1969) referred to tableaux vivants when he described one of the earliest attempts to capture the street scene of a large city, a short piece written by E. T. A. Hoffman, entitled "The Cousin's Corner Window." In this story an immobilized paralytic overlooks the urban crowd from his corner window. But, Benjamin explains, the observer's attitude toward the crowd is one of superiority: not only because he observes from an elevated window of his apartment house and is thereby raised above the throng, but because, due to his paralysis, he could never immerse himself in the crowd, to follow or be buffeted by it.

From this vantage point he scrutinizes the throng; . . . His opera glasses enable him to pick out individual genre scenes. . . . He would like, as he admits, to initiate his visitor into the "principles of the art of seeing." This consists of an ability to enjoy tableaux vivants. (p. 173)

Stallybrass and White (1986, p. 136) in *The Politics and Poetics of Transgression* suggest that the balcony in 19th century literature and painting takes on special significance as the place from which one could gaze but not be touched, could participate in the crowd yet be separate from it. This withdrawal of the senses from contact with the polluting masses even carried over to the bombardment of the senses that social critics saw resulting from the many phantasmagorias of the day. Forms of constructed space such as the arcades, department stores, the panoramas, the exhibition halls, the dazzling displays of electric lights were thought to flood the senses, overstimulating them and subsequently altering consciousness through sensory distraction. Flaubert claimed the Universal Expositions of the 19th century spread a delirium; Zola believed that department stores produced neurosis (Hamon, 1992, p. 9). These critical insights do not include the extent to which these phenomena also advertised the bourgeois city as an objective fact and established a social norm while additionally protecting their users from the actual street scene identified with contagion and contamination. In experiencing the city emotionally rather than rationally, the constructed nature of the city as artifice and the spectator's complicity in its construction both were displaced.

Benjamin's (1969) allusion to the spread of phantasmagoric places in 19th century Paris is an urban image that helps us interpret the figured city; in this case it becomes the precursor of an imaginary geography that underwrites the homogeneity of places detached from specific contexts, places that become in the end experientially closer to each other than to nearby abandoned spaces. In counterdistinction to the detached gaze seen from a balcony, Benjamin offers Baudelaire, who immersed himself in the big-city crowd, aimlessly wandering through city streets, parrying the shocks of the crowd as he was buffeted about, even while never feeling at home, always estranged and isolated no matter how familiar the scene. Baudelaire set up a traveling view: escape from boredom or a wishful desire just "to get away from it all." But in travel there is always something that can be lost and something to be gained . . . to lose oneself in the crowd, to journey into the metropolis leaving behind or losing one's homeland, implies a separation in space and time and can generate both nostalgia for what is remembered as left behind and estrangement from one's destination. Most important, for our purposes, this act of traveling at the same time implies the demarcation of a landscape or cityscape, the writing of place or topography, and the outlining of places on a map or a guidebook. Thus travel is both escape and coming home. It is wandering *and* marking a route that creates a particular kind of detached urban subject (Buck-Morss, 1992, p. 5).

The tableaux vivants and panoramas that became popular forms of entertainment before and during industrialization recaptured this thrill of experiencing the world as a visual adventure. These imaginary travels combined the adventure of detachment from the uncertain and exploitive nature of one's social position at the same time they provided all the comforts of traversing a familiar terrain. It was the sanitization of Baudelaire's flaneur: what today we might call the Disneyfication of the urban experience.

For instance, the late 18th-century *Eidophusikon*—or Representation of Nature—was a theatrical event in which deLoutherbourg re-presented on stage a series of quickly changing scenes that offered an illusion of travel; adjustable lighting simulated the times of day, season, and weather. Revealing that the age of simulated spectacles has a long history indeed, the *London Times* reported in 1785 on deLoutherbourg's presentation of scenes taken from the prints and drawings John Webber made during Captain Cook's third voyage to the South Pacific.

> To the rational mind, what can be more entertaining than to contemplate prospects of countries in their natural colorings and tints. . . . To bring into living action the customs and manners of distant nations! . . . To see exact representations of their buildings, marine vessels, arms, manufactures, sacrifices and dresses? These are the material that form the great spectacle before us—a spectacle the most magnificent that modern times has produced, and that most fully satisfy not only the mind of the philosopher, but the curiosity of every spectator. ("DeLoutherbourg and," 1962, p. 198)

The *Times* might have added: "in a safe and humane fashion." Rationally, the Western standard of humanity is identified here with travel in which one doesn't actually visit the sites experienced. The philosopher, an identity that again indicates highest human development, is fulfilled by a theatrical artifice made possible by the latest technology.

The panorama was yet another popular visual urban entertainment of the 19th century that used similar principles to gain the same effect as simulated travel. For example, Thomas Hornor's London Panorama was displayed in a specially designed building, the Colosseum, near Regent's Park in 1824. Spectators entered through a narrow passageway that led to a huge circular room where they climbed up to a balustraded circular platform. From this prospect spectators could look out on an engulfing canvas 46,000 square feet in extent (Altick, 1978). When St. Paul's dome was being repaired, Hornor climbed the scaffolding and. aided by telescopes and a camera obscura, painted a series of panoramic views. At the time the heart of the panorama's novelty lay in the manner in which all evidence that detracted from its illusion was erased. If the picture had discernible edges, if it had been flat and not circular, if it had not been so gigantic and overpowering, it would not have been so easy to take it for the real.

There were also panoramic wallpapers, planned as decorative diversions for the entertainment of diners, that presented unfolding scenes or episodes drawn from "The Travels of Captain Cook" or Hodges's "Views of India" or scenes from American landscapes and Parisian boulevards. As we shall see below, the answer to the question of when does travel not require travel is solved in an analogous fashion in the 20th century with the highly mediated terrain of the imaginary geography of redeveloped and energetically narrated urban destinations made possible by new levels of technological expertise.

There is an implicit politics in taking the picture for the real or the part for the whole that reinforces the logic of partiality in advertising discussed above. Again, the selectivity and spectacle that provide such satisfactory entertainment are based on presenting the appearance of a whole that obscures the viewer's connection to unpleasant aspects of the city scenery. The panorama turned cityscapes into pictures like those that hung in art galleries, a series of encircling spaces that contained their spectators, regulated their pleasures, and focused their gaze. The real city, never actually displayed, gradually disappears from view: its chaos, its class distinctions, its snares and vices, all of these lay outside the circular frame beyond the horizon that contains the spectator's gaze. Nothing unpleasant or disturbing could be found in the view. These panoramas were perfect reflections of a new sense of pride, which was part of the construction of the bourgeoisie's self-identity. People could marvel at the decorative and scenic look of their cities, which they now claimed responsibility for embellishing. Thus the panorama became the mirror image of the Panopticon: Both enabled spectators observing from a central tower a surface that revealed everything and said nothing.

Foucault's use of the Panopticon is often cited as a model for social/spatial forms of control that emerged at a certain juncture in European history. This was a time of increased population and shift of that population to urban areas, which themselves were changing. The new disciplines he describes "create complex [social and physical] spaces that are at once architectural, functional and hierarchical" (Foucault, 1977, p. 148). These spaces are real because they govern the disposition of things and ideal because they are projected over and constitute a particular arrangement of these things. Foucault explains that "the first of the great operations of discipline is, therefore, the constitution of 'tableaux vivants,' which transform the confused, useless or dangerous multitudes into ordered multiplicities" (p. 148). This is to say, the form of viewing, whether embedded within new scientific or social disciplines and professions or spatial productions, does many things at the same time. It organizes knowledge, makes objects available to observation, and also produces identities. What is relevant here is how Foucault joins construction and constraint: recognition and elevations of some and denial of other forms of existence are simultaneously defined by the Panopticon, the disciplines, and the urban tableaux vivants.

The struggle to stabilize the culture in flux is carried out by categorizing, by offering a stable and mappable form through a visual array or list. Replication and typification of what is thought to be best about it are strategies in the service of efforts to control. This is the same gesture that provided Paris with a new rational geography by mapping the city in the late 18th century into 20 districts or 20 sections, each with 20 houses per section and each floor numbered and a letter assigned to each door. Every building and person could be located on the spatial coordinates of this rationalized map, which in turn became all that was officially recognized as urban reality (Monleon, 1990, p. 25).

One board game of chance from the same period, "Paris Street Criers," was organized according to a similar scheme. The need to classify and depict in static form what was mobile and transitory occurred at the same time that ambulatory vendors were disappearing from the streets of the city. Their images were coded and codified into characteristic features and topical forms (Mullaney, 1988, pp. 16-18). Images that represented the old city view were nostalgically frozen into a typified view that was totally predictable and within control, all the more for not being real. These inventories helped the spectator to navigate as well as to enjoy the dangers and disorders of the urban terrain. Thus a city in flux was offered in terms of a stable and mappable representation through the visual array, replication, and typification of these Street Criers.

In an analogical manner, within the historic preserves and leftover remnants of the late 20th century, in cities that were recycled for upscale, upmarket residential, leisure, or work spaces in the 1970s and 1980s, the visual imagery of a city's past was literally reconstituted through the use of old photographs, paintings, lithographs, and former architectural styles and regulated through urban design codes, contextual zoning ordinances, and compositional plans. Images and traditional architectural forms have come to be the standard by which many contemporary cityscapes are now judged. In this leap backward over modernism, the nostalgic arts of city building and historic preservation operate like the 19th century genre of tableaux vivants and panoramas just discussed, that is, by presenting highly selective cuts on or reframings of urban reality. They too are related to a mix of commercial entertainment and travel that is static in form. They as well have confused and mixed the relationship between fine and popular art. As image spectacles, they are scenographic visions relying on an art of verisimilitude and the serial replication of well-known views, and they likewise derive from conditions of urbanization in flux. In their efforts to control, in part by distancing themselves from the masses, these contemporary iterations derive and contribute to the diminution of the public sphere. The notion of the city as a comprehensive whole and the necessary contact among all citizens that democracy requires are being outflanked by fragmentation into privatized visual environments of distinctive entertainment and consumption.

IS ANYBODY OUT THERE?
THE DIMINUTION OF PUBLIC SPACE

Walter Benjamin (1978) was hesitantly optimistic about the liberating potential of the new technologies of the camera and the cinema. He wrote in the 1930s:

> The "unclouded," "innocent" eye has become a lie, perhaps the whole naive mode of expression sheer incompetence. Today the most real, the mercantile gaze into the heart of things is the advertisement. It abolishes the space where contemplation moved and all but hits us between the eyes with things as a car, growing to gigantic proportions, careens at us out of a film screen. And just as the film does not present furniture and facades in completed forms for critical inspection, their insistent, jerky nearness alone being sensational, the genuine advertisement hurtles things at us with the tempo of a good film. . . . What in the end, makes advertisements so superior to criticism? Not what the moving red neon sign says . . . but the fiery pool reflecting it in the asphalt. (pp. 85-86)

Benjamin (1978) believed that a new potential for an awakened perception of experience arrived with the photograph and the film. Because these new technologies hit or bombarded the spectator with imagery, they acted on perception; thus the viewer no longer saw things passively but instead was forced to change his or her point of view. Benjamin also thought that camera and film fostered participation because they called attention to themselves as constructors of reality. By slowing down time, opening up hidden details of familiar objects, and through the principle of montage, they presented new synthetic realities. This potentially enabled observers to gain new insight into the constitution of things that governed everyday life and consequently allowed viewers to achieve a new level of awareness and find new fields for action.

Today there is less reason to be sanguine about the liberating potential of the new technologies of mass communication, because electronic communication seems to disrupt critical awareness—images, words, and sounds now flow along unleashing powerful serial repetitions that reframe commentary and forestall critical evaluation. Nevertheless, it is these figural forms stored in electronic audiovisual archives that we need to address; we need to become critically aware of how they structure our perception of the city and its figured/disfigured forms. With respect to the special imagistic power of our new technologies, Marjorie Perloff (1991), in *Radical Artifice: Writing Poetry in the Age of Media*, has explained that today language has given way to a medium that (to quote Charles Bernstein) is "constructed, rule governed, everywhere circumscribed by grammar and syntax, chosen vocabulary: designed, manipulated, picked, programmed, organized, and so an artifice, artifact—monadic, solipsistic, homemade, manufactured, mechanized, formulaic, willful" (p. 47). Perloff notes:

> Artifice, in this sense, is less a matter of ingenuity and manner of elaboration and elegant subterfuge, than of the recognition that a poem or painting or performance [or architectural design] is a made thing—contrived, constructed, chosen—and that its reading is also a construction on the part of its audience. (pp. 27-28)

To rethink the relationship between the city observed and the observer, therefore, means we must also account for the difficult situation facing architecture and city planning in the age of electronic media. Can architecture compete against the imagistic power of the computer, VCRs and compact disks, the art of advertising, the cinema, or television?

Indeed these artifices have leaped off the page and moved into the public realm: in ingenious advertisements, in the sign inflection of billboards, even in the poetics of greeting cards. Such powerful images challenge the artist to move beyond mere duplication. Because images are now sold by corporations, Perloff (1991) argues, the poetic image has become problematic—and the architectural image as well: "Given the sophisticated print media, computer graphics, signpost and advertising formats of our culture, all writing—and certainly all poetic writing—is inevitably 'seen' as well as 'seen through' or read" (p. 120). To see the latter not as phonemic but as ink on the page is to contest the status of language as a bearer of uncontaminated meaning.

An examination of the hypernarrated figured city suggests that both Benjamin and the critics of electronic communication have something to tell us about the political potential of 20th century reruns of the tableaux vivants. They do call attention to themselves as spectacle or artifice, but in a way that closes rather than opens up critical thought because the spectacle as spectacle is a complete and completed reality, a bracketed moment outside of time, foreclosing narrative possibilities. To quote *The New York Times* architectural critic Paul Goldberger (1992) perhaps the artifice

> has always been an essential part of architecture, an art that has long indulged in the fantasy that it was being more original than it really was. . . . Perhaps the real question to ask is *how much authenticity even matters anymore.* Is it an outdated idea in the age in which newness in itself is no longer a compelling concept? Is it that artifice well executed is the only authenticity our time is capable of creating? (p. 34, italics added)[2]

In other words, if we put Benjamin's optimism aside, the potential of modern media to call attention to themselves has completely overwhelmed any discursive space for reflection. Illusion is widely accepted to be the only thing, whereas authenticity is a question that no longer appears to have meaning in the spatial production of the figured city. For example, New York's Battery Park City is praised by one of its enthusiasts as "testimony to the irrepressible and timeless energy of the city to burst its seams" (Shepard, 1989, p. C19). On landfill jutting out into the Hudson River, an idealized city neighborhood has been put into place, combining the look of prewar apartment houses with Gramercy Park, Central Park lampposts and benches, and the views from Brooklyn Heights Promenade. In opposition a critic writes, "If this newest part of Manhattan called Battery Park City were a movie set, New Yorkers would laugh at its impossible concentration of city landmarks in reality" (Hinds, 1986, p. 1).[3] The point is that reality no longer matters—it is treated as constructable, a setup or artifice.

"Our society," de Certeau (1985) suggests, "has become a *narrated* society in a threefold sense: it is defined by *narratives* (the fables of our advertising and information), by *quotations* of them, and by their interminable *recitation*" (p. 152; italics in original). There is in addition a struggle for narrative ascendancy, a struggle waged inside the systems of mediation and artifice. The redevelopment of Times

Square is a case in point. There are at least three different narratives that could be constructed about the revitalization of Times Square. One would be a tale of the defeat and death of an exuberant multicultural entertainment spot that once was its fame. Another would narrate the adventures of real estate speculators who, over indignant protests and altercations, transformed the vital district into a mundane corporate office park as bleak as any darkened theater stage after the show has left town. By the end of the 1980s, at least nine new hotel and office towers were poking their heads above 43rd Street along the Broadway spine, and another seven or so office towers on the mid-blocks east of Seventh Avenue. All of these were accomplished without major public acknowledgment or protest, as the battle myopically focused on the massive four-tower redevelopment project proposed for the southern end of the square. Like the game of "capture the hill," it was hoped that blocking these structures would reclaim the entire square. But while the courts debated and trials deliberated, the ghost of Times Square departed (Huxtable, 1989; Lueck, 1992). Those who waged the battle to preserve the traditions of "The Great White Way" were seduced by a third narrative and the logic that justifies substituting partial improvement for political debate about the effects of the proposed redevelopment. The allure that accompanies the creation of every nostalgic theme park led them to focus on fixing its image, not reconstructing the context that made its image. Lest development sweep away the image—long after the way of life to which that image referred had been replaced—they set design codes and regulations for signs, lights, and setbacks expected to configure the look of the place. Now a decreed amount of *Lutses* (light units in Times Square), a measure used to calculate the mandated amount of illumination required on electric signs that must adorn each new structure in the Special Midtown District, spurt from the facades of new hotel and office towers that dot the area. By calling for flashy and outlandish signs, the regulations intend to hide the fact that Times Square has been reduced to a staid and underused corporate park.

Here the dynamics that overpower the development of a critical sense are themselves illuminated. The remaking of Times Square by lighting is an artifice based on the procedural codes of the computer. It mimics the "if . . . then" structure of commands: If we clean up the vice along 42nd Street then spectators will return to the Square. If we regulate billboard imagery then we can simulate the look of the Great White Way. If we store a prescribed set of codes that outline the architectural styles from yesteryear's faded images then we can generate virtual images in serial arrays by permutations on its set of variables. Yet like computer commands, the artifice is about its own logic, it repeats the mode of travel without travel, and it allows no thought to be given to the external, disfigured aspects of the city. The abstract design and development codes allow the city tableau to detail small spaces and to employ past architectural views for statements of distinction. Yet these selected sites, and the requirements of the forces that control them, never foster critical debate about the spatial politics that have restructured our cities in the 1980s and 1990s.

CONCLUSION

The efforts of urban design and historic preservation witnessed by the repetition of historic districts, revitalized waterfronts, recycled monumental structures, restylized public places, rebeautified Main Streets, and gentrified neighborhoods that first appeared in quantity during the last 2 decades have spread to almost every major city in the Western world. No matter how historically posed and trivialized these efforts sometimes appear, these historical and decorative tableaux are establishing our perception of what late 20th-century urban space looks like. A strange sense of urbanism now invades the city, full of inconsistencies, fractures, and voids. Homogenized zones valued and protected for their architectural and scenographic effects are juxtaposed and played off against areas of superdevelopment, while monumental architecture containers have turned the urban street inward and established their own set of public spaces and services within privatized layers of shops, restaurants, offices, and condominiums. In between and to the back of beyond, lie the areas of the city left to decay and to decline, until the day when they too will be recycled and redesigned for new economic and cultural uses.

Obviously there are rewards for the postindustrial mode of global capitalism, which seeks to identify all first-tier cities as equivalent locational decisions and all second-tier cities as more desirable destinations than their competitors. Cities are known by their amenities and self-promotional campaigns. Their urban spaces are generated as interchangeable parts, assuming that every city can establish progrowth coalitions that dominate local politics and provide livability attractions and mount the needed advertising campaign. As a matter of fact this strategy works *because* of the advertising dynamics whereby the part comes not only to stand for but to be better than the whole. And yet spatial restructuring engenders uneven development. As attention is focused on the upscale urban environment, it is simultaneously withdrawn from impoverished and abandoned territories, abandoning them further and making them even more impoverished. From the viewpoint of democratic governance, moreover, the imagistic face of economic restructuring is damaging because it tends not to be a matter of public debate. For structural reasons and given the boundaries of public discourse, related public policies such as locational incentive packages tend to be invisible. They are not so apparent nor politically accessible as the social welfare incentives that prodded cities during the 1950s and 1960s to focus on issues of poverty, low-income housing needs, and minority educational, health, and employment needs. Indeed progrowth advertising campaigns and locational incentives are considered private market endeavors, even though they target millions of public dollars to upper classes and well-to-do sections of cities and withdraw subsidies from the lower-class and poorer neighborhoods. Property and income tax abatements for home ownership, for historic preservation, for the renovation of older structures, which have underwritten the residential and commercial gentrification of historic and older areas of the inner city, are not considered public subsidies, even though they lower the city's overall revenue base. Nor are corporate income tax abatements and infrastructure provisions considered to be the result of direct public policy, although they sweeten the prospect for private enterprise to invest project by project in the construction of new convention centers, new sports arenas, new office complexes, new luxury hotels and residential structures, new retail and cultural centers.

These public expenditures are written off in the rhetoric of economic vitality as market incentives that have helped private enterprise to reinvest in the city. This privatization of public discourse parallels the privatization of public space. Both bypass, by denial and suppressed linkages, the source of social inequality and conflict. The politics of spatial restructuring are antipolitical in the sense that there is no overall public agenda or city plan and no forum for debate by those affected. Instead of constructing restructuring as a public issue, the spectacle of global capitalism and the power of multinational corporations capture our imaginations, even as they condition our everyday lives and bypass political accountability. Information technologies, which have enabled these corporations to create a worldwide decision-making base and market for their goods, simultaneously have eroded the national public sphere and municipal autonomy. Moreover, their investment effects are not always beneficial to the local economy. Often cities mount campaigns of imagistic revitalization at the same time they are experiencing declines in revenues, which will not be made up immediately, if ever, by the success of private/public ventures. This can compel cities to impose harsh service cuts in education, police, and other public services. In spite of all the progrowth rhetoric, booster imagery, and give-away packages of incentives, revenues from general corporation, financial corporation, and sales taxes are not guaranteed to grow as usually expected. Social services needs continue to grow, making those sections of the city that are already the most disfigured also the most likely to be the real bearers of fiscal austerity (Levine, 1989). These are some of the hidden costs to the imagistic practices of contemporary economic development. The figured city and the advertising rhetoric of cities for sale may frame our most optimistic thinking about urban space; nevertheless the interstitial spaces pushed through the sieve of spatial restructuring not only remain, but continue with yet undetermined relational connections to their actual creators.

NOTES

1. Young, Tracy. Courtesy *Vogue*. Copyright © 1989 by The Condé Nast Publications.
2. "Architecture View: 25 Years of Unleashed Elitism," by Paul Goldberger, Feb. 2, 1992. Copyright © 1992/1986 by The New York Times Company. Reprinted by permission.
3. "Shaping a Landfill Into a Neighborhood," by Michael deCourcy Hinds, Mar. 23, 1986. Copyright © 1992/1986 by The New York Times Company. Reprinted by permission.

REFERENCES

Altick, R. D. (1978). *The shows of London.* Cambridge: Harvard University Press.
Angus, I. (1989). Circumscribing postmodern culture. In I. Angus & S. Jhally (Eds.), *Cultural politics in contemporary American society* (pp. 96-107). New York: Routledge.
Benjamin, W. (1969). On some motifs in Baudelaire. In W. Benjamin, *Illuminations* (H. Zohn, Trans.) (pp. 155-200). New York: Schocken.
Benjamin, W. (1978). One-way street. In W. Benjamin, *Reflections* (E. Jephcott, Trans.) (pp. 85-86). New York: Schocken.
Buck-Morss, S. (1992). Aesthetics and anaesthetics: Walter Benjamin's artwork essay reconsidered. *October, 62,* 3-41.
Caplan, J. (1985). *Framed narratives: Diderot's genealogy of the beholder.* Minneapolis: University of Minnesota Press.
Crilley, D. (1993). Architecture as advertising. In G. Kearns and C. Philo, *Selling places.* Oxford, UK: Pergamon Press.
de Certeau, M. (1985). The jabbering of social space. In M. Blonsky (Ed.), *On signs* (pp. 146-154). Baltimore: The Johns Hopkins University Press.
DeLoutherbourg and Captain Cook. (1962). *Theatre Research/Researches Theatrical,* 4(2), 198.
Duchacek, I. D. (1986). *The territorial dimension of politics within, among, and across nations.* Boulder, CO: Westview.
Foucault, M. (1977). *Discipline and punish* (A. Sheridan, Trans.). New York: Pantheon.
Global reach gains edge over talent. (1987, May 5). *The New York Times,* p. D15.
Goldberger, P. (1992, February 2). 25 Years of unabashed elitism. *New York Times,* Section 2, p. 34.
Hamon, P. (1992). *Expositions: Literature and architecture in nineteenth century France* (K. Sainson-Frank & Lisa Maguire, Trans.). Berkeley: University of California Press.
Harvey, D. (1989). *The condition of postmodernity.* Oxford, UK: Basil Blackwell.
Hinds, M. D. (1986, March 23). Shaping landfill into a neighborhood. *New York Times,* p. B1.
Hobsbawm, E. (1983). Introduction: Inventing traditions. In E. Hobsbawm & T. Ranger (Eds.), *The invention of tradition* (pp. 1-2). Cambridge, UK: Cambridge University Press.
Huxtable, A. L. (1989, October 14). Times Square renewal (Act III) a farce. *New York Times,* p. 25.
Levine R. (1989, April 13). New York City faces bit cuts in services. *New York Times,* pp. B1, 7.
Lueck, T. J. (1992, March 4). Battling for tenants in a slow market. *New York Times,* Section 10, pp. 1, 11.
Lynch, K. (1960). *The image of the city.* Cambridge: MIT Press.
Monleon, J. B. (1990). *A specter is haunting Europe.* Princeton, NJ: Princeton University Press.
Mullaney, D. (1988). *The place of the stage.* Chicago: University of Chicago Press.
Perloff, M. (1991). *Radical artifice: Writing poetry in the age of media.* Chicago: University of Chicago Press.

Presbrey, F. (1968). *The history and development of advertising.* New York: Greenwood Press.

Pro bono. (1989, March 19). *New York Times,* p. D5.

Remaking cities conference [brochure]. (1988). Pittsburgh: American Institute of Architects and the Royal Institute of British Architects.

Robinson, C. M. (1911). *"Better Binghamton": A report to the Mercantile Press Club of Binghamton, New York.*

Ryans, J. K., Jr., & Shanklin, W. L. (1986). *Guide to marketing for economic development.* Columbus, OH: Publishing Horizons.

Shepard, R. F. (1989, May 19). Exploring Battery Park City: A guided ramble around the landfill. *New York Times,* pp. C1, C19.

Smith, P. (1989). Visiting Banana Republic. In A. Ross (Ed.), *Universal abandon: The politics of postmodernism* (pp. 128-148). Minneapolis: University of Minnesota Press.

Soja, E. W. (1989). The historical geography of urban and regional restructuring. In E. Soja (Ed.), *Postmodern geographies* (pp. 157-189). London: Verso.

Spanos, W. V. (1993). *The end of education: Toward posthumanism.* Minneapolis: University of Minnesota Press.

Stallybrass, P., & White, A. (1986). *The politics and poetics of transgression.* Ithaca, NY: Cornell University Press.

Study to cheer ad industry. (1989, April 11). *New York Times,* p. D25.

Vagnoni, A. (1988, November 21). Here's why you may be hearing "it's more New York, New York." *New York Observer,* p. 9.

Young, T. (1989, February). Trends. *Vogue,* p. 191.

5

◉

Black Politics on the Apollo's Stage

The Return of the Handkerchief Heads

◉

STUART ALAN CLARKE

With the exception of casual and often careless gestures, there has been little written on the relationship between race, politics, and postmodernism.[1] This absence provokes Cornel West's (1988) suggestion that "a thorough investigation into the content and character of postmodernism that takes seriously the role and function of black political and cultural practices will shed new light on the contemporary debate, revealing its blindnesses and silences" (p. 169).

West's position is certainly motivated in part by his understanding of the historically specific significance of black political and cultural practices. It also expresses a general annoyance at the frequent distance between speculations about postmodernism and observations and analyses of an explicitly political character. It is frequently difficult, for example, to locate the postmodernism of as political an observer as Frederic Jameson in any stable relationship to political developments on any palpable level.[2] Indeed, West's position on the celebrated Lyotard/Habermas debate aptly characterizes much writing on postmodernism: "interesting *philosophical* [italics in original] things are at stake there," he suggests, "but the politics is a family affair, a very narrow family affair at that" (interview with West in Stephanson, 1988, p. 273).

This frustration with the antipolitics of postmodern discourse is also evident in the feminism depicted by Linda Nicholson and Nancy Fraser (1990). Nicholson and Fraser argue that much postmodern thought functions quite poorly as social criticism because it originates in reflections on the condition of academic philosophy. By contrast, feminist thought, which is conditioned by the demands of political practice, results in a considerably more robust (if sometimes essentialist) social criticism.

This shared frustration is no coincidence. It is more troubling than ironic that as black and white women and black men begin to find themselves closer and closer to centers of power, we are smugly assured that the center does not hold and that power does not have the utility that we thought it had. In different but complementary ways, West and Nicholson and Fraser suggest that the experiences of women and persons of color can serve as both critique of, and corrective to, the political irrelevance (and arrogance) of much academic speculation about postmodernism.

In my view, the very best reason for speculating about postmodernism and race is to generate insights that might enhance our ability to engage in some type of dialogue with some kind of people other than ourselves. In this context, postmodernism is not a set of rules by which attempts at political analysis are deconstructed, nor a grid that properly identifies the significance of social patterns. Instead, postmodernism is a conceptual toolbox, offering resources for use in (power sensitive) conversations about political, cultural, and social practices. The point of these conversations is to facilitate the development of capacities to imagine, critically empowering alternative political practices—to open up discursive space for calculation, assessment, and strategy.

In order to be useful in the terms that matter to me, postmodern tools must be crafted so that their impact can be imagined, if not demonstrated. If this is to be done, then some description of the machine(s) upon which they might be exercised must be offered. Questions of shape and scale are all important here—too often postmodern critics seem to vastly overestimate the significance of tossing a monkey wrench into the workings of world historical systems.

Fred Pfeil (1990) has persuasively argued that "the value of a conjunctural analysis of postmodernism must lie in the usefulness and specificity of the strategic questions that analysis puts before us and the projects it suggests" (p. 118), and this perspective pushes us in the direction that I would like to go. My friendly amendment to Pfeil states that the value of postmodernism as a conceptual toolbox must lie in the usefulness and specificity of the strategic questions that those tools help us to unearth.

In particular, I am thinking of the usefulness of these tools in helping us to engage a relationship between political and cultural practices, to plunder possibilities for oppositional and resistive energy, and to scout out directions for discursive and practical interventions in extant economies of power.

None of the foregoing should be taken to suggest that there is no value in the attempt to describe the manner in which black political practices, discourses, and desires have been marked with the sign of the postmodern. However, such characterizations should be ventured with the utmost care. Certainly some of the circumstances that have come to be associated with postmodernism—difference, marginality, and the social construction of identity—are (or should be) difficult to talk about in the American context without considering the history of African American people. Nevertheless, as DuBois (1965) understood in 1903, there is a complicated relationship between African American history and developments in the dominant culture of America, and certain realities of African American life may be as much a function of a historically unique relationship to the claims and promises of modernity as of pervasive cultural shifts over time.

What will follow is a rudimentary attempt to develop an analysis of race and politics from something like a postmodern perspective. I take seriously the concern of West and Nicholson and Fraser to attend to the demands and character of political practice, as well as Pfeil's insistence on the centrality of useful strategic questions and political projects. In the service of these aims, the analysis will be kept as close to the ground as possible, for as long as possible.

There are three elements of the analysis that I am attempting to bring into a fruitful relationship with one another. First, there is the question of the relationship between cultural practices and political practices as they combine to constitute a multifaceted problematic of *representation*. Second, there is the question of the territory on which constructions of racial identity and racially significant political subjectivity are contested. Finally, there is what I will brazenly refer to as the *real* political and economic developments that condition life for the residents of New York City.

In the sections that follow I will: discuss a political event at Harlem's Apollo Theatre that is an example both of the cultural and political practices that West refers to and of a certain hegemonic racial discourse in New York City politics; offer descriptions of the political and symbolic economies of race in New York City and indicate the manner in which they are underwritten by this hegemonic discourse; speculate on the relationship between developments in the symbolic economy of race and the election of David Dinkins to the mayor's office, and, finally, offer an interpretation of Spike Lee's film *Do the Right Thing*, one possible element in the construction of a discourse of social criticism that might interrupt hegemonic racial discourses in New York politics.

STINKIN' DINKINS AND THE HANDKERCHIEF HEADS

So, we're giving a new interpretation to the civil rights struggle, an interpretation that will enable us to come into it, take part in it. And these handkerchief heads who have been dillydallying and pussyfooting and compromising—we don't intend to let them pussyfoot and dillydally and compromise any longer. (Malcolm X, 1964/1972, p. 992)

On Friday June 15, 1990, I attended a political event at the Apollo Theatre in Harlem, U.S.A. Billed as a benefit for black youth as an "endangered species," the ostensible purpose of the event was to focus attention on the frequency of violence against young black males in New York City. Although racial violence (in a variety of forms) is undoubtedly a common occurrence in most American cities, several high profile incidents in New York during the past few years have helped to create the impression that such violence is on the rise. The event was a combined rap concert and political rally, with the rap group Public Enemy and the New York representative of the Honorable Louis Farrakhan as the principal attractions.

The evening began with several musical groups, with the explicit politics following the intermission. Farrakhan's representative appeared on stage, backed by a group of New York City black activists, including Lenora Fulani, the Rev. Al Sharpton, C. Vernon Mason, Alton Maddox, and Moses Stewart. Fulani is the leader of the New Alliance Party. Sharpton, Mason, and Maddox are perhaps most widely known for their prominent and controversial roles in the Tawana Brawley affair. Moses Stewart is the father of Yusef Hawkins, a New York City youth slain last summer in the Bensonhurst section of Brooklyn by a gang of white teens.

Farrakhan's representative launched into a long entertaining rap of his own, running changes on traditional Nation of Islam themes like self-sufficiency, the general miseducation of blacks, and various nefarious white conspiracies designed to keep black folks down. The climax of his rendition was an attack on David Dinkins, the recently elected black mayor of New York City, an attack that contrasted "Stinkin' Dinkins's pallid temporizing with the stalwart examples of black leadership arrayed behind the speaker on the stage. In the midst of this attack, to the surprise and amusement of the young concertgoers in my section of the theater, the representative referred to Dinkins and other black leaders of his ilk as "handkerchief heads."

Among other things, the event was a brilliant example of effective grassroots political communication: offering a critique of black political leadership and situating that critique in a specific (and compelling) cultural and historical context.

As New York is understood by many to be the cultural capital of the United States, so Harlem has traditionally been considered the black promised land: the spiritual, political, and social capital of the diasporadic peoples of Afro America. Three generations ago the novelist and civil rights activist James Weldon Johnson (1930) wrote that throughout coloured America Harlem is the recognized Negro capital. [Indeed,] it is Mecca for the sightseer, the pleasure-seeker, the curious, the adventurous, the enterprising, the ambitious and the talented of the entire Negro world; for the lure of it has reached down to every island of the Carib Sea and penetrated even into Africa. It is almost as well known to the white world, for it has been much talked and written about. (p. 3)

Thirty years after Johnson, Harold Cruse (1967) considered Harlem to hold the promise for political and economic emancipation of Afro Americans, calling it the "pivot of the black world's quest for identity and salvation" (p. 12). And although today's Harlem has certainly lost no small amount of its promise, it remains a potent symbol of black pride in cultural and political achievement.

Within this promised land, the Apollo Theatre was clearly the cultural mecca. There is no other theater in the United States with the particular cultural history and resonance of the Apollo. In particular, the Apollo's world famous amateur night has spawned a reputation for tough audiences and unique standards of cultural achievement. Conditioned by a chauvinistic insistence on the cultural supremacy of black folks, this reputation asserts that although second-rate performers might achieve fame and fortune "downtown," only the best can hold the stage at the Apollo ("Amateur Night," 1988).

In his presentation, Farrakhan's representative drew on these collective memories to emphasize both the status of Harlemites (wherever they might be from) as the *true* judges of black leadership and the significance of extra-electoral spaces—such as the Apollo stage—as the sites in which their verdicts were rendered. He compared Sharpton, Mason, and Maddox favorably with the black leaders Malcolm X and Adam Clayton Powell Jr. These earlier leaders were distinguished by their ability to command a house like the Apollo, and in doing so they demonstrated their adherence to collectively embraced cultural conventions that underwrote their status as "true black leaders." In this manner the image of Harlem as the unofficial capital of black America combined with the Apollo's long-standing reputation for unique standards of performance to define *the Apollo stage* as a powerfully present conceptual space within which could be located a tradition of oratorically and spiritually gifted black leaders.

In constructing the Apollo stage as a metaphor for leadership validation, Farrakhan's representative conflated a conceptual space of political leadership with a physical space of exalted performance. Under the relentless scrutiny of an Apollo audience, downtown political polish dissolves, and titles and offices give way to the blunt challenge: Can you move *this* crowd?

Once established, the metaphor could (and did) effectively suggest that David Dinkins's low-key oratorical style spoke volumes about the political differences between himself and Sharpton, Mason, and Maddox. Once the standards of cultural presentation and political representation are conflated, the assertion that real black leaders can command the Apollo's stage becomes a tautology. As does the claim that handkerchief heads like Stinkin' Dinkins cannot.

These conflations and contextualizations were accentuated and elaborated through their association with rap music. Rap is a musical genre that often focuses on (among many other things) precisely the kind of leadership rifts—in the form of old school versus new school rivalries—that the representative was constructing, providing a powerful colloquial context. Rap also supports the emphasis on the performative component of leadership through which a David Dinkins fares poorly when compared with Sharpton, Mason, and Maddox. This relationship between leadership rifts and discursive riffs is constantly seen in rap music. Rakim's claim to leadership is predicated on his ability to move the crowd with his rhymes and his dj's (Eric B.) rhythms. The notion that the leadership function is validated by the performance function— indeed in this case that cultural presentation ought to precede political representation—is just another way of overlapping the physical and conceptual spaces of the Apollo's stage.

Finally, rap—at least as it is practiced by political rappers such as Kool Moe Dee, Rakim, KRS One, Queen Latifah, and Public Enemy— intends to employ and extend the tradition of vocal, militant black leadership from David Walker, through William Monroe Trotter, Ida B. Wells-Barnet, Hubert Harrison, Marcus Garvey, Malcolm X, and Angela Davis.[3] Farrakhan's representative's use of the term *handkerchief head* evokes this tradition, effecting a tropical convergence between Malcolm X and contemporary rappers in their shared use of culturally resonant but overdetermined images of denunciation.

Part of the power of the image (hence its overdetermined nature) rests in the fact that this intertextuality need not be recognized. It is likely that the fellas in front of me did not catch the reference to Malcolm's famous "The Ballot or the Bullet" speech. Nevertheless, if the term simply conjured up images of Aunt Jemima, or of Louis Armstrong—that ubiquitous photo with eyes popping, cheesing, with handkerchief mopping sweaty brow—handkerchief head functioned as a powerful representation of subservience, of political, material, and moral obsequiousness.[4] This representation condensed Malcolm's powerful denunciation of liberal electoral proceduralism, his implicit renunciation of Martin Luther King's optimistic faith in American democracy, and his profound insistence on the propriety of violence in self-defense. And the representation moved the crowd on the Apollo Stage.

FROM PROTEST TO POLITICS:
RACE AND REPRESENTATION IN NEW YORK CITY

On November 9, 1989, *The New York Times* heralded the election of David Dinkins as the first black mayor of New York with an editorial entitled "From Protest to Politics." Pointing out that blacks had previously been elected to office in municipalities where they were in a voting majority or where there was significant political division among whites, the *Times's* editorial writers argued that the willingness of New York City's whites to vote for David Dinkins was an indicator of their increasing maturity. The editorial went on to insist that Dinkins's election represented the fulfillment of the civil rights leader Bayard Rustin's generation-old hope that black Americans would move from "protest to politics."

Not surprisingly, the *Times* had seriously decontextualized Rustin's words and hopes. Although Rustin (1971) did call for a move from protest to politics, to be activated by precisely the kind of coalition that Dinkins was able to mobilize ("Negroes, liberals, labor unions and religious groups"), this transition was to be made in the service of what he considered to be "radical objectives."

> We are challenged now to broaden our social vision, to develop functional programs with concrete objectives. We need to propose alternatives to

technological unemployment, urban decay, and the rest. We need to be calling for public works and training, for national economic planning, for federal aid to education, for attractive public housing—all this on a sufficiently massive scale to make a difference. (p. 122)

Rustin's belief that radical political objectives might be realized through traditional political avenues was noble but naive. This naivete was recognized by political scientist Robert Smith (1981) in another installment in this "protest to politics" discourse written almost 20 years after Rustin's. Smith wrote of Black Power as the symbolic catalyst that forged the kind of group solidarity necessary to underwrite the mobilization of blacks as a political interest group, thereby facilitating the "entry by blacks into the pluralist political arena" (p. 433).

In comparing this process to earlier historical processes—from the agrarian crusade of the 1890s to the farm lobby of the 1920s or from the labor movement of the 1930s to the contemporary labor lobby, Smith (1981) proved alert to the deradicalizing character of political incorporation.[5] In particular, he did not believe that this transformation would involve the absolute disappearance of street protests, but rather their subordination to and manipulation by a black political lobby that was likely to have a middle-class agenda.

The political scientist Martin Shefter (1986) uses the term *extrusion* to describe the process by which previously excluded political groups purge those of their members who are ideologically problematic as the group becomes incorporated into the political system. Shefter's research indicates that extrusion can have explicitly racial manifestations. With respect to the emergence of Adam Clayton Powell Jr. on the New York political scene, Shefter writes:

> The circumspection with which the major parties approached issues of potential concern to blacks, their caution in nominating black candidates, and their reluctance to mobilize large numbers of blacks into the electorate left New York's Negro population open for mobilization by leaders who did not have ties to the regular party organization, and who relied upon racial and or radical appeals. (p. 86)

I would suggest that the converse of the proposition stated here holds as well; that is, if the absence of political incorporation allows space for racial appeals, then incorporation itself usually tends to have a deracializing effect on political rhetoric and practice. The relationship between the deradicalizing and deracializing effects of political incorporation is usually effected through ideological maneuvering. Thus the *Times*'s (Editorial, 1989) deradicalization of Rustin's legacy is yoked to the propagation of a model of black political development whereby the black gains of the 1960s with respect to the opening up of the polity provoke a rationalization of black political behavior, a rationalization that would presumably lead to a fully modern polity underwritten by a liberal narrative—that is to say, a political narrative in which for purposes of political subjectivity, race is ultimately dissolved into citizenship. Hence the *Times*'s enthusiasm over the "fact" that Dinkins ran as a "politician who is black, not as a black politician" (p. A34).

Both in general and in the particular case of New York, the process that the *Times* applauds can be seen to produce results that are quite the opposite of Rustin's hopes. Using Rustin's words to underwrite this process effects Shefter's extrusion at the discursive level, and it constitutes an ugly revision of the old assurance that the capitalists would sell the rope by which they themselves would be strung up.

THE POLITICAL ECONOMY OF RACE IN NEW YORK CITY

It is no coincidence that the *Times*'s (Editorial, 1989, p. A34) insistence that the political transcendence of race is "worth celebrating and fighting to preserve"should come in the context of an explosion of race in American politics. Indeed, the *Times*'s ideological offensive is matched by a diverse intellectual countermobilization. Jesse Jackson's presidential campaigns, racial violence on college campuses and in city streets, and black nationalist developments in popular culture combine to assert the significance of race in American life and politics with a force that would even seem to be attracting the notice of political scientists. Much recent attention of American political science to race insists on its primacy for understanding American politics (Allen, Dawson, & Brown, 1989; Bobo & Gilliam, 1990; Carmines & Stimson, 1989; Henry, 1990; Huckfeldt & Kohfeld, 1989; and especially Marshall, 1990). At the same time, many activist scholars are issuing calls for a movement from politics to protest in the form of social and political mobilizations that take race consciousness and racial subjugation as analytical and strategic points of departure. The political environment that underwrites much of this attention to race is primarily one of disappointment: a recognition of the failed promise of electoral activity.

If political incorporation is to be measured in terms of electoral success, then there is no question about the significance of the gains made by black folks since the early 1970s. There are presently 7,370 black elected officials in the United States, 4,955 of whom are in 16 southern and border states and the District of Columbia. In 1970 there were 48 black mayors—in 1987 there were 303. These impressive gains have been enhanced at the perceptual level by national power embodied in Ron Brown, William Gray, Colin Powell, Doug Wilder's governorship in Virginia, and particularly high-profile victories in significant cities like Chicago, Philadelphia, Baltimore, and most recently New York.

However, there is almost unanimous agreement that these municipal victories do not result in the kind of political and economic gains for blacks that might have been expected. Susan and Norman Fainstein argue that during the 1970s, there appeared to be a close connection between the general economic trajectories of cities and the proportion of their populations that were black. That is to say, cities such as San Francisco and Boston with relatively small black populations were relatively successful at converting their manufacturing economies to service-based economies, whereas cities with large black populations were considerably less successful.

Throughout the 1980s this pattern appeared to change as cities such as Baltimore, Chicago, and New York produced strong, service-sector-led economic growth. Fainstein and Fainstein (1989) insist that this change does not represent a declining significance of race for the urban political economy, but instead represents the fact that "in a majority of political jurisdictions, blacks had been isolated sufficiently to become irrelevant to aggregate growth" (p. 188).

This containment had two dimensions: residential segregation and political demobilization. Residential segregation by race allows middle- and upper-income white households to isolate themselves and their tax bases from the large numbers of black residents who are poor, and the shift from a political agenda of social justice to one of economic restructuring and development in the mid-1970s resulted in a significant demobilization of black political activity. Both factors significantly reduced the burden of black political and economic demands on aggregate growth. With respect to the electoral gains of blacks, Fainstein and Fainstein (1989) write "racial containment has not been seriously threatened by the great expansion in the number of black elected officials" (p. 189).

Adolph Reed (1988) has persuasively presented the ironic dynamic that helps to account for this representational gap. The same structural and demographic factors that condition the rise of black regimes also severely constrain them with respect to addressing the needs of their black constituencies.

At the same time that American cities have experienced a substantial in-migration of blacks and other minorities, they have suffered considerable suburbanization and a substantial out-migration of manufacturing jobs. The result has been the development of a corporate city: a center city economy fueled by the provision of services to its corporate tenants.

The imperative to reproduce the conditions conducive to the sustenance of this corporate city is underwritten by progrowth governing coalitions: business and political forces allied to keep tax burdens low and to coordinate state-subsidized development activities.

Reed (1988) sees three major problems with this dynamic for the prospects of black political representation. First, the same factors that make possible the empowerment of a black regime—the movement of minorities into the inner city and the movement of manufacturing jobs and well-off white residents out—also results in the economic and political marginalization of a significant segment of the black population of inner cities. Second, the logic of progrowth politics (that essentially boils down to a fire sale of the city to real estate developers and corporate tenants in the hope that expanded tax revenues and jobs will result) does not include within its set of policy options a broad and progressive redistribution of social resources. Finally, black regimes often wind up governing polities in which there is a zero sum relation between principal electoral and governing coalitions.

It is important to note that the black regime/progrowth dynamic is not only structural and demographic, but it is strategic as well. For if the rules of the game are that corporate citizens are to be exempted from serious civic sacrifices on the assumption that an equitable distribution of municipal burdens will provoke them to take their toys and go elsewhere, then those sacrifices must ultimately (and disproportionately) be borne by the unpropertied residents of the city. As urban areas become blacker and blacker, the value of a political leader with natural communicative and persuasive advantages increases. Felix Rohatyn puts the case delicately, but definitively:

> On balance, people in the business community think that reduced tension has to be the highest priority; that it's impossible to govern with any requirement for sacrifice unless the people who are being asked to sacrifice feel they are being treated fairly. Dave (Dinkins) *has a lot of personal qualities* [italics added] that lend themselves to that kind of approach. (1989, p. B2)

The consequences of all this with respect to the ability of black regimes to effectively represent their black constituencies is summed up by Reed (1988):

> They are, by and large, only black versions of the progrowth regimes that they have replaced, distinguished in part by the asymmetry of their campaign rhetoric and their practice of governance. They are in one sense even more attractive to junior members in the progrowth coalition because of their peculiar skill at derailing opposition to developmental initiatives and cultivating the loyalty or acquiescence of the growth machine's victims. (p. 50)

All of these dynamics are at work in conditioning the political and social environment in New York City, the environment against which black denunciations of David Dinkins take place. New York has experienced enormous demographic changes over the past 2 decades. From 1970 to 1980 New York City became 26% less white and 11% more black; one fourth of the city's black population is foreign born compared with 5% in 1960. As a percentage of total city employment from 1950 to 1980, manufacturing has dropped from 30% to 11.2%, whereas financial activities have increased from 9.7% to 14.6%. Extending back to 1980, the city has lost 28% of its manufacturing jobs (Mollenkopf, 1988).

These factors combine to create a certain crisis of political representation in three interconnected ways. The needs of blacks and other minorities conflict with the policy preferences of the city's governing coalitions, and for demographic and structural reasons blacks and other minorities are especially ill-positioned to address this divergence.

First, the political calculus wrought by the economic changes has created a gap between the city's policies and the needs of large numbers of its minority residents: the progrowth logic has proven seriously faulty in New York City. Despite a 6-year period of economic growth—inspired in part by the growth in the financial services industry—the percentage of the city's population living in poverty rose in 1989 to 23.25%, erasing a 3.4% drop reported for 1986—33.85% of the non-Hispanic blacks in the city live in poverty, as do 41.6% of the city's Hispanics. Samuel M. Ehrenhalt, regional commissioner of labor statistics for the U.S. Department of Labor, argues that as the city begins to feel the effects of the October 1987 stock market crash (16,000 jobs lost in the financial services industry), it will become ever clearer that the city has lost the opportunity to draw thousands of black, Hispanic, female, and teenage residents into the workforce.

The numbers have hung there without a major reduction while New York's economy was undergoing the best period of growth in the private sector since World War II. This challenges some cherished notions of the past that economic growth would be adequate to pull people out of poverty (see DePalma, 1989; Levine, 1989; cf. Rosenberg, 1987; Tobier, 1984).

Second, the demographic shifts have created a certain gap between the electorate and the resident population. Although whites are only half of New York's population, they made up almost three quarters of the 1980 presidential general electorate, because they are older than other groups, and more likely to be citizens, to be registered voters, and to turn out on Election Day (Mollenkopf, 1988, p. 242; see also Roberts, 1989a). The maintenance of this gap will depend in part on whether black electoral turnout stabilizes at the 30% level seen in the Dinkins and Jesse Jackson campaigns or falls back to the 23% level seen in Denny Farrell's campaign for mayor in 1985.[6]

If sustained political mobilization within the black community is to help close this gap, it will have to counteract the third factor, the enervation of traditional agencies for political mobilization of new social groups: reform forces and regular party channels. The corruption scandals of the Koch regime have severely damaged the efficacy of regular party structures in a way that may have assisted Dinkins, but the situation opens up a certain mobilizational vacuum particularly with respect to immigrant groups in the city. The ascension of reformers such as Ruth Messinger, Elizabeth Holtzman, and Mark Green to municipal office may not bode well for the reform tradition in New York City politics.

The problems for representation posed by these structural shifts have been exacerbated by the relatively rigid institutionalization of progrowth politics through the reorganization of the city's politics after the 1975 fiscal crisis.

As Martin Shefter (1985, pp. 149-193) has indicated, political power in New York has crystallized around a triangular formation involving the mayor, a municipal union/financial center nexus, and the public creditors and fiscal watchdog agencies. The accommodations necessary to extricate the city from its fiscal crisis include a statutory role for agencies like the Financial Control Board to exercise an explicit veto over social spending, which could only be implicitly vetoed in many other cities.

David Dinkins's successful campaign for mayor clearly illustrates the gap between electoral coalition and governing coalition written of by Reed. Dinkins was able to achieve the mayoralty by creating a coalition of African Americans, liberals, and organized labor and by healing (or at least papering over) traditional rifts between black politicians in Harlem and those in Brooklyn (Lynn, 1989b, 1990a; Roberts, 1989b). For the Democratic primary, blacks and organized labor provided substantial financial assistance: as of August 10, 1989, organized labor had contributed $218,000 of Dinkins's $1.9 million campaign treasury, and contributors "with Harlem addresses" had contributed another $270,000 (Lynn, 1989b, 1990a). As significant was the manpower provided by organized labor and the capacity to evade the new city campaign financing law.[7] According to a chart on p. B4 of The New York Times, September 14, 1989, David Dinkins wound up winning the Democratic primary with 93% of the black vote and 29% of the white vote, 32% of white union households, 97% of black union households, 30% of white city government employees, and 96% of black city government employees. Dinkins's ability to capture 29% of the total white vote, and to provoke a black turnout that almost matched that of Jesse Jackson in the Democratic presidential primary in 1988 (29% vs. 32%) ensured his trouncing of incumbent Mayor Ed Koch with 51% of the vote (to Koch's 42%) (Lynn, 1990b).

After the primary, Dinkins began to build his governing coalition. As he headed toward the general election, the business establishment in New York City and liberal and black Democrats outside the city began to replace unions and local blacks as the primary financial supporters of Dinkins's campaign (Lynn, 1989a, p. 40).

With his election, Dinkins moved to further reassure the business community of his loyalty by establishing important relationships with people like Arthur Levitt, Norman Steisel, and Philip Michael, ultimately submitting a budget that, according to Colleen Woodell, the associate managing director for Moody's Investors Service, was quite similar to a budget that Mayor Koch might have submitted (Barsky, 1990). Facing a fiscal crisis that some have compared to those in 1974 and 1975, painful budgets are likely to be the norm.

The difficulty that these factors pose for a significant amelioration of the condition of the proportion of the black population of New York City that is poor constitutes the political economy of race in New York City. The question of black political representation in New York must reach beyond the attainment of electoral office to include the ability to facilitate changes in this political economy.

THE SYMBOLIC ECONOMY OF RACE IN NEW YORK CITY

The barriers to effective representation for blacks in New York are not located merely in the structures of fiscal power. There is a symbolic economy of race in New York City that affects issues of black political representation in vital ways.

This symbolic economy of race includes the historical traditions and collective memories that underwrite politics on the Apollo stage; the culturally dominant constructions and representations by which race is defined, and by which races are mobilized for political purposes, and the words, images, and symbols through which contemporary black people live their various lives as black people.

Indeed, political theater on the Apollo stage, although conditioned, supported, and in important respects *legitimated* by the realities of the political economy of race, is nonetheless most directly a bid for a redistribution of power in the *symbolic* economy of race. Whereas the social and political environment constitutes the backdrop against which black criticism of Dinkins takes place (and must therefore be taken into precise account), it is within the system of contestation and struggle over the meaning and significances of race—struggles that involve the negotiation among these three components—that this criticism is most immediately situated.

These struggles are politically important because although the quality of political representation for blacks must be measured at least in part by their capacity to effect change in the structures and distributions of power in the political economy, that capacity itself (as well as the character of the changes sought) rests in part on the fertility of the representations through which black folks are politically mobilized. The more arid and one-dimensional are the tropes by which black folks are politically mobilized as a race, the less likely it is that they will be able to mobilize the political resources necessary to effect real change in a progressive and emancipatory direction.

This relationship between political representation and cultural representations can be seen in the fact that the character of the representations through which black folks are politically mobilized will affect the range of black people who will be effectively empowered as political agents. At the one extreme, black politics is a strictly male, upper-middle-class affair, as an undifferentiated notion of race becomes rather easily articulated to the most politically and economically powerful fraction of the black population.[8] At another extreme are political activity and mobilizations that are coded in racial terms and at least attempt to address the manner in which, as lived experience, race is increasingly complex and multifaceted, refracted through economics, status, culture, gender, sexuality, and politics.

As the gap between an electoral coalition and a governing coalition is an indication of political extrusion and measures deficiencies in political representation, so a gap between race as an arid and one-dimensional category of political mobilization and race as a discursive distillation of cacophonous lived experiences is also an indication of political extrusion, and likewise measures deficiencies in political representation.

In this context, the meaning of race in terms of lived experience in a place like New York is constantly a point of contention and political struggle—both within and across racial boundaries. As I suggested above, the piece of political theater on the Apollo's stage with which this article begins must be situated within these struggles. The symbol of the handkerchief head is an effort to write a dimension of militance and independence into the political definition of race—a point that can be seen in the explicit distinction between "real black leaders" and handkerchief heads. Moreover, the attempt to present young black males as an endangered species is certainly a profound effort to invert culturally dominant representations—from Tom Wolfe's *The Bonfire of the Vanities*[9] to some of the more lurid coverage of the trial of the Central Park rape case[10]—of the young black male as the most dangerous species in urban America.

The celebrated trial of the Central Park rape case is an especially illuminating instance of contestation over the meaning of race; in particular it illustrates the danger of collapsing the contemporary complexity of black identity into discursive gestures that draw their power from collective memories and historical traditions.

Village Voice writer Greg Tate (1989) was correct when he said that both black and white media coverage were characterized by transparent efforts to deny the extent and seriousness of racism and sexism in American society. Whereas much of the mainstream media in New York City has tended to focus on the inhumanity of the jogger's attackers, a good deal of the black press has insisted that the accused are getting the expected raw deal from the criminal justice system. This latter accusation is implicit in the constant comparison of the defendants to the Scottsboro Boys, a gesture that condenses an entire historical narrative about the assertion of an imperative to defend white womanhood as an excuse to trample on the rights and lives of black men.[11]

This perspective has been particularly trumpeted in New York's *Amsterdam News*, the city's premier black newspaper.[12] In a series of editorials, the *Amsterdam News* has insisted that the trial essentially amounts to a "legal lynching." The *Amsterdam News* editorial writers have repeatedly argued that the city's criminal justice system is prepared to unjustly convict those accused of the rape simply in order to satisfy those who perceive the case as a litmus test on crime and the punishment of black men accused of raping or assaulting whites.[13]

A similar position has rather consistently been taken by talk show hosts on the city's black radio station WLIB. In both instances, WLIB and the *Amsterdam News,* pains are taken to acknowledge the tragic suffering of the jogger, but at the end of the day any question of sexism, or violence against women, is entirely dissolved in the implicit insistence that "the black community" close ranks around the racial (read: endangered black male) aspects of the case.

Enacted through all of this is a symbolic contest over the meaning of race and racial violence. But it is a contest between boys who own newspapers that leaves women in general, and black women in particular, in the familiar position of struggling to establish discursive space that is not infected by the paternalistic and duplicitous interests of black and white men. On the one hand are culturally dominant representations of black male criminality that focus the horror of city residents on the ever-present dangers to white womanhood. On the other hand are culturally resonant representations of black male victimization that attempt to mobilize black populations to close ranks against the historically substantiated transgressions of the oppressor.

In the midst of this contest over the meaning of race and racial violence, Lisa Kennedy and Joan Morgan, black women writers for the *Village Voice,* reflect the real life pains of black women, recognizing the threats that appear from both sides, struggling to carve out a definition of self that acknowledges necessary allegiances as well as unavoidable antagonisms. These women understand the historical and contemporary truth in the Scottsboro Boys analogy, but the everyday dangers posed by male members of their own black communities is also a reality that they "cannot not know." In a perceptive and important article, Joan Morgan (1989) wrote of her pain at the assumption of an aggressive male privilege on the part of many black men. She wrote of those who seemed to feel they had the right to stop her on the street to demand her name, address, telephone number, and "pussy"—and moreover had a right to verbally abuse her when she dared to ignore them.

At the same time, both Morgan and Kennedy are particularly sensitive to the manner in which the city's collective outrage over the jogger's situation seems to diminish the public significance of the obscene numbers of women of color who are subjected to various forms of male violence in New York City every single day. Kennedy (1990) writes how as a black woman, she finds herself torn between her blackness and her femaleness, wondering what happens to the quality of her blackness if she accepts the media coverage's implicit premise that the jogger's rape is more heartbreaking than all of the rapes that happen to women of color.

The problem is that as the symbolic economy of race in New York City is currently structured, the efforts of these women and others like them to open up the conceptualization and representation of race continue to be relegated to a narrow discursive margin.

Although efforts to rewrite culturally dominant representations of young black males are vital and necessary, it nevertheless remains the case that those engaged in these efforts enjoy a certain limited hegemony in the symbolic arena themselves. As a category of electoral political mobilization, race tends toward an especially static life within which most of these efforts fit quite comfortably. The predominant and politically relevant contest is between nationalist and liberal conceptions of race, both of which distort lived experience and enervate political possibilities. The former obscures differences within race, collapsing gender, sexuality, and class into a unified racial subjectivity. The latter obscures differences across races, collapsing diverse (and often divergent) historical and cultural traditions into a unified American citizenship.

The mass-mediated construction of a tradition of racially significant political subjectivity through the canonization of couplets—Booker T. Washington and W.E.B. DuBois, Martin Luther King Jr. and Malcolm X, or, as in *The New York Times* editorial celebrating Dinkin's victory, David Dinkins and Jesse Jackson[14]—facilitates the maintenance of this narrow symbolic contest. The binary character of this discourse has three consequences for political representation. First, it makes it easy for the boys who own newspapers and radio stations and barbershops to choose up sides, a game with which we are especially familiar. Second, it facilitates the articulation of racial struggle to a pluralist model of political incorporation, simplifying racial interests into a binary opposition that accords well with a winner take all electoral structure. Finally, as we shall see it offers strategic opportunities for black politicians in the way in which it poses stark alternatives to sometimes skittish white electorates.

This discourse helped to underwrite the election of David Dinkins and has a powerful if unexpected relationship to his ability to maintain a political economy of sacrifice in New York City. First, as the *Times* editorial indicates, the opposition around which the discourse is constructed helps in the characterization of David Dinkins as the lesser of two evils. Second, the fact that the discourse is propped up by individuals (most of whom are dead and can therefore neither repudiate nor affirm their employment in this manner) with mythically potent but historically ambiguous political roles encourages it to float along at a distance somewhat removed from the terrain of real political economy. This makes it easy to reduce the nationalist interest to symbols that traditional black political forces in New York are in a peculiarly powerful position to satisfy.

A LITTLE FINGER-POPPING MUSIC

The theatrical business on the Apollo stage is an example of the perpetuation of this truncated discourse around race and political leadership and illustrates the propositions about its utility for the maintenance of political power. There are two elements that are especially striking here. First is the pervasive gesturing backward toward a golden age of black political (and masculine) assertion that would seem ironic in the face of the real political gains achieved over the last 20 years. This feeling is certainly attributable to the omnipresence of icons like Malcolm X, Adam Clayton Powell Jr. and Martin Luther King Jr. in the rhetoric of black political activism, but it is also carried in the style and posture adopted by contemporary black activists. When Al Sharpton took over the Brooklyn Bridge in a "Day of Outrage" to protest racial violence in New York City, the reference to Martin Luther King on the Pettus bridge in Selma was not just in my imagination. In this computer age, there seems to be a conscious effort at achieving authenticity by association with past victories, an association that is activated through mental photographs and recordings that recall an earlier technology of political assertion. It is almost as if an investment in political leadership requires a return in the form of a fat pay envelope, not some computer transfer of funds.

The Apollo event is also an example of the commodification of political criticism through the production and distribution of nationalist images and icons. This is especially significant in New York City today, given Percy Sutton's critical role in both political and symbolic economies of race.

Both elements of the discourse have rather obvious consequences for its critical power. When social criticism is offered and political leadership defined in terms of dehistoricized mythopoetic figures and events, there is little ground for critical engagement with structures and procedures that produce contemporary social and political conditions. And when leadership is reduced to the production and distribution of powerful images and mental photographs, political desire can be satisfied without seriously challenging extant distributions of power.

None of this is new, or unique to racial politics. What is new, at least in New York, is the context in which it takes place and the functions that it serves. The black political regime in New York is new and, as I have suggested, neither unique nor circumstantial, but instead it develops directly out of economic and demographic shifts that have become identified with the postindustrial society.

At issue, then, is the function of this criticism/theater relative to this regime. In order to understand this, there is an irony that must be grasped. The irony is that the Apollo Theatre, site of this critical practice, is owned by Percy Sutton, David Dinkins's political mentor and right-hand man (Lynn, 1989b, p. 29). More important is Sutton's ownership of WLIB, the black radio station that served as the platform upon which most of the black activists on stage that evening established their citywide reputations. It is in this sense that Sutton plays a pivotal role in both political and symbolic economies of race in New York City.

WLIB is an AM radio station with a predominantly talk format. Broadcasting from the stage of the Apollo Theatre from 9 a.m. to 12 p.m. Mondays through Thursdays (and from its studios in New Jersey at other times), the station has readily opened its microphones to black activists and black activist agendas. Throughout much of the Tawana Brawley affair, some combination of Mason, Maddox, and Sharpton could be heard almost daily, promoting their case and attacking the statements and characters of the state Attorney General and the police officials in Wappingers Falls. Announcements of community meetings, rallies, and protest marches are a staple on WLIB, usually ending with the slogan of Al Sharpton's National Youth Movement: "No Justice, No Peace."

Black activists in New York—from Sharpton, Mason, Maddox, Sonny Carson, and Elombe Brath to Herbert Daughtry, Calvin Butts, and David Patterson—believe WLIB offers the most direct and unmediated access to the black community. When Sharpton was publicly accused of cooperating with the FBI to spy on other black leaders, he turned to WLIB to make his defense, arguing that WLIB offered him the fastest, most direct, and least censored access to the black community (Shipp, 1988, p. B1).

Perhaps the most compelling evidence of WLIB's significance to the black activist community came to light when it was revealed in July 1987 that the New York City Police Department had engaged in the practice of recording and preparing summaries of WLIB radio call-in shows, ostensibly for the purpose of finding out more about planned protests in the black community (Purdum, 1987a, 1987b).

In spite of its evident support for black activism in New York, WLIB not surprisingly played an important role in the more traditional politics of the mayoral campaign.[15] On the day of the Democratic primary, Jesse Jackson presided over the microphone at the station, urging its listeners to go out and vote.[16] However, I would suggest that as a crucial site for the reproduction and dissemination of nationalist images and iconographies, WLIB's (as well as the *Amsterdam News*, *The City Sun*, and other black media) role in the election of David Dinkins went beyond its explicit get-out-the-vote effort.

In maintaining a constant and sharp awareness of racial difference and division, the station served two important functions. First, by promoting a brand of militant, vocal, theatrical black leadership, the station enhanced Dinkins's appeal as healer and conciliator by raising the stakes of race relations in the city. By the primary, campaign coverage and commentary seemed to suggest that the single most important problem faced by the city was race relations, and Dinkins's presumed ability to manage racial tensions became, in some quarters, sufficient reason to vote for him. This situation certainly owed much to Koch's belligerence, as well as to the racial killings in Howard Beach and Bensonhurst, but Mason, Maddox, Sharpton, and other black activists did their parts to keep the specter of social disorder alive.

At the same time, the ongoing dialogue about race helped to sustain interest and energy among segments of the black electorate who might otherwise have correctly recognized that *no* mayoral candidate was likely to have much of a salutary impact on their lives if elected. For these folks WLIB dispensed and promoted political performances that satisfied a real desire to be entertained and affirmed through politics.

Given their emphasis on racial difference and division, these performances were quite often subversive of Dinkins's campaign rhetoric and strategy. However, at the end of the day, they were themselves subverted by WLIB's larger ideological thrust of "keeping the business in the family." This standard pro-black-business ideology generally manifests itself in gestures like the station's distribution of WLIB family cards, redeemable for discounts at participating businesses. In this instance, keeping the business in the family could, and apparently did, have an explicitly political meaning: In whatever ways David Dinkins might be a disappointing black leader, he was nevertheless better than *any* white alternative.

In this manner, a discourse whereby political subjectivity and racial leadership are alternatively conceived in liberal and nationalist modes underwrites a black political comedy. The nationalists entertain their audience by railing at the liberal as an imposter: a disgrace to the tradition of leadership that they themselves represent. The liberal nods at the brushfires the nationalists have been starting and confidently waves his big hose. Sporting Malcolm X T-shirts, black folks file into the voting booths by any means necessary.

This symbiotic relationship between the nationalist rhetoric and performance and the liberal rhetoric and practice is perhaps best characterized by Percy Sutton's comments about his two radio stations, the money-making all-music WBLS and the break-even all-talk WLIB. Sutton says that although WBLS provides the revenue that allows his operation to maintain itself, his heart really belongs to the talk and news format of WLIB. Indeed he seems to take real pleasure in the way that WBLS's "finger-popping music" subsidizes WLIB's politics (Smothers, 1989).

SPIKE LEE AND THE BLACK POLITICAL (W)HOLE

We are confronted, then, with what appears to be a black political (w)hole that consumes the opposition that it spawns: symbolic contests that interact with political interests to ultimately secure the

hegemony of a bourgeois, progrowth political leadership. It is therefore tempting to dismiss the opposition thus generated as illegitimate.
This temptation is strengthened by the fact that we have a fancy
vocabulary of postmodernism with which to expedite the dismissal
and a nostalgic desire to pursue pernicious distinctions between high
and low forms of popular culture.

However, an interest in the development of a robust mode of
African American social criticism would insist that such a dismissal
is counterproductive. The production and distribution of powerful
mental photographs and recordings is a partial and potentially manipulative project, but it will remain intricately connected to the way
in which most people experience their politics, regardless of our
preferences. If one wants to be in the business of social criticism in
anything but an academic way, this practice partially defines the
terrain upon which the only game in town is played.

The problem that must be faced is the hegemony exercised over the
terms upon which the elements of the symbolic economy of race get
negotiated. In the two dominant competing modes of oppositional racial
construction, the operative strategy is the same: In order to counter
culturally dominant representations, we must all pull in one direction,
putting our collective strength behind certain historical representations
and contemporary images. The fact that these representations and
images may actually work to disenfranchise many of us is an unfor-
tunate consequence that will be addressed once we have sufficiently
redrawn the distribution of power in this symbolic economy.

The appropriate response to this assertion of power (because that
is surely what it is) is not to cede the field either through acquiescence
or dismissal. Instead, the proper response is to attempt the construction of a hegemony that overcomes this one. In this context, Stuart
Hall's (1982) suggestion is a useful one: "the first thing to ask about
an organic ideology," he says, "is not whether it is false, but what is
true about it" (p. 12; see also Hall, 1987). This is what must be
remembered about handkerchief heads and the Scottsboro Boys
analogy—as troublesome as they may be, and as surely as they may
facilitate distorted and exclusionary notions of race and racial leadership, it is nevertheless the case that *there is something true about
them*. They resonate with a certain historical power, something that
moves the crowd, and as such they provide a place to start.

The development of new modes of social criticism, therefore, involves exploding narrow discursive boundaries, constructing new discursive space in a manner that can both critique and draw upon the energy that cultural and historical representations exercise, and challenging representations that suppress differences that matter.[17] In other words, what is called for is a social criticism that can establish an ongoing conversation among representations that carry the power of historical traditions, cultural conventions, and collective memories, representations that bear the pleasures and pains of contemporary African American life as it is lived by vastly different contemporary African Americans and representations that engage the realities of the political economy of race.

There are many places to begin this work of exploding that discursive space. One of these might be with the motion picture *Do the Right Thing*. Spike Lee's motion picture seems both a likely and an unlikely candidate for this job. The film's depiction of racial tension and police violence in New York City certainly reflects a good deal of the history and future of social order in New York City. Much of the criticism that the film provoked touches on the issues that I have been discussing in this article. In particular, the relationship between performance and leadership—cultural presentations and political representation—is addressed in Lee's stated desire for the film to have an effect on the mayoral campaign, as well as in the response of critics like *New York* magazine's Joe Klein (1989), who suggested that Lee's movie might have a deleterious effect on David Dinkins's electoral aspirations.

The relationship between cultural presentation and political representation is also evident in the extent to which Lee is accorded a certain leadership status, with media brokers such as Ted Koppel and Bryant Gumbel underwriting Lee's ambition to, in Stanley Crouch's (1990) words, "take on the position of race leader, cloaked in slogans and using the manner of a rap star, the nappy-headed Napoleon seeking the seat at the big table reserved for the boy who's paid to be bad" (p. 243).

Despite these factors, there are important respects in which the film would seem an unlikely candidate for a progressive role in my screenplay. *Do the Right Thing* has been roundly criticized for proffering empty manipulative images that conceal a narrow, impotent political vision behind a cheap but colorful nationalism.

Moreover, there are important respects in which the film would seem to be simply an extension of the discursive space to which I have been objecting: the canonization of black male historical figures as the embodiment of alternative avenues of political subjectivity.

The central conflict of the film involves the desire to replace pictures of prominent Italians on Sal's wall of fame with pictures of "brothers." The political salience of the conflict is underlined in the way in which it is uneasily resolved: Smiley enters the burning pizzeria and affixes a photo of Malcolm X meeting Martin Luther King Jr. onto the wall (recalling, of course, James Baldwin's comments on being integrated into a burning house). The controversial closing of the film juxtaposes quotes from Malcolm X and Martin Luther King Jr. on violence and racial struggle.[18]

In spite of all of this, I would want to suggest that the film allows an interpretation that subverts the binary, iconographical discourse of race. In the film's depiction of the ubiquity and multifaceted character of urban violence, Lee exposes the falseness of the choice between violence/Malcolm and nonviolence/ Martin and the consequent aridity of the discursive terrain that is bounded by that choice.[19]

As W. J. T. Mitchell (1990) has written, "Negative reactions to the film tend to focus obsessively on the destruction of the pizzeria, as if the violence against property were the only 'real' violence in the film" (p. 896). However, it seems obvious that the film depicts an urban setting that offers a variety of different forms of violence. When Da Mayor enters Sal's pizzeria looking for a handout and Sal says to him, "Choose your weapon," Da Mayor chooses the broom and proclaims that Sal will have the cleanest walk in Brooklyn. The charge to choose your weapon provokes reflection on the variety of different weapons used in the film. The broom used by Da Mayor recalls Booker T. Washington's insistence on the power of the toothbrush in fighting white stereotypes and disrespect. There is the cultural assertion of Radio Raheem's boombox; the all-American property-preserving/ destroying violence of Sal's baseball bat; the attempt at economic violence in Buggin' Out's boycott; the verbal violence of the racial epithets that black, Hispanic, and Korean characters fling at one another—all weapons of the cultural, economic, and political violence that effectively defines the urban landscape in places like New York City.

In this context the violence/nonviolence choice as represented by Martin Luther King and Malcolm X seems considerably less salient than Sal's admonition to choose your weapon. And the space defined by this new choice seems characterized by a more complicated, complex landscape requiring new maps and new cognitive landmarks.

To suggest that the film may subvert a hegemonic racial discourse and open up new discursive space is not to exaggerate its potential. Lee's political vision is blurry at best—he offers no answers. Of course, in his inability to offer a compelling postnationalist, postliberal vision of black political practice he keeps good company with every other black political scientist, social critic, and politician that I am aware of.

Moreover, there are deep problems with the work, not least of which is Lee's unwillingness to render black women in anything but the most narrow and stereotyped fashion. Nevertheless there is much that is true about the account offered in *Do the Right Thing*, indeed for me part of the film's power lies in the way in which the limitations of Lee's vision are illuminated by the veracity of his account: His depiction of the multiplicity and complexity of the forms of violence that define the urban landscape exposes the emptiness of the political choice that he seems to be offering.

CONCLUSION(S)

In this chapter I have offered an analysis of race and politics in New York City from a postmodern perspective. In sketching the relationship between the political economy of race and the symbolic economy of race, I have shown the way in which a narrow hegemonic discourse about race underwrites the articulation of racial politics to a progrowth model of urban management.

This is a postmodern analysis not because of its deployment of fancy and arcane vocabularies, but because it attempts to address the problematic of *representation* as it is constituted by the intersection of politics and culture. And it attempts to do this in a way that issues in suggestions for strategic interventions.

I have suggested the need for critical discourses that contest the hegemony of narrow, binary constructions of black leadership and black political subjectivity. Such discourses must engage texts like the film *Do the Right Thing* and spaces like the Apollo stage, for these are the vehicles that carry the culturally resonant representations upon which mass mobilization seems to rely.

In its broad outlines, the problem that an African American social criticism faces is this: how to address racial oppression (carried in the culturally dominant representations of race) without succumbing to the temptation to suppress differences that matter in the interest of the (w)hole. This will always be a difficult project. One thing that it would seem to require would be the constant demystification of the unitary racial subject. The myth that fragmentation necessarily equals weakness must be subverted. Donna Haraway's (1988) suggestion that the fragmented self offers a shifting ground of political possibility is a principle upon which such subversion might be premised, and novelist Octavia Butler's creation of the Oankali species, whose survival depends on its ability to embrace difference, offers a vision toward which such subversion might be directed.[20]

Haraway (1988) turns from the celebrated postmodern death of the subject toward a more reasonable perspective that recognizes that the subject was always partial anyway: "never finished, whole, simply there and original; it is always constructed and stitched together imperfectly, and therefore able to join with another, to see together without claiming to be another" (p. 586).

In *Adulthood Rites* Butler's (1988) Oankali aliens have saved the Earth from itself. Their compensation is a constant genetic exchange with humans, an exchange that is necessary for their survival, because

> Oankali crave difference. Humans persecute their different ones, yet they need them to give themselves definition and status. Oankali seek difference and collect it. They need it to keep themselves from stagnation and overspecialization. . . . When you feel a conflict, try to go the Oankali way. Embrace difference. (p. 80)

NOTES

1. But see Winant (1990) and West (1988, p. 169).

2. On Jameson's postmodernism and political analysis see Jacoby (1987, pp. 166-172) and Pfeil (1990).

3. In this regard it is important to note that, media misrepresentations to the contrary, neither tradition—contemporary rappers or vocal militant black leadership— is an exclusively male preserve. This needs to be emphasized because of the tendency to represent both traditions as such. The claims that rap music is, at its essence, boy-talk and macho posturing are legion. Likewise, it is often suggested that what is especially significant about prominent political figures like Malcolm X and Jesse Jackson is their embodied contestation of socially constructed notions of black masculinity. C. Gerald Fraser, executive editor of *Essence* magazine, argues that the upsurge of interest in Malcolm X can be attributed to the fact that he was "a consummate figure of male strength" ("The Voice," 1990, p. B3). Compare this to G. Early's (1989b) statement:

> What makes (Jesse) Jackson so vitally important for our culture is precisely that on a public stage he is trying mightily and sometimes nobly to work out on moral and psychological levels what human commitment is and, on political and pragmatic levels, what black male ambition means. (p. 28)

4. See Early (1989a):

> One shudders to think that perhaps two generations of black Americans remember Louis Armstrong, perhaps one of the most remarkable musical geniuses America ever produced, not only as a silly Uncle Tom, but as a pathetically vulnerable, *weak* old man. (p. 292)

Louis Armstrong as handkerchief head is doubly salient; not only are his "Tom" credentials intact, but Minton's Playhouse, on 118th Street in Harlem, was the site of the bebop revolution that involved (obviously among many other things) a repudiation of Armstrong's obsequious style. James Lincoln Collier (1983) quotes Dizzy Gillespie: "if anybody asked me about a certain public image of him, handkerchief over his head, grinning in the face of white racism, I never hesitated to say I didn't like it" (p. 305).

5. On the transformation of the agrarian crusade see Goodwyn (1978); on labor see Davis (1986) and Moody (1988).

6. The Dinkins turnout was undoubtedly aided by incidents of racial violence in Bensonhurst and Howard Beach, as well as by the rapprochement between Harlem and Brooklyn black politicians.

7. Monies spent by labor unions to lobby their own members were not considered campaign expenditures for the purposes of the new campaign finance law. In this manner, candidates (like Dinkins) with substantial support from organized labor were in a position to have money spent on their behalf that other candidates could not.

8. The best description of this process is still Reed (1986). See also Marable (1987).

9. This quote from *The Bonfire of the Vanities* (Wolfe, 1987) provides an example:

> All at once Sherman was aware of a figure approaching him on the sidewalk, in the wet black shadows of the town houses and the trees. Even from fifty feet away, in the darkness, he could tell. It was that deep worry that lives in the base of the skull of every resident of Park Avenue south of Ninety-sixth Street—a black youth, tall, rangy, wearing white sneakers. Now he was forty feet away, thirty-five. Sherman stared at him. Well, let him come! I'm not budging ! It's my territory! I'm not giving way for any street punks! (p. 17).

10. On April 19, 1989, a white 28-year-old female jogger was beaten, raped, and left for dead in Central Park by a gang of mostly black and Hispanic youths. The brutality of the crime combined with issues of race and class to focus the attention of New York media on the dangers of life in urban America. The crime provoked real estate developer Donald Trump to take out full-page ads in the four major daily newspapers in New York, calling for the return of the death penalty. Trump's advertisement can be found in the May 1, 1989, edition of *The New York Times*, Part 2, p. 11.

11. On the Scottsboro Boys see Carter (1969). On the relationship between allegations of rape and the institution of social control over black men and white women, see Wells (1969), Davis (1981), and Hall (1983).

12. The *Amsterdam News* is edited by Wilbert Tatum. In 1973 Tatum was a top official in the office of Manhattan Borough President Percy Sutton. After his election as Mayor of New York City, Abraham Beame indicated that he would appoint Tatum the first black deputy mayor in the city's history. Concerned that this move would provide Sutton with privileged access to City Hall, black elected officials opposed the appointment, and Beame changed his mind. See Shefter (1985, p. 243, n.34).

13. "The jogger trial: Backdrop for a Lynching" *Amsterdam News*, Vol. 81, No. 28, Sat. July 14, 1990, p. 12; "The Legal Lynching Continues: The Police Write the Script," Sat. July 21, 1990, p. 12; "Jogger's Trial: Lynching, or Reasonable Doubt?" Sat. July 28, 1990, p. 12.

14. According to the *Times* (Editorial, 1989), the fact that Dinkins was willing to reject the help of Jesse Jackson in his election campaign was evidence that Dinkins thinks of himself as a politician who happens to be black rather than a black politician.

15. This is a general trend. See Schmidt (1989).

16. Mollenkopf, (1989, p. 51) acknowledges the political significance of the station.

17. Cf. Haraway (1990): "Some differences are playful, some are poles of world historical systems of domination. Epistemology is about knowing the difference" (p. 203).

18. King: "Violence as a way of achieving racial justice is both impractical and immoral. It is impractical because it is a descending spiral ending in destruction for all. The old law of an eye for an eye leaves everybody blind. . . . Violence ends by defeating itself"; Malcolm X: "I think there are plenty of good people in America, but there are also plenty of bad people in America and the bad ones are the ones who seem to have all the power and be in these positions to block things that you and I need. Because this is the situation, you and I have to preserve the right to do what is necessary to bring an end to that situation, and it doesn't mean that I advocate violence, but at the same time I am not against using violence in self-defense. I don't even call it violence when it's self-defense, I call it intelligence."

19. This reading of the film is deeply indebted to (although different from) Mitchell (1990).

20. The works in Octavia Butler's Xenogenesis Trilogy are *Dawn*, *Adulthood Rites*, and *Imago*, all published by Popular Library.

REFERENCES

Allen R., Dawson, M. C., & Brown, R. E. (1989). A schema-based approach to modeling an African American racial belief system. *American Political Science Review*, *83*(2), 421-441.

Amateur night at the Apollo: Boo birds and happiness. (1988, February 28). *The New York Times*, Section II, p. 28.

Barsky, N. (1990, February 2). Dinkins sets four-year financial plan with "painful elements" for New York. *The Wall Street Journal*, p. A6A.

Bobo, L., & Gilliam, F. D., Jr. (1990). Race, social political participation, and black empowerment. *APSR, 84* (2), 377-393.

Butler, O. (1988). *Adulthood rites.* New York: Popular Library.

Carmines, E. G., & Stimson, J. A. (1989). *Issue evolution: Race and the transformation of American politics.* Princeton, NJ: Princeton University Press.

Carter, D. (1969). *Scottsboro; a tragedy of the American South.* Baton Rouge: Louisiana University Press.

Collier, J. L. (1983). *Louis Armstrong: A biography.* London: Michael Joseph Ltd.

Crouch, S. (1990). *Do the race thing: Notes of a hanging judge.* New York: Oxford University Press.

Cruse, H. (1967). *The crisis of the Negro intellectual.* New York: Arno Press.

Davis, A. Y. (1981). *Women, race and class.* New York: Random House.

Davis, M. (1986). *The fall of the house of labor: Prisoners of the American dream.* London: Verso.

DePalma, A. (1989, January 11). Boom ends as minorities in the region lag behind. *The New York Times*, Section II, p. B1.

DuBois, W. E. B. (1965). The souls of black folk. In J. H. Franklin (Ed.), *Three Negro classics.* New York: Avon. (Original work published 1903)

Early, G. (1989a). "And I will sing of joy and pain for you": Louis Armstrong and the great jazz traditions. In *Tuxedo junction: Essays on American culture* (pp. 291-300). New York: Ecco Press.

Early, G. (1989b). Jesse Jackson's black bottom, or, crossing the roads at Tuxedo Junction. In *Tuxedo junction: Essays on American culture.* New York: Ecco Press.

Editorial. (1989, November 9). *The New York Times*, p. A34.

Fainstein, S. S., & Fainstein, N. I. (1989). The racial dimension in urban political economy. *Urban Affairs Quarterly, 25*(2), 187-199.

Goodwyn, L. (1978). *The populist moment: A short history of the agrarian revolt in America.* New York: Oxford University Press.

Hall, J. D. (1983). The mind that burns in each body. In A. Snitow, C. Stansell, & S. Tompson (Eds.), *Powers of desire: The politics of sexuality* (pp. 328-349). New York: Monthly Review Press.

Hall, S. (1982). The battle for socialist ideas in the 1980s. In *The Socialist Register 1982* (pp. 1-19). London: Merlin Press.

Hall, S. (1987). *The hard road to renewal.* London: Verso.

Haraway, D. (1988). Situated knowledges: The science question in feminism and the privileging of partial perspective. *Feminist Studies, 14*(3), 575-599.

Haraway, D. (1990). A manifesto for cyborgs. In L. Nicholson (Ed.), *Feminism/postmodernism* (pp. 190-233). New York: Routledge.

Henry, C. P. (1990). *Culture and African American politics.* Bloomington: Indiana University Press.

Huckfeldt, R., & Kohfeld, C. W. (1989). *Race and the decline of class in American politics.* Urbana: University of Illinois Press.

Jacoby, R. (1987). *The last intellectuals: American culture in the age of academe.* New York: Basic Books.

The jogger trial: Lynching, or reasonable doubt? (1990, July 28). *Amsterdam News*, p. 12.

The jogger trial: Backdrop for a lynching. (1990, July 14). *Amsterdam News*, p. 12.

Johnson, J. W. (1930). *Black Manhattan*. New York: Knopf.

Kennedy, L. (1990, May 9). Body double. *Village Voice*, p. 35.

Klein, J. (1989, June 26). Spiked? *New York*, 14-15.

The legal lynching continues: The police write the script. (1990, July 21). *Amsterdam News*, p. 12.

Levine, R. (1989, February 28). New York City's economic growth fails to curb rise of "new poverty." *The New York Times*, p. A1.

Lynn, F. (1989a, October 15). Dinkins' money base keeps getting broader. *The New York Times*, p. 40.

Lynn, F. (1989b, August 6). Labor forms potent alliance for Dinkins. *The New York Times*, p. 27.

Lynn, F. (1990a, August 10). Black candidates find a fortune since '77 election. *The New York Times*, p. B1.

Lynn, F. (1990b, September 13). Dinkins sweeps past Koch for nomination. *The New York Times*, p. A1.

Malcolm X. (1972). The ballot or the bullet. In P. Foner (Ed.), *The voice of black America*. New York: Simon & Schuster. (Original work, a speech delivered April 3, 1964, at the Cory Methodist Church in Cleveland)

Marable, M. (1987). Black politics and bourgeois democracy. *Black American Politics*. London: Verso.

Marshall, D. R. (1990). The continuing significance of race: The transformation of American politics. *American Political Science Review, 84*(2), 611-616.

Mitchell, W. J. T. (1990). The violence of public art: *Do the right thing*. *Critical Inquiry, 16*, 880-899.

Mollenkopf, J. H. (1988). The postindustrial transformation of the political order in New York City. In J. H. Mollenkopf (Ed.), *Power, culture, and place: Essays on New York City* (pp. 223-258). New York: Russell Sage Foundation.

Mollenkopf, J. (1989, September 17). Blacks started Dinkins bid in a symbolic river crossing. *The New York Times*, p. 51.

Moody, K. (1988). *An injury to all*. London: Verso.

Morgan, J. (1989, May 9). The pro-rape culture. *Village Voice*, p. 39.

Nicholson, L., & Fraser, N. (1990). Social criticism without philosophy: An encounter between feminism and postmodernism. In L. Nicholson (Ed.), *Feminism/postmodernism* (pp. 19-38). New York: Routledge.

Pfeil, F. (1990). "Making flippy-floppy": Postmodernism and the baby boom PMC. In *Another tale to tell: Politics and narrative in postmodern culture* (pp. 97-125). London: Verso.

Purdum, T. (1987a, July 3). U.S. judge tells police to preserve inquiry Record. *The New York Times*, pp. B1, B2.

Purdum, T. (1987b, July 2). Ward discloses a secret inquiry on black group. *The New York Times*, p. B1.

Reed, A., Jr. (1986). The black revolution and the reconstitution of domination. In A. Reed Jr. (Ed.), *Race, politics and culture: Critical essays on the radicalism of the 1960s* (pp. 61-95). Westport, CT: Greenwood Press.

Reed, A., Jr. (1988). The black urban regime: Structural origins and constraints. In M. P. Smith (Ed.), *Power, community, and the city* (pp. 138-188). New Brunswick, NJ: Transaction Books.

Roberts, S. (1989a, July 22). New York's immigrants aren't rushing to politics. *The New York Times*, p. 27.

Roberts, S. (1989b, June 21). Rich in political power, labor joins Dinkins "mayoral effort." *The New York Times*, p. A1.

Rohalyn, F. (1989, September 26). Dinkins gaining support among business executives. *The New York Times*, p. B2.

Rosenberg, T. J. (1987). *Poverty in New York City: 1980-1985*. New York: Department of Research Policy and Program Development.

Rustin, B. (1971). From protest to politics: The future of the Civil Rights Movement. In *Down the line: The collected writings of Bayard Rustin* (pp. 11-122). Chicago: Quandrangle Books. (Original work published 1964)

Schmidt, W. E. (1989, March 31). Black talk radio: A vital force is emerging to mobilize opinion. *The New York Times*, p. A1.

Shefter, M. (1985). *Political crisis/fiscal crisis: The collapse and revival of New York City*. New York: Basic Books.

Shefter, M. (1986). Political incorporation and the extrusion of the Left: Party politics and social forces in New York City. *Studies in American Political Development, 1*, 50-90.

Shipp, E. R. (1988, January 22). WLIB: Radio "heartbeat" of black live. *The New York Times*, p. B1.

Smith, R. C. (1981). Black Power and the transformation from protest to politics. *Political Science Quarterly, 96*, 431-443.

Smothers, R. (1989, July 3). Station offers perspective of black New Yorkers. *The New York Times*, p. B2.

Steinberg, S. (1989). The underclass: A case of color blindness. *New Politics, 2*(3), 42-60.

Stephanson, A. (1988). Interview with Cornel West. In A. Ross (Ed.), *Universal abandon? The politics of postmodernism*. Minneapolis: University of Minnesota Press.

Tate, G. (1989, May 9). Leadership follies. *Village Voice*, pp. 33-34.

Tobier, E. (1984). *The changing face of poverty: Trends in New York City's population in poverty: 1960-1990*. New York: Community Service Society.

The voice of Malcolm X has an audience again. (1990, February 20). *The New York Times*, p. B3.

Wells, I. B. (1969). *On lynchings*. New York: Arno.

West, C. (1988). Postmodernity and Afro America. *Prophetic fragments* (pp. 168-170). Trenton: NJ: African World Press.

Winant, H. (1990). Postmodern racial politics in the United States: Difference and inequality. *Socialist Review, 20*(1), 121-147.

Wolfe, T. (1987). *The bonfire of the vanities*. New York: Farrar, Straus, Giroux.

6

◉

The Rise of the New Walled Cities

◉

DENNIS R. JUDD

APPROPRIATING THE SYMBOLS OF PUBLIC SPACE

Historically, the public city has found expression in two primary landscapes: the marketplace and the residential community. These two forms are the sources of most of our images of urban life, past and present. The medieval marketplace provided a setting for "free, familiar contact among people" (Bakhtin, 1968, p. 100),[1] a space devoted equally to commerce and culture, a venue for festivals and fairs, theater, the exchange of books, pamphlets, and ideas. Over the past 200 years, market squares have been replaced by commercial

AUTHOR'S NOTE: I am grateful to Lynne Silverman for conducting research and drafting early material for this chapter. An earlier version of this chapter was presented at the Albert A. Levin Lecture Series, Cleveland State University, February 20, 1991. I am grateful to Susan Fainstein, Helen Liggett, and David C. Perry for carefully reading earlier versions and making helpful suggestions.

streets, but the image of the marketplace as an organic entity beyond the control of any external authority except the "invisible hand" has not only endured but has become the sacred icon of capitalist culture.

The idea of community has also been central to representations of the historic city. Residential communities traditionally have been portrayed as constantly changing, free-flowing networks of human relationships centered in home and family. Imagine a crowded street, someone shouting from a window, several people visiting on a front stoop or talking on a street corner. In the United States, embellish these images with a Norman Rockwell painting of a New England town meeting or a suburban village. What these scenes share in common is an assumption that community is constructed of voluntary, not externally imposed, interactions.

The image of the public marketplace has been appropriated by the builders and promoters of modern shopping malls. Their corporate owners frequently refer to malls as the new "medieval marketplaces" and "town squares." Far from rejecting the images associated with the historic marketplace, the promoters of the new enclosed commercial environments resurrect them as useful themes in public relations and advertising copy. The developers of malls and their kin, the "entertainment cities" such as the South Street Seaport in New York, try to create an ambience evoked by "authentic reproductions" of Main Street, frontier towns, and colonial villages (Boyer, 1992, pp. 189-190).

An equally conscious appropriation of the idea of community has been used by residential developers. By the late 1980s about 40 million Americans, or one person in eight, lived in some form of Common Interest Development (CID) (McKenzie, 1989, p. 257). CIDs are often referred to as the "new walled communities" or "gated communities" because of a passing or imagined resemblance to the walled cities of the Middle Ages (Louv, 1985, p. 85). Because CIDs are governed by their own residential associations, developers are fond of promoting CIDs as pure expressions of local democracy and community.

The enclosure of commercial and residential space is becoming a defining and ubiquitous feature of American cities. To understand the impact of this development on urban life and culture, it may be useful, as a starting point, to consider the promoters' claims that they are merely reproducing the marketplace and the democratically organized community. I argue that the recent enclosure of urban space replaces organic processes of the marketplace and residential community with hierarchical control by corporate bureaucracies and developers. Because the authoritarian control characteristic of enclosed, privatized space cannot be sold on its own terms, its promoters describe it, ironically, as its exact opposite.

THE RETURN OF THE WALLED CITIES: SHOPPING MALLS

Kansas City's Country Club Plaza can plausibly be regarded as the first modern shopping center built in the United States. It was begun in 1923 by the suburban housing entrepreneur, Jesse Clyde Nichols (Jackson, 1985, p. 123). Anyone seeing Country Club Plaza today can immediately recognize that Nichols already possessed most of the ingredients making up the formula for a successful shopping center. Nichols certainly thought so; in 1945 he distilled what he had learned over the years into an Urban Land Institute monograph, *Mistakes We Have Made in Developing Shopping Centers.* With its Spanish-Moorish architecture—white stucco buildings and walls inset with multicolored tile mosaics, red-tiled roofs, towers and gables—all set amid flower gardens, walkways, waterfalls, and fountains, Country Club Plaza artfully romanticized a Spanish cityscape. It concentrated together a mixture of shops, professional offices, and services with plenty of parking. Were it not for the economic disruptions of the Great Depression and World War II, shopping centers would surely have proliferated in the 1930s and 1940s. However, by 1946, only nine, including Country Club Plaza, had been built.

The first enclosed mall, Southdale, opened on October 8, 1956, in Edina, Minnesota. It was enclosed for the practical reason of the hard Minnesota winters, but according to its architect, Victor Gruen, it was also designed as "an antidote to suburban sprawl" and as a "mechanism for creating community centers where there were none" (Kowinski, 1985, p. 120). By the 1970s enclosed malls began to compete seriously with open-air shopping centers. Developers liked the malls because enclosure allowed them to compose a total ambience uncontaminated by external influences, a complete integration of surveillance, security, climate control, pedestrian flow, and aesthetics.

Most enclosed malls were originally built in the suburbs, but they now also exist in every American city of consequential size. Indeed they have become a principal weapon used by central cities to compete with the suburbs. A downtown shopping mall is a part of every mayor's "trophy collection," along with an atrium hotel, a restored historic neighborhood, a domed stadium, an aquarium, new office towers, hotels, and a redeveloped waterfront (Frieden & Sagalyn, 1990, p. 43). Frequently, a new convention center and a light rail system are thrown in to complete the set.

Many of the enclosed malls built in big cities have accreted block by block, with tubes and skyways connecting atriums, arcades, food courts, and hotels. In Minneapolis the downtown mall has grown by eating away the insides of the historic buildings, leaving only the historic facades intact. In Montreal and Dallas, veritable underground cities have formed through a network of molelike tunnels. The mall's assault on Atlanta has been much more direct: A huge complex of connected buildings has replaced the historic downtown completely. In core cities and in suburbs, malls have been the fastest-growing form of shopping for almost 2 decades, drawing 172 million adults annually by 1990 (Barbour, 1990, p. A42). Unlike the shopping centers of the 1950s and 1960s, malls constitute more than a mere collection of stores. The larger of them interconnect shopping, recreation, hotels, restaurants, office towers, and, sometimes, condominiums and apartments. The malls increasingly engulf and centralize activities that were formerly spread throughout the urban community at large. Often they also contain stores and activities that corporations have developed solely for mall environments. As described by a developer of a California plaza, his project, like others, is "a city within a city, from high-rise to commercial, from arts and sciences to residential, you name it, it'll have it" (Kowinski, 1985, p. 280).

The Mall as Marketplace

A medieval saying went, "city air makes people free" (Sorkin, 1992, p. xv). According to the literary critic Mikhail Bakhtin (1968), the medieval marketplace "enjoyed a certain extraterritoriality in a world of official order and official ideology, it always remained 'with the people'" (p. 154). The cries of booksellers, hawkers, and merchandise sellers mingled. The language of the marketplace was coarse and rough. Bakhtin suggests that it provided the inspiration for Rabelais's use of language and imagery in his novel, *Gargantua and Pantagruel*. It inspired, as well, Adam Smith, who derived the abstract images of unfettered capitalism from his observations of marketplaces in English towns.

The mall as marketplace is the exact opposite of the medieval market square. Malls are constructed by the same calculus that produces advertising—"pure imageability" (Sorkin, 1992, p. xiv). Many of them derive their images from reconstructed fragments of city life. A sad irony is a necessary component of such efforts: the corporate planners go to great "pains to assert . . . ties to the kind of city life [they are] in the process of obliterating" (Sorkin, 1992, p. xiv). Typically they reproduce a stylized, romanticized, even fairy-tale interpretation of city architecture and culture. They attempt to make perfect that which is flawed. The tableaux they construct are meant to evoke feelings of nostalgia for a school textbook image of cities, or for a utopian city of the imagination. These representations seem better than the actual scenes they mythologize; homeless streetpeople, the din of traffic, deteriorating buildings, litter, and dirt, "all are erased and ignored in the idealized city tableaux . . . set up as an entertaining show" (Boyer, 1992, p. 191).

Despite the power of the images thus invoked, the new walled cities do not replicate the public cities they are replacing. Nor are they merely innocuous facades standing in for the real thing, like Disneyland's three-fifths-scale Main Street America. Rather than being an integral part of a larger urban tapestry, in order to succeed, malls must keep the actual city at bay. When he went back to his hometown of Greensburg, Pennsylvania, William Kowinski, the author of *The Malling of America*, was struck by the irony of the Greengate Mall's ability to keep the town at a far remove, yet idealize its charm:

> The mall not only acted like a main street, it was designed to be one. But not the real one—an archetypal Main Street, designed to fulfill wishes and longings and to allay fears; it was meant to embody a dream and keep out the nightmares. So Greengate Mall's Main Street was an idealization of Greensburg's Main Street, with just the right touch of obvious artificiality to make it permanently extraordinary. It was also cleaner, dryer, more

comfortable, more convenient, better scaled and designed for walking, apparently safer, brighter—and in the final irony, more nostalgically reminiscent of small-town Main Street life. (Kowinski, 1985, p. 68)

The environment of malls is meticulously regulated to ensure absolute predictability. Each type of mall is defined by its mix of shops, design features, and clientele. There are a few standard variations: the luxury hotel/tourist/office and restaurant complexes, such as John Portman's sprawling Peachtree complex in downtown Atlanta; the festival markets, such as James Rouse's Faneuil Hall in Boston; malls that concentrate on exclusive, upscale, high fashion stores; malls that cater to the "typical" middle-class family; and major brand discount malls. For every region of the country and from city to city, within these themes the activities, the mix of exhibits, the tenant stores, atmosphere, and customers are remarkably uniform. A suburban mall in Alabama will have basically the same stores as one outside San Diego, with perhaps a nod in the direction of regional tastes and preferences in gift and curio shops and restaurants. Rouse's Union Station in St. Louis will seem familiar to anyone who has been in Boston's Faneuil Hall. In this respect malls are like the fast-food chains described by Margaret Visser (1987):

When you travel, [they] provide the links that render your route as predictable and as secure, as protective and as limiting as swaddling bands. . . . travel as far as you like, and it will always be as though you were still at home, in the arms of the parent company. Space loses its association with change and surprise. [Down the road] you can without difficulty seek out the identical ambience. (p. 118)

Of course, what is excluded from malls is as important in creating an ambience as the particular mix that defines them. "Undesirable" characters and activities are prohibited—no pawn shops, liquor stores, beer halls, or second-hand stores here, and no going-out-of-business, bankruptcy, or damaged goods sales either. Bell-ringing Salvation Army Santas and their Christmas kettles are not considered the right kind of image and are barred from many malls (Blumenthal, 1989, p. B9). Obvious noncustomers, such as bag ladies, the homeless, or in some cases, teenagers, will be asked to move on or will be thrown out.

Teenagers, who represented a growing $56 billion market in 1990, present a revealing dilemma for mall managements; some of them are customers, and their parents are surely customers, but they pose a potential threat to the mall's controlled atmosphere. A seminar sponsored by the International Council of Shopping Centers considered the problem of teenagers under the rather disingenuous (indeed, dishonest) title, "Hanging Out: Whose Mall Is It Anyway?" (Barbour, 1990, p. A44). Most malls have instituted policies designed to limit the contact between adult customers and free-roaming teenagers, and some have gone farther. North Randall Mall in Ohio requires all teens to be escorted by an adult, even to enter its movie theaters. Park Fair Mall in Omaha has banned all persons under 18 years of age. Almost all malls have increased security measures targeted at teens (Barbour, 1990, p. A44).

Mall managers are particularly militant about forbidding any activities that call attention to social issues. When the Galleria in suburban St. Louis opened in August 1990, a group of gay men tried to enter wearing shoulder sashes imprinted with "Queer Nation-St. Louis." They were, predictably, thrown out (Klamer, 1991, p. 8). The East Town Mall in Madison, Wisconsin, permitted military recruiters to set up displays of military vehicles but refused to allow the antinuclear dance troupe, Nu Parable, to perform. In Arizona, mall owners sued a group of citizens who gathered petition signatures for the recall of Governor Evan Mecham. In 1988, a 71-year-old man received a 1-year prison sentence for entering a mall and distributing leaflets that urged world peace (Hagedorn, 1989). Virtually all malls display notices that activities protected in public areas are not necessarily protected in the mall. Posted near the entrances are notices similar to the Lerner Company's sign, which says: "Areas . . . used by the public are not public ways, but are for the use of the tenants and public transacting business with them. Permission to use said areas may be revoked at any time."

Although mall promoters appropriate the image of the public marketplace, they assert that malls are private places where people do not have the constitutional rights guaranteed in public places. The courts have generally agreed with this interpretation.[2] In 1968 the U.S. Supreme Court, under Chief Justice Earl Warren, ruled that there was a right to free speech in spaces that were essentially public, although privately owned (*Food Employees Local v. Logan Valley Plaza, Inc.*). However, only 8 years later, the same court, now under Chief Justice Warren E. Burger, overruled that decision *(Hudgens v. NLRB*, 1976). In 1979 the California Supreme Court, citing language in the state constitution, ruled that malls in California were required to allow restricted rights to speak, picket, and distribute leaflets (*Robins v. Pruneyard Shopping Center*, 1979). That decision was affirmed by the U.S. Supreme Court (*Pruneyard Shopping Center v. Robins*, 1980). Five states allow some political expression in malls; for most of the country malls are regarded, before the law, as strictly private places (Glaberson, 1992, p. A10). Thus, although the image of the organic, free marketplace informs the rhetoric about malls, their users are defined narrowly as passive consumers.

The Mall as Carnival

The medieval marketplace was the scene of the numerous feasts, fairs, and carnivals that occurred throughout the year, the occasions when "the unofficial folk culture of the Middle Ages and even of the Renaissance" found expression (Bakhtin, 1968, p. 154). These wild and often bacchanalian celebrations functioned as a safety valve in medieval society. Elaborate rituals turned the rigidly enforced ecclesiastical and social hierarchy upside down. The liberal use of profanity and debased language, exaggerated and even grotesque ceremonies, skits that mocked sacred rituals and crowned paupers as kings, the throwing of excrement and urine allowed the masses to escape, however temporarily and symbolically, the rigidly enforced hierarchical relationships of everyday life.

The writer Tom Wolfe once described architect John Portman's Peachtree Center in downtown Atlanta as "great theater" (Oney, 1987, p. 184). A lover of kitsch, Portman sprinkles his lobbies with Japanese streamers, giant mobiles, bronze and glass elevators outlined in lights, even, in Peachtree Plaza, a Liberace-style bandstand with a white grand piano. To the affluent consumers of the new city-within-a-city, Portman's developments feel much like carnival midways.

A carefully nurtured carnival atmosphere pervades all of James Rouse's festival malls, such as Faneuil Marketplace in Boston, Union Station in St. Louis, and Manhattan's South Street Seaport. Rouse has said that his aim is to give "a medieval sense of the marketplace" by mixing specialty shops, clothing stores, restaurants, and food stands and by employing musicians, jugglers, acrobats, and mimes to entertain shoppers. Community activities figure prominently in Rouse malls. Portside Mall in Toledo adopted the city's ballet company, which did the ballet and the city little good. The mall went bust. Faneuil Hall took over the function of displaying art during the remodeling of Boston's art museum. Symphony orchestras, school pageants, and theater groups are invited into Rouse malls.

Mall developers and managers may go to great pains to project a carnival atmosphere, but malls are precisely the opposite of the carnival as a historic phenomenon. The carnival atmosphere nurtured in festival malls is hardly spontaneous or "of the people." Immaculately clean, brightly lit, sometimes deafeningly loud, if some malls feel like carnivals, it is because this impression is meticulously choreographed. The lobbies and atriums, arcades, fountains, pools, waterfalls and sculptures, the trees, flowers, and landscaping, the piped-in music and entertainment, all are coordinated to the last detail. The corporation that manages the mall manages the carnival, if there seems to be one. The stimulation provided in these encompassing environments is precisely like television: the consumer is the passive object of a kaleidoscope of images and impressions. Rather than questioning or challenging the hierarchical relationships of modern capitalism, the version of carnival presented in malls silences consumers with an overwhelming corporate presence.

The Mall as Fortress

The historic image malls most faithfully project is the medieval city as fortress. Malls are "the castles of our own prosperous but anxious times" (Kowinski, 1985, p. 393). The most dramatic and faithful renditions of the fortress theme are John Portman's projects—Peachtree Center in Atlanta, the Renaissance Center in Detroit, the Hyatt at Embarcadero Center in San Francisco, the Bonaventure Hotel in Los Angeles, the Marriott Marquis on Times Square. When Peachtree opened in downtown Atlanta in 1967, it was an instant hit with architectural critics, the media, and the public. By the late 1980s Peachtree Plaza had swallowed up an entire downtown. Sixteen buildings clustered around the aluminum cylinder that housed the Marriott Hotel, anchoring the "honeycomb complex" of Atlanta's constantly expanding, enclosed downtown business district (Oney, 1987, p. 183). The 46-story vaulted atrium that serves as the hotel's lobby sweeps upward toward a skylight. Ranks of balconies ascend into the vast space. The corridors that run along these balconies seem to cling precariously to the sheer walls of a canyon; they are lined with lights and mirrors to enhance the impression.

There is a stark juxtaposition between Peachtree Center and the public streets that run below and around it. Because nearly all activity in downtown Atlanta has moved indoors, the city streets are left almost deserted to pedestrian traffic, especially by nightfall. They seem narrow and confining, an impression provoked by the parabolic curves of the sheer granite and concrete walls of the Peachtree complex as they rise from the edges of the sidewalks. Entrances are few; most of them serve as the grand porticos of hotels, closely monitored by uniformed bellhops. Portman's own interpretation of his enterprise confirms the inescapable impression that Peachtree Center stands as a rejection of the city around it. He has said, "I'm building a city that will become the modern Venice. The streets down there are canals for cars, while these bridges are clean, safe, climate controlled. People can walk here at any hour" (Oney, 1987, p. 184). Portman's design reflects his philosophy that "downtowns are dangerous, that what they lack are 'oases'" (Oney, 1987, p. 184). However, such an interpretation may serve as a gloss for less positive sentiments. Portman has also said, "My idea is I just couldn't see abandoning the cities to the poor" (Oney, 1987, p. 184).

Peachtree Center sits astride downtown Atlanta like a colossus. Little is left of the 19th-century brick business district. The downtown's main tourist attraction is symptomatic of Atlanta's transformation. Once a seedy but fascinating network of jazz and blues clubs, restaurants and bars, tourist shops and the occasional tattoo parlor and prostitute, by the time it closed in the mid-1970s it was dingy and dangerous. In its latest incarnation, it is as squeaky clean, plastic, contrived, and, of course, safe, as any festival mall.

The glassed-in skyways that connect the various atriums and lobbies isolate the inhabitants of Peachtree from the street below. There is a pure segregation between the consumers of the private space inside and the public space shared by people using the streets. This understanding was summed up brilliantly one night by a cab driver as he was delivering this author and some of his friends to the Hilton Hotel. "What do you think of all this?" He replied, "See those tubes up there? We call them 'honky tubes.'"

As city streets become less trafficked the contrasts between public street and privatized enclosure become ever more pronounced, creating a "spatial apartheid" separating the white middle class from the black and poor (Whyte, 1988, p. 203). As the second-story skywalks, atriums, and shops become the preserve of office workers, tourists, and suburban commuters, the streets below are left to minorities and those who ride the bus. In a few cases—Montreal and Dallas, for instance—the enclosed city runs its maze below rather than above. In Dallas, an underground system of walkways attracts the affluent, leaving the sidewalks to "students, minority, and poor people" (Whyte, 1988, p. 204). Whether vaulted above or buried below, the "sealed realm" of the enclosed city is utterly removed from the city outside the walls (Boddy, 1992, p. 125).

The new megastructures constitute "fortified cells of affluence" (Davis, 1992b, p. 155) that divide gilded private enclaves from increasingly degenerated public space. Enclosed malls "filter away the middle classes from downtown streets," thus emphasizing and helping to create two worlds, one within the walls, the other without (Boddy, 1992, p. 151). In this way modern cities begin to seem remarkably similar to medieval walled cities, as described by Umberto Eco (1983):

> In the Middle Ages a wanderer in the woods at night saw them peopled with maleficent presences; one did not lightly venture beyond the town; men went armed. This condition is close to that of the white middle-class inhabitant of New York, who doesn't set foot in Central Park after dark. (p. 79)

One way in which modern cities differ from the medieval cities described by Eco is that the maleficent presences of the Middle Ages were often identified with nature. In contemporary cities they have become one's fellow citizens.

THE RETURN OF THE WALLED CITY: HOUSING

In the early 1980s, the building industry adopted the term *common interest development* (CID)—it sounds better than the term lawyers use, *association-administered servitude regimes*—to describe "a community in which the residents own or control common areas or shared amenities," and that "carries with it reciprocal rights and obligations enforced by a private governing body" (Louv, 1985, p. 85).[3] Upon buying a condominium or home in a CID, the buyer, by virtue of ownership, agrees to abide by a variety of covenants, contracts, and restrictions (CC&Rs). The buyer also shares spaces and amenities "in common" with other home owners. The CC&Rs and common properties, amenities, and services are administered by a home owners association, to which all deed holders belong.

The number of CIDs, which include New Towns, cooperative apartments, condominiums, and single-family houses constructed by a single developer, exploded from about 1,000 in the early 1960s to well over 80,000 by 1984 (Rosenberry, 1989, p. 69). In 1982, one fourth of all housing starts in Florida were condos; by 1990 condos outnumbered single-family dwellings. By the early 1980s, "common interest housing had become a standardized product like cars or televisions sets, offered in a finite range of models" (McKenzie, 1994, p. 182). By the next century CIDs in some form will have become the principal form of new home ownership in most metropolitan areas.

Compulsory-membership home owner associations began to be important mechanisms for enforcing CC&Rs in the 1950s. It is no accident that they began to serve this function in the wake of the U.S. Supreme Court's *Shelly v. Kraemer* decision of 1948, which struck down the enforceability of racially restrictive real estate covenants. The housing industry and the federal government still wanted some means of maintaining the homogeneity of neighborhoods. Although Robert H. Wilson, an economist with the U.S. Department of Interior, denied that "these developments are . . . a product of any systematic philosophy of well-defined public policy" (Nelson, 1989, p. 51), it is clear that CIDs did become the means of continuing the housing industry's and the federal government's decades-old policies that segregated residential areas by income, social class, and race.

In the 1940s and 1950s income and social class segregation was efficiently achieved by building subdivisions of uniform lot sizes and housing cost. Suburbia was virtually synonymous with low-density tract housing, an equation that reflected the developers' success in marketing the suburbs as an escape from the cities (Judd & Swanstrom, 1994, pp. 179-200). By the 1960s, this version of the suburban dream began to yield lower returns. Builders found that the market for single houses constructed on individual lots was diminishing. Huge demographic and income groups that might move to the suburbs if only costs could be brought down remained as vast untapped markets. However, the constantly rising price of suburban land meant that developers could only build lower-priced homes if they could achieve much higher densities. Accordingly the housing industry initiated a campaign to sell a new version of the suburban dream that would include rowhouses and apartment buildings. In the 1960s the American Society of Planning Officials, the Urban Land Institute, developers, and the Federal Housing Administration (FHA) became sudden critics of "gridiron" development and large-lot, low-density zoning. The CID idea anchored a campaign to convince local governments and consumers that higher density development was compatible with the maintenance of property values and exclusion in suburbia (McKenzie, 1994, pp. 158-164).

For more than half a century, the housing industry had sold the idea that exclusion was synonomous with low-density development. It is interesting how fast the same principle was placed into service in behalf of the cause of high-density development. In a report published in 1963, the Urban Land Institute pointed out that CIDs could achieve exclusion better than any alternative form of development: "Existing as private or semi-private areas they may exclude undesirable elements or trouble-makers drifting in" (quoted in McKenzie, 1994, p. 158). The FHA agreed to insure loans for condominiums in multiunit buildings in 1961. Two years later the FHA released its first manual explicitly encouraging developers to build planned units that would be governed by home owner associations. In 1964 the FHA and the Urban Land Institute copublished a 400-page volume describing the history of CIDs and setting forth detailed directions on how to establish restrictive covenants and home owner associations to administer them (McKenzie, 1994, pp. 163-164).

Developers, mortgage lenders, and the federal government promoted CIDs as a way to stabilize land uses and property values. Since
the early 1970s the two biggest secondary mortgage purchasers, the
Federal National Mortgage Association and Federal Home Loan Corporation, have insisted on formulating and reviewing guidelines for
residential associations before purchasing the loans on properties
that will be governed by them. In only 2 decades the institutional
pressures applied by the housing industry and the federal government fundamentally changed the face of the suburbs.

Home Owners Associations
as Expressions of Local Democracy

The fact that home owners and condominium associations elect
their own governing boards led the executive director of the Community Association Institute to proclaim home owners associations to
be a "classic form of democratic government. It's right out of Civics
1" (Stevens, 1988, p. A18).[4] However, there are several ways that
home owners associations do not fit civics-textbook notions of democracy. Perhaps most important, these organizations are invariably
established not by the residents through voluntary agreement, but by
a developer, who sets up a residential association and all of its
governing procedures and bylaws before the first piece of property is
sold. Indeed, even the Community Association Institute itself, which
purports to represent all the home owners associations in the country, was established by the National Association of Home Builders
and the Urban Land Institute in 1973, as a means of marketing CIDs
to a reluctant public.

Home owners cannot buy property in the development without
becoming a member of the residents' association or without, by virtue
of owning property, agreeing to abide by its rules. Further, the
association cannot be dissolved or its bylaws changed without a
unanimous vote of all the members. It exists, effectively, in perpetu-
ity. The covenants and restrictions enforced by residents' associations may dictate minimum and maximum ages of residents, hours
and frequency of visitors, color of paint on a house, style and color
of draperies hung in windows, size of pets and number of children
(if either is allowed), parking rules, patio and landscaping—the list

can be staggering in its length and detail. The restrictions may be dozens of pages long—if, that is, they exist in printed form at all.

Studies have shown that a large proportion of buyers are not familiar with the rules that govern them and sometimes are unaware of any restrictions at all (Winokur, 1989, p. 87). Builders and developers are not required in all states to fully disclose restrictions and covenants; indeed, they may not be required to provide any information about them at all. Even so, except where disclosure is explicitly required by state law, restrictions and covenants are binding even if buyers have not been told they exist (Winokur, 1989, p. 87).

Residents' associations have a tendency toward autocratic rule making, all the more so because they are not required to observe rights of self-expression, free association, and free speech. The residents of CIDs often bridle at the rules, and lawsuits against developers or community associations over their enforcement are frequent. One study of 600 home owners associations found that more than 44% of the boards had been threatened with lawsuits in a year's time (Winokur, 1989, p. 88). Home owners nearly always lose their cases. The courts generally uphold the right of association boards to enforce property contracts and their accompanying restrictions on the ground that buyers voluntarily accepted the terms when they signed a deed.

The litigation to contest restrictions generally involves seemingly trivial minutiae, necessarily so because the restrictions themselves are so numerous and detailed. Litigation has been initiated over the mounting of a basketball hoop, the picking up of dog droppings, untrimmed bushes blocking ocean views, for-sale notices, and flying of the American flag (Klein, 1988; McKenzie, 1989, p. 259; Miller, 1989). In Orange County, California, an association banned fighting by spouses after 11 p.m. The rule was later rescinded, possibly because it was so peculiarly open to ridicule. These and other rules governing daily life are a common feature of residents' associations, and they illustrate the near absence of limits on the powers of home owner associations. The rules and regulations that govern the residents of CIDs are designed to specifically prevent the complex, voluntary interactions, the change and flux, that compose the symbols of urban community and lay the foundation for democratic processes.

CIDs as Community

Kenneth Jackson (1985) has observed, "Throughout history, the treatment and arrangement of shelter have revealed more about a particular people than any other product of the creative arts" (p. 3). Current trends in housing can be regarded as the bellwether of a society that is achieving a remarkably efficient social segregation, even by the standards of the segregated living patterns that have historically characterized urban America.

The new walled cities are planned as spatially segregated environments. Most of them are developed and marketed to sort out home buyers into different income groups. Green Valley, Nevada, a massive gated community just outside Las Vegas, is sectioned not only by different architectural styles, but by the cost and size of houses (Guterson, 1992). Each of these "villages," as the developer calls them, carries the accoutrements of community: a name (Silver Springs or Valle Verde), a community center, a school, a recreational center, perhaps a park (Guterson, 1992, pp. 60-61). However, these are not communities in any sociological sense, because rather than constructing rich networks of relationships, residents tend to isolate themselves in their homes. Rather, the concept of community has been commodified, marketed whole-cloth and in standardized units just like shoes, clothes, cars, and any other consumer product (Guterson, 1992, p. 60). Developers go to great lengths to ensure that the purity of the community-as-commodity they have packaged will not be tampered with by the home buyers. This is the purpose of the detailed regulations and restrictions that they impose.

Whereas historical notions of community evoke images of organic complexity and change, developers have learned to fine-tune their projects to achieve segregation and isolation. The costs of the housing and amenities offered in individual gated communities virtually guarantee that the people living in them will represent a narrow subset of the urban population. Many gated communities are marketed to extremely specialized groups; for example, to retirees, golfers, singles, even nudists. One developer praised this trend as "positive ghettoism," saying,

I think it's fantastic . . . Think of a community where all the people interested in the performing arts live with other people like themselves, or
people who are interested in horticulture live with other horticulture
hobbyists. Or fine arts or culinary interests . . . it's the us against-them idea.
(Louv, 1985, p. 115)

Such a conception of community redefines it to mean less, not more,
interaction, escape from democracy rather than involvement.

CIDs as Fortress

The new gated communities are remarkably like the walled cities
of the medieval world, constructed to keep the hordes at bay. CIDs
are marketed by promising a bundle of goods. These include security,
exclusiveness, and an extraordinary level of amenities. The promise
of security is nestled at the center of all advertisements for the new
walled cities. Typical are these two from an advertising supplement
to *The New York Times Magazine* (November 18, 1990):

The new Southwinds Ocean House offers apartments of 3,000 sq. ft. with
all the advantages of a single family home. A resident manager and security
gate ensure care-free living. You may laze by the pool/gazebo, exercise in
the lap pool, or stroll the miles of sandy beaches at your doorstep. (p. 13)

Sailfish Point is an idyll celebrating your achievements. Its numbers add
up to a lifestyle without compromise . . . . Jack Nicklaus designed our par
72 membership only course to stimulate and challenge but not intimidate
. . . Yachtsmen delight in our private sea-walled marina . . . . The St. Lucie
Inlet puts boaters minutes from deep-sea fishing and blue-water sail-
ing . . . . Natural seclusion and security are augmented by a guarded gate
and 24-hour security patrols. (p. 13)

As the contrast between public and private space becomes more
stark, the psychological lure of defended space becomes ever more
enticing. The media beat a daily drum of hysteria about violent crime.
National and local news stories obsessively chronicle daily drug
busts, drive-by shootings, and murders. American culture is saturated with images of violence. Prime-time television shows such as
America's Most Wanted and *Unsolved Mysteries* profile actual crimi-
nals on the loose and reconstruct heinous crimes while inviting

viewers to phone in any tips to hot lines manned around the clock. As in the anticommunist crusades of the late 1940s and 1950s, citizens are exhorted to watch their neighbors for signs of suspicious activity. It can come as no surprise that no matter where they live, a high proportion of people fear that they will victimized, and the fear of crime has increased since the mid-1960s (Liska & Baccaglini, 1990).

The emphasis on security in some CIDs seems akin to a state of war. Leisure World, a California retirement community, is surrounded by 6-foot walls topped with barbed wire. Quayside, a planned community in Florida, blends the atmosphere of a Norman Rockwell small town of the 1920s with the latest in high-tech security: laser beams sweep the perimeter, computers check the coded entry cards of the residents and store exits and entries against a permanent data file, and television cameras continuously monitor the living and recreation areas (Louv, 1985, pp. 121-125). Members of the security force can wake up or talk to any resident through a housing unit's television set. When the chief of the security police was asked if his employees would also be able to spy on people, he replied, "Absolutely not. There's laws that prohibit that kind of thing. Of course not" (Louv, 1985, p. 125).

In such bunker-style communities, the walls, moats, guarded gates, and security cameras convey an impression of a fortress and of a menacing presence beyond the walls. A fixation on security amplifies fear. A traveler in Albania in the late 1980s commented on the hundreds of gun emplacements he saw in fields and the rows of steel spikes set atop posts in vineyards, meant to impale enemy paratroopers if they tried to land. He wondered about their real objective:

> Of the military worth of these artillery emplacements I cannot speak; I do not know whether Albania has sufficient men or arms to defend them, or indeed whether they are defensible against modern weaponry. But as a constant message to the peasants in the fields that foreigners are enemies, to be guarded against at all costs, the gun emplacements are unrivalled. (Daniels, 1991, p. 6)

The trappings of security that impregnate the new walled communities must have a similar effect, reminding the inhabitants, constantly and repetitively, that the world beyond their walls is dangerous. In both malls and gated communities, "'being inside' becomes a power-ful symbol for being protected, buttressed, coddled, while 'being outside' evokes exposure, isolation, and vulnerability" (Boddy, 1992, p. 139).

Oscar Newman's (1980) study of the residential associations of the private streets of St. Louis, formed in the 19th century, sheds some light on the psychological effects of living in insulated environments. Newman found that the private streets provided "a self-selection of like-minded economically similar and committed residents" (p. 130). The residents reported that the closure of their street made them feel less vulnerable to changes going on in the city around them. "Those gates are not so much barriers as they are signs. We have a need for . . . symbols, signs and arches that say our street is different," said one resident (p. 132). When asked to define "their neighborhood" most residents defined the boundaries as congruent with their own street. In contrast, few residents of public streets limited their defi-nition of neighborhood to only their own street (Newman, 1980, p. 133).

The boundaries of CIDs separate the private from the public world both physically and symbolically. The relative affluence and security of the protected realms creates a stratified culture of separation that makes public space less and less desirable. In this regard, as with so much else, Los Angeles may be the harbinger of the urban future (Davis, 1992a). In Southern California, fortress enclaves have become a ubiquitous feature of suburban development. In search of hi-tech security, architects working for the rich "are borrowing design fea-tures from overseas embassies and military command posts," build-ing hardened walls, secret passages and doors, and installing a dazzling array of sophisticated electronic surveillance devices (Davis, 1992b, p. 173). The middle classes, who can afford a lesser panoply of security gimmicks, are avid customers. There is a heavy demand for gated communities in the Los Angeles area; they are rapidly replacing all other kinds of development. In the suburbs of Los Angeles, the urban future can already be read into the landscape: vast, sprawling clusters of gated communities are connected to one another and to fortress buildings, enclosed malls, and sports stadiums by a web of freeways and interchanges. Urban dwellers learn to negotiate the labyrinth of walls like rats in a maze.

THE NEW CITY ON THE HILL

For years, "container" and "greenhouse" architects have sketched their visions of the city of the future. In the early 1970s the late Buckminster Fuller (1981), inventor of the geodesic dome, produced plans for what he called "Old Man River City"; he wanted, he said, to build a dome over the entire city of East St. Louis. Constantine Doxiadas (1967) envisioned a single worldwide city with an interconnected network of urban communities called Ecumenopolis. Princeton University physicist Gerard O'Neill (cited in Brown, 1989) has proposed orbiting self-sustaining cylindrical communities that operate on solar power. Just as Henry Ford said that the automobile would be the answer to urban problems by predicting, "we shall solve the city problem by leaving the city" (Jackson, 1985, p. 78), these visionaries—or prophets—discern that the solution to urban problems will be a withdrawal to new environments.

The seeds of the future city are planted in fortress enclaves and in gated residential communities. The next logical step will unite these two versions of the new walled cities into enclosed, comprehensive economic and social networks. Architect Dennis Mann, professor of Architecture at the University of Cincinnati's College of Design, Architecture, Art and Planning, predicts that by the year 2000 housing will routinely be built within the enclosed malls: "Apartments will be connected to shopping areas by walkways or built above them, elevating down to lobbies with transitional areas featuring restaurants, grocery, and drug stores and other services used by residents and shoppers" (quoted in Lubinger, 1991, p. 23).

Mann (quoted in Lubinger, 1991) says that home buyers will be attracted by the "commercial components," and retail tenants will also flock to the "built-in market." As housing is incorporated into malls and these structures accrete outward through expanding systems of skyways and tunnels, they are likely to grow into full-fledged cities within cities that privatize and enclose much of what is now located on public streets.

If a future dystopia rises on a foundation of the new walled cities of today, it will be sustained by an antidemocratic, authoritarian politics suited to it. The shrinking of public space is accompanied by a rapid retreat from public institutions of all kinds. A segregation and isolation impelled by fear and anxiety are becoming fixed in urban culture. In cities, the problems of drugs, violent crime, and other problems associated with concentrated poverty are escalating. Rising numbers of the homeless roam downtown streets. One way to deal with these outcasts—it is appropriate to reference the literal meaning of that term—is to wall them out. The architects' visions of the cities of the future may provide a clue to the political response that will be considered appropriate for solving such social problems—and to a possible future response to ecological and environment problems as well. Toxic chemicals, acid rain, global warming, and the erosion of the ozone layer can, at least for a time, be cordoned off, just as urban problems have been. Even if such strategies of escape ultimately fail or backfire, surely they will be tried. The corporate marketplaces and new gated communities of the late 20th century, by enclosing the commons within a protected sphere, reveal a contemporary version of the walled cities of the Middle Ages, albeit a different one from that described by the builders and promoters of today's enclosed and privatized commons.

NOTES

1. I would like to thank Arthur Sabatini, of Arizona State University-West, for guiding me to the works of Mikhail Bakhtin. At the time he suggested I read Bakhtin, I was having trouble framing my study. Arthur suggested that I go beyond the political analysis that came easily to me as a political scientist and also consider the historic images of urban life, as conveyed through Rabelais and critiqued by Bakhtin.

2. I thank Evan McKenzie for informing me about the legal cases on shopping malls. I have shamelessly borrowed from a letter he wrote me, in which he summarized the cases.

3. For an extraordinary account of gated communities, I refer readers to Evan McKenzie, *Privatopia* (1994).

4. Copyright © 1988 by the New York Times Company. Reprinted by permission.

REFERENCES

Bakhtin, M. (1968). *Rabelais and his world* (H. Iswolsky, Trans.). Cambridge: MIT Press.
Barbour, J. (1990, December 9). Malls taking gentler approach toward teens. *Los Angeles Times*, pp. A42-A45.

Blumenthal, R. G. (1989, December 11). Salvation Army kettles are shut out by some malls in bid to control access. *The Wall Street Journal*, p. B9.

Boddy, T. (1992). Underground and overhead: Building the analogous city. In M. Sorkin (Ed.), *Variations on a theme park: The new American city and the end of space* (pp. 123-153). New York: Noonday Press.

Boyer, M. C. (1992). Cities for sale: Merchandising history at South Street Seaport. In M. Sorkin (Ed.), *Variations on a theme park: The new American city and the end of space* (pp. 181-204). New York: Noonday Press.

Brown, A. (1989, July). Japans moonhouses. *Omni*, p. 17.

Daniels, A. (1991). *Utopias elsewhere: Journeys in a vanishing world*. New York: Crown.

Davis, M. (1992a). Fortress Los Angeles: The militarization of urban space. In M. Sorkin (Ed.), *Variations on a theme park: The new American city and the end of space* (pp. 154-180). New York: Noonday Press.

Davis, M. (1992b). *City of quartz: Excavating the future in Los Angeles*. New York: Vintage.

Doxiadas, C. A. (1967, March 18). The coming era of ecumenopolis. *Saturday Review*, pp. 11-14.

Eco, U. (1983). *Travels in hyperreality* (W. Weaver, Trans.). New York: Harcourt Brace Jovanovich.

Food Employees Local v. Logan Valley Plaza, Inc., 391 US 1 308 (1968).

Frieden, B. J., & Sagalyn, L. B. (1990). Downtown malls and the city agenda. *Social Science and Modern Society*, *27*(5), 43-47.

Fuller, B. (1981). *Critical path*. New York: St. Martin's Press.

Glaberson, W. (1992, April 21). In malls, protest and politics are as welcome as crime. *The New York Times*, p. A10.

Guterson, D. (1992, November). No place like home: On the manicured streets of a master-planned community. *Harper's*, pp. 55-64.

Hagedorn, A. (1989, February). Shopping malls becoming free speech battleground. *The Wall Street Journal*, p. 1.

Hudgens v. NLRB, 424 US 507 (1976).

Jackson, K. (1985). *Crabgrass frontier: The suburbanizaton of the United States*. New York: Oxford University Press.

Judd, D. R., & Swanstrom, T. (1994). *City politics: Private power and public policy*. New York: HarperCollins.

Klamer, K. (1991, August 7). Out shopping. *The Riverfront Times* (St. Louis), pp. 7-13.

Klein, D. (1988, October 28). Democracy or chaos? The power of homeowner associations. *Los Angeles Times*, pp. 1, 15, 36-39.

Kowinski, W. S. (1985). *The malling of America: An inside look at the great consumer paradise*. New York: William Morrow.

Liska, A. E., & Baccaglini, W. (1990). Feeling safe by comparison: Crime in the newspapers. *Social Problems*, *37*(3), 360-365.

Louv, R. (1985). *America II: The book that captures Americans in the act of creating the future*. New York: Penguin.

Lubinger, B. (1991, March 23). Mall housing is on horizon, Cincinnati professor predicts. *Cleveland Plain Dealer*.

McKenzie, E. (1989, Spring). Morning in privatopia. *Dissent*, pp. 257-260.

McKenzie, E. (1994). *Privatopia*. New Haven, CT: Yale University Press.

Miller, J. (1989, May 19). Condo warfare. *The Wall Street Journal*, p. R26.

Nelson, R. H. (1989). The privatization of local government: From zoning to RCAs. In
   Advisory Commission on Intergovernmental Relations, *Residential community
   associations: Private governments in the intergovernmental system?* (Publication
   A-112). Washington, DC: Advisory Commission on Intergovernmental Relations.
Newman, O. (1980). *Community of interest.* New York: Anchor Press.
Oney, S. (1987, June). Portman's complaint. *Esquire,* pp. 182-189.
Pruneyard Shopping Center v. Robins, 100 Ct. 2035 (1980).
Robins v. Pruneyard Shopping Center, 23 Cal. 3d. 899 (1979).
Rosenberry, K. (1989). Condominium and homeowner associations: Should they be
   treated like "mini-governments?" In *Residential community associations: Private
   government in the intergovernmental system* (pp. 69-73). Washington, DC: Advi-
   sory Commission on Intergovernmental Relations.
Shelly v. Kraemer, 334 US 1 (1948).
Sorkin, M. (1992). Introduction: Variations on a theme park. In M. Sorkin (Ed.),
   Variations on a theme park: The new American city and the end of space (pp. xi-xv).
   New York: Noonday Press.
Stevens, W. K. (1988, September 1). Condominium owners grapple with governing
   themselves. *The New York Times,* p. A18.
Visser, M. (1987). *Much depends on dinner: The extraordinary history and mythology,
   allure and obsessions, and perils and taboos of an ordinary meal.* New York:
   Collier.
Whyte, W. H. (1988). *City: Rediscovering the center.* New York: Doubleday.
Winokur, J. L. (1989). Association-administered servitude regimes: A private property
   perspective. In *Residential community associations: Private government in the
   intergovernmental system* (pp. 85-89). Washington, DC: Advisory Commission on
   Intergovernmental Relations.

7

Regulation and Flexible Specialization as Theories of Capitalist Development

Challengers to Marx and Schumpeter?

RICHARD A. WALKER

The Regulation and Flexible Specialization Schools are currently the leading contenders for theoretical hegemony in economic geography. Both have been part of a vigorous and salutory debate about the nature of contemporary capitalism and a stimulus to new ways of thinking about industrial and social history—to which I readily acknowledge a considerable debt (cf. Storper & Walker, 1989). Despite this contribution, both schools are seriously flawed in their

AUTHOR'S NOTE: Thanks are due to the ideas of Bob Brenner and Marc Glick, Gerard Duménil and Dominique Levy, and Andrew Sayer and Richard Florida, from which I have borrowed freely—in recognition that the gift is returned from time to time.

understanding of the structure and dynamics of capitalist development and cannot sustain their theoretical ambitions to replace the
classical tradition of political economy, particularly the systems of
Marx and Schumpeter, as a coherent foundation for understanding
the revolutionary evolution of the capitalist mode of production.[1]

This is not to say that we simply go back to the Marxist verities for
all the answers to questions that now perplex us about the changing
face of capitalism across the world today; but I do insist that we not
hastily reject a large body of deep insights into the workings of the
capitalist economy. Marx had a number of things right about the
nature of capital, such as his grasp of class, accumulation, and the
labor process. Schumpeter ("the bourgeois Marx") never succeeded
in overthrowing the Marxian system, but his attention to technological development, industrial epochs, and business cycles continued
more in the tradition of historical materialism than he would have
liked to admit. As circumstances change, we must continue to amend
and update important parts of the tradition to keep abreast, as the
world economy shifts into a new post-Fordist epoch. But it will not
do to jettison too many useful tenets of political economy in the
search for a plausible reevaluation of the past or a shining new image
of the capitalist future.

I wish to condense, from the vast range of disputes raised in
connection with the movement from Fordism to post-Fordism, four
elements of a theory of capitalist development seen through the lens
of Marxist theory, with a Schumpeterian twist. After an introduction
to the Regulation and Flexible Specialization Schools, I begin with
the importance of industrial revolutions in providing a foundation
for major historical epochs of capitalist growth, and I contrast this to
the truncated versions of history presented by the two schools,
centering on the rise and fall of Fordism and mass production. This
is followed by the case for the a broad-based industrial revolution
taking place today, using the concept of the labor process as a way of
organizing the discussion in a way that is more wide-reaching than
the concept of labor process used by the Regulation School and more
grounded than the vague notion of *technological paradigm* employed
by the Flexible Specialization writers.

Next, I argue that industrial revolutions are necessarily entwined
with the uneven geographic development of capitalism. Regulation

and Flexible Specialization theories recognize the importance of geography, but chiefly as a container for variants of national Fordism and local industrial districts. In my view, new methods of production and renewed relations of production grow up together and diffuse with the rise and fall of industries and territorial production complexes, at various spatial levels from the local to the national. Finally I consider the process of economic growth and crisis, by which one epoch of expansion dies out, to be followed by another. The Regulation School has an impoverished theory of growth and crisis, and the Flexible Specialization School has none worthy of the name. In contrast, Marx's theory of the destabilizing drive to accumulate and advance the forces of production offers a better fit with the historical evidence.

These are all daunting fields of economic theory and historical-geographic research to which one can hardly do justice in a brief chapter. Nevertheless they need to be posed in one sweep in order to grasp what the fierce debates over Regulation and Flexible Specialization, Fordism and post-Fordism, are ultimately about. And the fundamental challenges to Marxism—and all classical political economy—have to be admitted, with the proviso that there are things about all the above issues that remain poorly understood by everyone, regardless of their theoretical and political allegiances.

Regulation theory and Flexible Specialization theory are now well-known, but their overall intentions and position in relation to Marxism and prior economic theory need to be indicated. Both are grand theories of capitalism that attempt to grasp the dynamics of economic change in new ways and to reperiodize the last 200 years. I shall indicate their relevant propositions about the economy as the argument of the chapter unfolds, but some general observations can be made at this point.[2]

Regulation theory has two central concepts, the regime of accumulation and the mode of regulation. *Regime of accumulation* refers to the basic economic conditions of production method, income distribution, and effective demand, whereas *mode of regulation* signifies the institutional framework by which balance and stability are maintained, in order that the accumulation process can proceed for a period without structural crisis and transformation to a new regime. Regime of accumulation and mode of regulation play a role analogous to forces and relations of production in Marxist theory, and most of the key concepts deployed by Regulationists, such as Gramsci's Fordism, are taken from the Marxian corpus.[3]

Regulation theory has allowed a critical debate on the nature of contemporary capitalism to take place without anyone having to say the troublesome name of Marx and without having to flog to death old horses such as crisis theory and value theory. Methodologically, the Regulationists have been keen to avoid the relentless determinism and overgeneralization of so much Marxist theorizing, as well as the neglect of intermediate concepts that link the structural logic of capital with the many concrete forms of capitalism. Theirs is the language of the middle ground.[4] Regulation theory makes considerable sense on this score, yet an open-minded methodology serves to frame theory and cannot substitute for theories that seek to explain events. The Regulationists are aware of this, but ardent followers may easily forget that a litany is no substitute for hard answers to difficult questions (cf. Walker, 1989c).

Flexible specialization (Flex Spec) theory has also called Marxist orthodoxy into question on several crucial points. It has challenged the ideas that mass production, large firm concentration, geographical dispersion, and the deskilling of labor are necessarily the culmination of capitalist laws of production and accumulation, thereby forcing a reappraisal of some poorly theorized tenets of Marxian faith. In particular, Flex Spec has helped to recover a lost history of craft work and small-firm industrial districts as complements to Taylorized production in large factories and giant corporations. However, it goes further, in claiming that flexible specialization and mass production are alternative paradigms and that flexible specialization has reemerged as the dominant form of production in the late 20th century, after passing over a "second industrial divide." Flex Spec offers a more technologically supple form of economic development, but it needs to be nurtured through careful institution-building to promote interaction and trust at the regional level (see, e.g., Brusco & Sabel, 1983; Piore & Sabel, 1984; Sabel, 1989; Sabel & Zeitlin, 1985; Scott, 1988a, 1988b; Scott & Storper, 1990; Storper, 1989; Storper & Scott, 1988).

Flex Spec theory cannot compare in scope with Regulation theory, despite its ambitions. Its indifference and even antagonism to Marxist foundations are a serious handicap, insofar as they deny the relevance of concepts such as class, mode of production, or laws of historical development (e.g., Piore & Sabel, 1984; Storper, 1987). Advocates of flexible specialization share with Regulation theorists a concern for middle-level concepts that allow for geographic divergence and temporal breaks in the trajectory of development, and they stress turning points in history in place of the grinding logic of much orthodox historical materialism. Nevertheless, methodological openness often turns into a voluntarism and eclecticism, which comes closer to advocacy than explanation.[5]

INDUSTRIALIZATION AND EPOCHS
OF CAPITALIST GROWTH

Regulation and Flex Spec theories portray capitalist history in a remarkably similar fashion: It all turns on the emergence of mass production, and in each there are three long periods. For the Regulationists, an early epoch of extensive accumulation or competitive regulation, up to about 1914, is followed by the explosion of mass production derived from Frederick Taylor's and Henry Ford's revolution in working methods, and a neo-Fordist epoch is emerging in our own time. The middle period is divided in two, with an early interregnum in which Fordist production methods are put in place, but no comparable Fordist mode of regulation exists to balance production with mass consumption; this comes with the post-World War II labor accords and social welfare state (Aglietta, 1979; Boyer, 1986b; Lipietz, 1987).

The Regulation School's theory of capitalist growth rests on three precepts: that capitalists try to expand productivity (to extract more surplus value); that consumption must balance production (to sell a given output and realize its value); and that large firms have come to dominate industrial production and distribution (a centralization of capital). Fordism is defined by its characteristic methods of high-productivity labor (Taylorist division of labor and the assembly line), means to absorb the output of mass production (the rising, productivity-linked wage), and mode of competition (oligopoly among large firms).[6]

The key period in the scheme is the postwar "Golden Age" of High
Fordism, which is preceded by an epoch of Fordist production without the corresponding regulatory mechanisms of mass consumption.[7]
The theory of Fordism was a response to the postwar situation in
Europe, which was swept by the triad of Fordist production, the giant
corporation, and mass consumption coming from North America.
Aglietta (1979) then read this experience back in time in his path-
breaking treatment of U.S. history. Unfortunately, Aglietta and his
followers fall into three glaring errors in their analysis of capitalist
development, clearly visible in the evidence from the economic
history of the United States. First, they misread 19th-century economic history as lacking in significant mass production and mass
consumption, when it is shot through with technical advances and
the consumption of industrial goods. Second, they take 1929 to be a
crisis of underconsumption—that is, mass production outrunning
mass consumption—when consumption was high and rising in the
1920s. Third, they portray monopoly capital, CIO-type industrial
organizing, and the Keynesian state as necessary to regulation, when
the correspondence between production and consumption has been
achieved through other methods, such as agroindustrialism and
suburbanization (Brenner & Glick, 1991; Duménil & Lévy, 1989b;
Page & Walker, 1991; Walker, 1977).[8] I will take up these shortcomings again later in the discussion.

Flexible specialization theory's history of capitalist epochs is vaguer,
but it amounts to this: an early period of craft production up to the
mid-19th century is gradually replaced by the mass production paradigm and modern corporation, which are eventually stabilized at
their peak by the Keynesian policies of the welfare state. All this is
overthrown in the era of flexible specialization, beginning in the
1970s—the key historical moment in this scheme. This is capitalist
history reduced to a trilogy of a distant craft era (a virtual Virgilian
Golden Age), a well-known Middle Age of mass production, and an
emergent future of Flex Spec. It is a myth.

Both schools center their story on a not terribly original view of
mid-20th-century capitalism, shared with Keynesians and business
historians (e.g., Chandler, 1977; Fraser & Gerstle, 1989; Marglin &
Schor, 1989). In this view, the modern corporation, Taylorist work
study methods, and the Fordist assembly revolution spread rapidly

through the 1920s; mass consumption by workers began in the 1920s but was aborted by the Depression and only secured after World War II; and the state adopted a Keynesian focus on supporting effective demand. It should be said, however, that Regulation theory was a welcome break with the then-dominant Marxist School of monopoly capitalism (Baran & Sweezy, 1966; Braverman, 1974) and its obsession with long-run stagnation—which could not explain the postwar boom satisfactorily. Yet economic history virtually stops for the Regulationists with High Fordism, whereas the Flex Spec School was vigorously trying to convince people that dramatic changes were in the offing by the 1970s.

The reason for the very spare histories drawn by the Regulation and Flex Spec Schools is that neither theory has a strong dynamic component that is able to explain the forward motion of capitalist economies. The historic breaks necessarily come as something of a surprise. Flex Spec makes a virtue of this necessity by theorizing the "industrial divide" as an unpredictable moment when the economy lurches onto a new pathway.[9] Regulation theory does not take its own precepts about raising labor productivity seriously before or after the Taylor-Ford revolution, which is virtually sui generis. It is, rather, occupied with the quietest notions of balance between production and consumption and establishing stability through a mode of regulation. It is closer to neoclassical equilibrium theory than Marxian dynamics (Brenner & Glick, 1991).

According to Marx, capitalist development rests fundamentally on the way this mode of production accelerates advances in the forces of production, a process usually called *industrialization*.[10] By industrialization I mean qualitative advances across a broad front in methods of working, products, divisions of labor, base technologies, and leading industries. The evolution of the forces of production yields periodic transitions sufficiently thoroughgoing to be called *industrial revolutions*. For Marx this story only goes as far as the emergence of what he called "Modern Industry," including the factory system and the making of machines with machines. It had to be left to others, especially Schumpeter, to push the matter farther along into the 20th century. Certainly the advent of Taylorism and Fordist assembly were leading components in the industrial revolution of 1890-1920, but they were not the only significant advances of the time. Electrification (especially motors and controls), hard alloys and high-speed machining, and better cost accounting, among other things, played a big part. Similarly, the period around World War II brought a whole new phalanx of technologies to the fore, such as high-power tubes, transitors and computers, catalytic cracking, plastics and petro-chemicals, and general adoption of the multidivisional corporation.

Those revolutions—or shifts in technical frameworks—occur across groups of leading industries and spread widely during the course of a regime of accumulation. This is why a history of capitalism is necessarily a history of its industries, not just of modes of regulation (Storper & Walker, 1989). Because industries develop on different technical foundations and generate widely disparate kinds of prod-ucts, they are not revolutionized at the same time or in the same way, and we must therefore be very attentive to uneven development as a counterpoint to the sweeping tale of industrial revolutions (Rosenberg, 1972; Walker, 1989a). There are "base technologies," such as machin-ing in the 19th century (Rosenberg, 1976) or microelectronics today (Perez, 1985), which cut a wide swath across many sectors; Fordist assembly was one such revolution in methods, which touched on everything from consumer durables to World War II shipyards. But the Regulationist account of Fordism oversimplifies the evolution of mass production and the unity of 20th-century production.

In my view, the old Kondratieff cycle/long wave periodization of capitalist development, first enunciated fully in Schumpeter's (1939) masterpiece, *Business Cycles*, provides a more satisfactory historical framework than either the Regulationist or Flex Spec visions.[11] It is possible to speak of at least five industrial revolutions that have structured the long periods of capitalist growth since the late 18th century—not the one or two of the Regulationist and Flex Spec accounts. One can do this without the Schumpeterian notion that technological change is a matter of sudden waves of innovation and the first cause in capitalist growth (cf. Mandel, 1975; Storper & Walker, 1989).

Driving these productive advances is the logic of the capitalist mode of production. That task master, accumulation, and its over-seer, competition, provoke capitalists to try to increase the rate of surplus value (improve labor productivity in several ways; intensify labor effort), reduce constant capital (materials saving), reduce the turnover time of capital (eliminate idle time of labor, materials, machines, and finished products), improve realization (better distribution, tighter links to consumers, improved product performance), and open up new areas of value production and realization (offer up new commodities). Regulation theory has surprisingly little to say about the causes and process of technical change other than the refinement of Taylorism (Faucher & DeBresson, 1990). Flex Spec theory has equally little interest in technology, other than pointing out new forms of computer-aided machining for batch production. In general, theories of industrial divides and modes of regulation pay far too little attention to the forces of production, in relation to politics and organization.[12]

The forces of production do not operate as deus ex machina. I take the dialectic of forces and relations of production seriously, and I hold to the Marxian precept of the dominance of class relations of property and exploitation as the defining characteristic of a mode of production. Rapid technical change and industrial revolutions require the right social context, not everywhere to be found; certain social situations and capitalist class relations are more conducive to technical change than others. The 19th-century American Midwest, for example, with its wide access to land and means of production for new producers, was once a hotbed of rapid development (Page & Walker, 1991). The pace of Japanese industrialization cannot be understood without reference to class upheavals of the Meiji revolution and the defeat and occupation brought on by war (Moore, 1966). The relative slowness of British development, by contrast, rests firmly on its immobile class relations (Anderson, 1987). At the same time, industrial revolutions have a massively unsettling effect on social relations. They frequently usher in new production regimes, which are the foundation for new regimes of accumulation. The developing forces of production in crucial ways set the terms for the successive modes of regulation (Storper & Walker, 1989).

Furthermore, the exploitation of labor remains a cornerstone of capitalist production. New sources of super-exploitable labor, such as immigrants in Southern California or women in the Third Italy, and new forms of exploitation, such as temporary hiring, can cause surplus value to gush forth like a freshet amid the most worn technical clichés. Regulation theorists (e.g., Boyer, 1988a; Leborgne &

Lipietz, 1990) and Flex Spec theorists (e.g., Christopherson & Storper, 1988; Scott, 1988b) are quite right to worry about the struggle for more humane forms of flexible work and employment in the post-Fordist era (see also Standing, 1992). Nonetheless, capitalist development rests fundamentally on the creation of relative surplus value and elevation of productivity, which no amount of intensive exploitation can equal in the long run (Brenner, 1977). The character of the epoch rests in part on the core employment relation between capital and labor, but it cannot be defined in those terms alone, as Regulationist theory implies (e.g., Leborgne & Lipietz, 1988).[13]

Industrial revolutions are, I repeat, qualitative advances across a broad front in the ability of humankind to master the forces of nature to useful ends. This includes new methods of working, new products, new divisions of labor, new materials, even whole new base technologies. The postwar period saw not only a spread of Taylorism and Fordist assembly methods, but revolutions in agriculture, petrochemicals and synthetics, aircraft design, and metallurgy that owed little to Ford's achievements, vast though they were (Freeman, 1982; Rosenberg, 1972).

The Labor Process and the Contemporary Industrial Revolution

Industry is a highly diverse set of activities that cannot easily be reduced to a single term. Economic theorists have tried in various ways to boil it down to "utility" or "energy flows," but the yardstick to which everyone usually returns is human labor. The reason is that whatever else production may be—horsepower, metallurgy, bioengineering—it is still a human-initiated, conceived, and conducted transformation of nature for human ends. The guiding hand of industry is human, notwithstanding the implicit contributions of nature (i.e., dependence on natural forces) and the fantastic enhancements achieved through the use of accumulated human technology. In order to comprehend industrial development, then, there is still good reason to build on the labor process approach of Marx.

The analysis of industrial progress is similarly vexed without a core concept of human labor. For example, many writers seem to use quantity of output as the defining element of industrial development, as in the terms *mass production* and *batch production* used liberally by Regulation and Flex Spec theorists. To begin with, the crucial relation behind these terms is not mere quantity (after all, the women who sew baseballs in Haiti produce a tremendous number of them), but productivity—the ratio of output to inputs. However, measuring productivity raises a whole host of difficulties (Perlo, 1982). Above all, it requires an index of *total factor productivity* that aggregates a host of unlike things—products, materials, machines, buildings, and people. Both major indices in use, the productivity of labor and the productivity of capital, are subject to doubt, owing to the heterogeneity problem.[14] Nonetheless, the bottom line in industrial advance is ultimately the productivity of labor—as indicated by its continuing general use for international and intersectoral comparisons of industrial capability and progress.

Flex Spec writers have mistakenly substituted *flexibility* for *productivity* as the key variable in contemporary industrialism. Not only is the term used indiscriminately, in contrast to *rigidity* (Sayer, 1988), but it centers on a response to consumer demand, not on enhancing production in the interest of accumulation.[15] Flexibility is seen principally as a defensive strategy of risk avoidance in the face of fragmenting demand, increasing competition, and a stagnant world economy rather than as a means of competitive advantage and the development of the forces of production in an expanding system.[16]

Furthermore, flexible specialization is portrayed as an alternative rather than a complement to mass production (Piore & Sabel, 1984). Mass production is presented as a *technological paradigm*, as if it were merely an idée fixe, rather than a predictable consequence of successful expansion of output and productivity—the universal goal of capitalist commodity production—wherever demand and technical conditions allow. There is no evidence that mass production has been eclipsed today, only that the methods of achieving higher output and productivity of a wider variety of goods have improved (e.g., Donaghu & Barff, 1991). The challenge is not mass versus batch production, but improvements in both.[17]

Regulation theorists are correct to build on labor process theory, but they have taken over largely intact the narrow and one-sided interpretation of Marx put forth by Braverman (1974), as well as his obsession with Frederick Taylor's role in defeating craft workers in certain key industries at the turn of the century (e.g., Aglietta, 1979;

Coriat, 1983). Thus Fordism is defined as "Taylorism plus mechanization" (Leborgne & Lipietz, 1990). This is wholly inadequate. To begin with, it does not distinguish Fordism from any other period of capitalist industrialization: Taylor was building on a long tradition of work rationalization and detail division of labor going back to the manufacturing era of the 18th century; and mechanization had been applied to factory production from the first industrial revolution. Both developments were amply discussed by Marx (1863/1967)(Brenner & Glick, 1991).[18] In addition, Fordist assembly goes well beyond Taylorism and mechanization; it was, in fact, a very specific set of accomplishments in interchangeable parts, elimination of "fitting," rationalization of work flow, dedication of specialized machinery, and, finally, automation of the moving line (Hounshell, 1984).[19]

Furthermore, the Regulationist definition of Fordism ignores the breadth of technical change outside metal-working and assembly industries, as previously indicated. Without a broader understanding of the labor process, we are blind to the dynamics and richness of the process of technical change.[20] There are five dimensions to the labor process: direct labor, machinery, materials/products, indirect labor, and collective labor. Each lends a twist to the development of the forces of production.[21]

- The direct actions of labor—processing, assembly, transfer, regulation, and integration (Walker, 1989a)—can be improved by detail division of labor, rationalization of effort, better sequencing, improved flow, careful measurement and feedback, learning, and skills acquisition. Taylor emphasized the first two kinds of strategies; Ford attended most to the next three (Hounshell, 1984); the Japanese have added close attention to worker cooperation and learning (Sayer, 1986).

- Machinery can be applied to the actions of labor to enhance the performance of the worker or to replace some workers altogether. However, there is no one path to mechanization: Higher productivity might be achieved through either automated flow, computer-regulated feedback, or simply larger, faster individual machines (Walker, 1989a).

- Materials can be improved so the same effort yields better results. Materials are transformed according to the nature of the substances themselves; hence, progress in steel making has rested in large part on advances in metallurgy—not on Fordist-type improvements in direct labor. This is even more dramatically the case for the chemical industries or electronics.

- Improvements in indirect labor contribute to productivity by enhancing such activities as design, engineering, and software (Walker, 1985a). Furthermore the multiplication of new products, new inputs, and complementary activities generates external economies, owing to specialization, learning, efficient scope, flexibility, and so forth (Scott, 1988a; Storper, 1989).[22]
- The fragments of the division of labor must be reintegrated into functioning labor systems (Marx's "collective worker") through systems of industrial organization, which are themselves subject to repeated improvements in management methods and ways of cooperative working (Walker, 1988b).

The Regulation School borrows heavily from traditional French Marxist theory of state monopoly capitalism in emphasizing a restricted set of large firms and nation-states as the means of economic "régulation" (Boyer, 1986b). Flex Spec theory broke with this orthodoxy to insist on the positive contribution of small firms, regions, and networks of firms, but has been unduly wedded to the *industrial district* as the principal mode of organization today (Sabel, 1989; Scott, 1988b).

The technical basis of the current industrial transition has been touched upon from many angles, yet almost no one has tried to pull the scattering of insights together in one argument about a major advance in the forces of production on several fronts. There has been, in my view, a qualitative shift in the nature of capitalist industrialization—a new industrial revolution, whose key elements are:[23]

1. More efficient and creative uses of human labor
2. New and improved machinery, and especially machine monitoring
3. Better understanding, preparation, and use of materials
4. New divisions of labor in products, design, circulation, and so on
5. New forms of industrial organization and production integration.

It is not possible here to do more than provide an indicative list. Nonetheless, it is impossible to maintain the thesis that industrial methods are little changed from the high tide of the post-World War II epoch (cf. Gertler, 1988; Williams, Cutler, Williams, & Haslam, 1987). At the same time, the new industrial revolution cannot be reduced to a detached technical phenomenon, as in the popular neo-Schumpeterian

theme of the "microelectronics revolution" or "information revolution" (Forester, 1987; Perez, 1985). There is a much wider scientific-
technical push taking place, which includes radically new materials
as well as faster communications, better administrative techniques
as well as machine capacities. Recall that Ohno's just-in-time/total
quality control system evolved entirely in the absence of computers,
using kanban boards (Cusumano, 1985; Sayer, 1986).

The new industrial revolution crosses the whole domain of labor,
and cannot be confined to the shop floor or the mechanical industries
such as machining and auto assembly. Nonetheless, improvements in
direct, hands-on labor are a big part of it. Better work rationalization
and intensification are important, of course, but this is not simply
neo-Fordist, after the fashion of the early Regulation theorists (Aglietta,
1979).[24] Flexibility in the application of labor and in interfirm relations
is a part of it, but so are rigidities of new forms of fixed capital, organizational networking, and mass retailing (Johanson, 1989; Schoenberger,
1990). Better learning and directly anti-Taylorist methods of creative
application of labor are important, too, but there is not by any means
a general revival of craft work using flexible work stations, in the
manner of Piore and Sabel (1984), nor a thoroughgoing shift toward
intelligent work, in the hopeful scenarios of Hirschhorn (1984) and
Kern and Schumann (1987). It cannot be forgotten that many capitalists continue to rely on extreme exploitation through lower wages or
driving workers harder (Christopherson, 1988; Leborgne & Lipietz,
1990; Sassen, 1988). In short, there are several competing and complementary paradigms of production available (Sayer, 1988).[25]

Certainly, capitalists have had to come to grips with limits to the
Taylorist problematic: This means often junking simplistic notions
of individual work rationalization and extreme division of labor and
backing off from high automation and top-down managerial control
in order to reassess the organization of labor—one step back and two
forward, down different (often surprisingly different) lines of approach (Walker, 1989a). Having discovered that you can never get the
labor out of production systems as a whole and that more sophisticated processes and machines benefit from more intelligent application of human labor, many capitalists have been forced to rethink
how best to use workers.

The same is true of Fordist notions of rigidly linked and unstoppable flows, backed up by large inventories available "just-in-case" something goes wrong (Sayer, 1986). These have proven to be wasteful of circulating capital and expensive to retool, owing to large amounts of fully dedicated fixed capital. They are particularly inappropriate in the face of unstandardized demand or rapidly shifting technologies. Ford's revolution in mass production was so immense that capitalists often lost sight of an older principle of fitting supply to demand as a way of increasing sales, rather than the other way around (Forty, 1986). GM's Sloan was the first to demonstrate the vulnerability of Ford's Model T to product variation (Hounshell, 1984), but today this principle has been taken much further, as the Flex Spec theorists have indicated.

The relation between ordinary labor and technical innovation has become a greater focus of capitalist attention in this period, as well. As technology progresses, industrial engineers and capitalists have become increasingly aware of the rewards of pushing those possibilities as far as possible, and they have tried to build more continuous innovation into their organizational plans and ways of working. This means that the strategies of putting thought to work, harnessing indirect to direct labor, and linking today's work to tomorrow's product should be highlighted as increasingly explicit parts of capitalist rationalization of production. Yet a serious note of caution needs to be raised with regard to the oft-heard claim that the rate of innovation has gone up (e.g., Sabel, 1989). The level of technical sophistication has repeatedly risen over the course of industrialization, and the latest industrial revolution does not mean that things are moving faster; rather, because greater capability keeps pushing up against bigger and harder problems, maintaining the same rate of innovation requires a more systematic approach to technical change as a part of the complete labor process (Florida, 1991).[26]

Uneven Development and the Specificities of Time and Place

These improvements are not being applied equally nor everywhere at once. This is why we commonly speak in terms of new "models" of production developed in particular places. These models combine different pieces of the new industrial revolution into concrete packages of innovation and workable production. In short, the geographic specificity of industrial activity and technical change must be confronted directly (Storper & Walker, 1989).

For example, the Emilia-Romagna model of flexible specialization in metal working is the result, in good part, of improvements in machinery for batch production, better attention to product design, development of labor skills, and better interaction among a network of workshops. The Japanese model of just-in-time production is a way of reducing idle time for capital, increasing work effort (especially the intelligent application of workers' time), and more effective sales (through product quality control and response to demand), among other things. The Silicon Valley model, if you will, is one of harnessing creativity to the exploration of the possibilities of the technological base of designing and etching microcircuitry on silicon chips, coupled with explorations in computer design and programming (software), to the end of multiplying commodity offerings, improving commodity performance, and lowering costs.

There are other important models besides the Holy Trinity. There is Fujitsu's link of product design and manufacture within one big firm (Kenney & Florida, 1988)[27]; the California model of industrial agriculture (Fitzsimmons, 1986); the West Los Angeles model of armament production involving hyperinnovation of limited-production military products (Markusen, Hall, Deitrich, & Campbell, 1991); the Korean model of large ship building (Amsden, 1989); the German model of steady skill development, especially in metal working (Katzenstein, 1989); or the Ikea-Benneton model of merchant subcontracting and targeted retailing (Gardner & Sheppard, 1989).

There are thus a great many important areas of advance in capitalist industry that the Italian model of flexible specialization does not comprehend, contra Sabel's (1989) embracing sweep of everything into that particular basket. Japanese mass production methods are not reducible to anything like flexible specialization, as Friedman (1988) argues (Dohse, Jurgens, & Malsch, 1985; Sayer, 1988). Nor am I convinced that microelectronics is adequately handled in Flex Spec terms (e.g., Saxenian, 1991): Its mining of the Silicon Lode is based on a technological breakthrough of an historical magnitude quite beyond anything the Third Italy can boast. I'm suspicious of Storper's (1989) case for Hollywood as flexible specialization, tout court:

Television, video cassettes, and audio technologies have fundamentally conditioned the breakup of the studio system. I also find it improbable that German industry's long and continuing vitality is reducible to flexible specialization along Baden-Wurtemburg lines (Sabel, Heerigel, Kazis, & Deeg, 1987). And, finally, the big gains of the newly industrializing countries have often come in sectors such as steel, ship building and chemicals, and through modes of state planning and repression, which owe almost nothing to flexible specialization—or Fordism, for that matter (Amsden, 1989; Harris, 1986).

The preceding arguments about the new industrial revolution and its internal diversity form the basis for a more general theory of uneven development. Industrial revolutions are spatial revolutions. To their credit, Regulation and Flexible Specialization theorists have contributed to the rediscovery of the geographic in social theory and political economy in the 1980s (Soja, 1989). But each has decided shortcomings.

Abstractly, Regulation theory notes the specificities of time and place as part of its refusal of overgeneralization: Capitalism takes on varied forms as it develops throughout the world (Aglietta, 1982; Boyer, 1986a). The intention is to preserve the dialectic of the whole and the parts that is lost in world-system and globalization theories (Boyer, 1986b). Nonetheless, Regulationist thinking revolves chiefly around variants of Fordism at the level of the nation-state (Lipietz, 1987).[28] Advocates of Flex Spec, by contrast, have focused on the regional basis of flexible production (Becattini, 1987). This fills in an important dimension below the nation-state; but Sabel (1989) takes this much further, arguing that the regionalization of economies is supplanting national economic integration. Scott (1988b) pushes the argument in another direction, noting the formation of new industrial spaces of flexible production outside the Fordist heartlands.

I would like to pick up on the themes of localization and new industrial spaces in uneven development, while avoiding four pitfalls into which enthusiasm for flexible specialization and industrial districts can lead. First, there is no reason to think that new industrial spaces are singularly identified with Flex Spec; they have been apparent even in Fordist industries such as automobiles around Detroit. Second, the local, national and global are all important territorial levels in the rolling process of uneven development. But the case for a strictly globalized, international division of labor under the dominion of the multinational corporations was never very strong, and the local needs to be recovered (Jenkins, 1987; Walker, 1989b).[29] Third, regionalism was never dead. Even within a place as homogeneous as the United States, regions such as the Midwest or California were always distinct (Page & Walker, 1991). Sabel (1989) exaggerates the contrast between past and future by using the same globalization thesis for the era of mass production as his critics. Fourth, territorial production complexes can have quite extensive external linkages, without this denying the significance of localized divisions of labor, networks, and governance mechanisms (Gordon, 1991).

The geographic theory of industrial growth and change can be developed in a way different from either the theory of Regulation or Flexible Specialization. The process of *geographical industrialization* (Storper & Walker, 1989) has the following principles:

- Key industrial breakthroughs tend to be sector- and site-specific because technological progress is strongly tied to practical competence, based on the accrual of experience and learning, and to the space for collective puzzle solving, passing on ideas, and developing the possibilities of a technological framework. Fordism's birthplace was the American Midwest for reasons that go deeper than one man's inspired madness (Hounshell, 1984; Page & Walker, 1991).
- New industrial locales have the ability to develop in unlikely places, thanks to both the rapid rates of accumulation and the experimental nature of their growth process. Industrialization produces new places, to be added to the growing and shifting geography of the developed world. The ossification of managerial and engineering practices in existing industrial areas frequently works against innovation, whereas the implementation of new industrial methods often proceeds most easily with fresh labor forces without acquired habits of work, labor organization, or self-identification.
- New industrial implantations are often sites of innovation in class and labor relations, involving new levels of exploitation, as well as new ways of working and managing. The geography of accumulation is made up of the accretion of many such local capitalisms.
- Growing industries build up extensive territorial concentrations of related activities, while at the same time spinning off growth peripheries to capture markets, conquer competitors, or exploit new supplies of labor and/or materials. Growth peripheries bring with them social practices

adhering to the new industrial base, by means of which the class relations and institutions of accumulation are substantially overhauled.

- Given the common technological and social foundations of broad industrial revolutions, the space-economy of capitalism has undergone repeated upheavals, as Marshall (1987) has shown for Britain.
- The local becomes the global as the effects of new industrial systems spread through large segments of the national and international economy and transform the larger capitalist system.

Regulation theory, by contrast, overstates the necessity of national and international consolidation of a mode of regulation (cf. Brenner & Glick, 1991). As late as the 1970s, the unions in the United States were still fighting corporate end runs to southern branch plants or through southern-controlled congressional committees in an effort to salvage a declining U.S. Fordism (Clark, 1989; Schoenberger, 1988). Similarly, the regime of Italian Fordism, centered in the north, was never successful in conquering either the center or the south (Sabel, 1982). Consolidation of any regime at the international level is even more problematic, as the interwar years show (Mistral, 1986). Today's situation is very much open, with no clear hegemonic form of production yet established (Sayer, 1988; Leborgne & Lipietz, 1990).

More important, even where a core national economy sits safely atop the world, it presides over a system of uneven development in which the parts are moving at different rhythms and speeds. Just-in-time delivery and computer-guided machines were gestating in the belly of Fordism, beginning to kick up a disturbance before erupting full-born on the world stage. This represents more than different sectoral growth rates and their disturbing influence on accumulation; it means nurturing potential new forms of employment and class relations, which serve as a political as well as economic challenge to the hegemonic order. Geography is deeply indicted in this drama of capitalist regicide, placing the crucial contradictions often just beyond our field of vision. One has to return to the place of Japan again: its growth rate has far exceeded all other developed nations, whereas its experience of crisis has been much milder (Gordon, 1988; Lipietz, 1987). A most profound struggle is now being played out as Japan— now the wealthiest nation—shoulders its way to the top.[30]

The Dynamics of Accumulation and Crisis

The great postwar boom in global capitalism—whether it is called High Fordism, the Golden Age, or something else—fell on rocky times after 1970. Growth rates have generally been slower in the last 20 years than in the previous 20, business cycles more marked, unemployment and poverty more persistent (see e.g., Brenner & Glick, 1991; Devine, 1986; Marglin & Schor, 1989). What caused this economic slowdown and instability? More generally, what is the process by which any industrial epoch comes to an end, to be transcended by another?

Every period of rapid economic growth, or accumulation of capital, eventually slows as the conditions for balanced expansion disintegrate. As things come apart, the economy usually goes into some form of open crisis, such as the bankruptcy of many companies, collapse of major banks, and sudden widespread layoffs of workers. The precept that such crises are generated by the internal logic of the economy is shared by Marxist, Schumpeterian, and Keynesian theorists but rejected by neoclassicals, for whom the balancing mechanisms of the market are entirely self-regulating, absent large external shocks such as OPEC's raising of oil prices in the early 1970s. Regulation theory falls into the first camp, whereas Flex Spec is essentially neoclassical (or noncommittal) in its treatment of the end of the era of mass production.

Marxist crisis theory has had a fruitful intellectual history, but one long on disputation and short on consensus. One can understand the impatience with what has often degenerated into a scholastic debate. Regulation theory can be seen, in this light, as an effort to get round the Vs and Cs and get on with filling in the middle level of treating the contours of growth and crisis in greater richness: the "diversity of their exact forms" (Boyer, 1986b, p. 15). Yet Regulation theory explicitly acknowledges the Marxian precept that the initial wellspring of crisis, however it may be compounded by middle-level forces, lies within the accumulation process itself, not in happenstance (Boyer, 1986b, p. 69). In fact, Regulation theorists have been in the midst of a flurry of recent research into the exact course of the economy leading up to the great crises of the 1930s and 1970s, which brought the two long periods of expansion in the 20th century to an end.

There is a growing body of evidence to support the classic Marxian idea that the slowdown of accumulation is led by a falling rate of profit.[31] For the postwar era, it appears that profits fell rather steadily from a point circa 1950 through the 1960s and have revived somewhat (but variably) since (for reviews see Cherry et al., 1988; Devine, 1986; see especially Duménil & Levy, 1989b; Shaikh, 1987; Webber & Rigby, 1986).

The principal cause of the postwar fall in the rate of profit was, according to the Regulationists, the stagnation of Fordist production methods (Aglietta, 1979; Boyer, 1988b; Lipietz, 1986). Fordism, it is said, ran up against the technical and social limits of the basic framework (cf. Schoenberger, 1988). Increasing detail division of labor created mismatches among the cycle times of various subprocesses, dedicated machinery became too unadaptable, delays or failures in one part of the system could jeopardize the whole of articulated assembly lines, and so forth. At heart of the failure of Fordism was a porousness in the application of labor (Aglietta, 1979). Concomitantly, the intensification of labor and of mind-numbing Taylorist work rationalization generated worker absenteeism, resistance, and poor work quality.[32]

Some sort of exhaustion of any technological framework is to be expected at some point (Sahal, 1981; Walker, 1985b). But the evidence for a general exhaustion of mass assembly processes is poor. For example, Japanese productivity in auto assembly was rising fast throughout the last 40 years, and Japanese car makers eventually overtook U.S. and European producers in volume on a world scale (Abernathy, Clark, & Kantrow, 1983; Mair, Florida, & Kenney, 1988). The more "exhausted" portions of the industry were outcompeted and displaced to a large degree. As for technological stagnation in general, it is almost impossible to make such a case. The Regulationists are here reproducing a pure Schumpeterian theory of growth and crisis, in which waves of technical innovations trigger epochs of growth and exhaustion of those innovations lead to crisis, until a new wave of innovations bursts on the scene. This theory has been amply researched in recent years (Mensch, 1979) and rejected by the neo-Schumpeterian School itself (Freeman, Clark, & Soete, 1982).

On this much we agree: that the rate of technological change is a fundamental variable in any analysis of growth and crisis tendencies in capitalism. But to me it is essential to locate the source of crisis in the forward movement rather than the stagnation of the forces of production. My reading of Marx's analysis of the falling rate of profit is that he was trying to make his theory of capitalist development consistent with crisis. That is, he wished to show that the principal dynamic force in capitalist expansion—the drive for relative surplus value by revolutionizing the labor process—was at the same time capable of undermining accumulation as it proceeded. Technological dynamism ought to figure in major crises in the capitalist system, then, but in what way? We shall return to this in a moment, but consider first the Regulationists' treatment of the early 20th century.

The Great Depression of the 1930s is explained by the Regulationists as a crisis due to the rapid growth of productivity combined with the rapid spread of Fordist methods, uncompensated by a parallel growth of consumption due to suppression of working-class organization after World War I (Aglietta, 1979; Boyer, 1986b, 1988b; Lipietz, 1987; see also Devine, 1983).[33] Here the problem is not stagnation but rather too-rapid technological change. The key failure of the system is portrayed as the lack of an appropriate mode of regulation (especially the wage accord). Thus the Regulationists have two theories of crisis for the whole century-long period of Fordist mass production: underconsumption in the 1920s and technical stagnation in the 1970s. This may be a sign of open-mindedness, or an intellectual shell game.

The underconsumptionist view of the 1920s has been sharply challenged (Brenner & Glick, 1991; Duménil, Glick, & Rangel, 1987; Duménil & Lévy, 1989b). There is no clear evidence in the aggregate statistics on U.S. consumption to show that it lagged behind production in the 1920s, even though there are indications of rising productivity from World War I onward. The fallacy in the argument is to think that a shift in aggregate income distribution away from the working class took place, and that this meant mass consumption sagged. Rather, profits fell more than wages, middle- and upper-class consumption roared ahead (much of it on credit), the consumption of investment goods by capitalist firms proceeded apace up to the crash.

Meanwhile the idea that either technical stagnation or underconsumption lay behind previous crises in accumulation is, for the case of the United States at least, far-fetched. The Regulationist history of capitalist development in the United States turns on a decisive break from extensive accumulation to intensive accumulation around the turn of the century, thanks principally to Taylorism and Ford's assembly line. This is pure myth. U.S. development had been intensive from the late 18th and early 19th century, as the first industrial revolution spread and was enhanced by additional American innovations in everything from grain milling, saw milling, and cotton ginning to house building, machining, and integrated textile fabrication (Hounshell, 1984; Rosenberg, 1972). At the same time, mass consumption of industrial goods had been steadily expanding, thanks to the relatively well-off farm population, thorough commercialization of social relations, effective merchandising and retailing, and cheapening of products (Porter & Livesay, 1971; Tedlow, 1990; Williamson, 1951). The United States was Fordist before Fordism or, rather, thoroughly capitalist and rapidly developing on that basis before the 20th century (Page & Walker, 1991).

In fact, the aggregate data on technical progress (productivity growth) and mass consumption (retail sales) for the United States mark out a surprisingly smooth curve of steady exponential growth (Duménil & Lévy, 1990). Even though I am inclined to divide industrial history over the last 200 years into four epochs, or long waves, with a fifth in the offing, there is no clean break in the technical or aggregate income records at such points as 1787 or 1900.[34] Only with hindsight is it possible to reconstruct the kinds of substantial technical innovations that allow this amazing rate of growth to be sustained again and again, and to see that the industrial system did move through a sequential of epoch-making changes from one set of structures to another (cf. Rosenberg, 1972; Sahal, 1981; Schumpeter, 1939).

The principal flaw in Schumpeterian theories of technological exhaustion is to ignore the dynamics of investment (Harvey, 1982). If one is to take Marx and Keynes seriously, as the Regulationists purport to do, then investment has to be allowed to play a leading role in accumulation (Walker, 1988a). Investment is the critical element in the addition of new capacity, the application of new equipment, the opening up of new product lines, the creation of new firms, and so forth. It is easy to generate models of growth swings (expansion followed by crisis of overinvestment) with a few simple assumptions, for example:

- Capitalists invest in an effort to expand their market share.
- Demand is growing at a given rate and can be saturated.
- The future cannot be anticipated perfectly.
- Competition drives every capitalist to try to expand at the expense of the others.
- Fixed capital (in equipment, structures, etc.) is necessary to production; it has a long life (e.g., 10 years) and cannot be adjusted downward instantaneously (without loss).
- Capitalists expand investment when profits rise and cut back on investment when profits fall.

In such a model, investment accelerates until supply outruns demand due to overinvestment in fixed capital, precipitating a falling rate of profit on now-underused capacity; this triggers a downward spiral of investment (and unemployment) until excess fixed capital is retired (for a review, see Van Duijn, 1983). If we allow the additional assumptions that investment can occur in new firms and through credit formation, then overinvestment will show up in these forms, as well: too many firms (excess competition) and too much debt (excess fictitious capital). Marx calls such overinvestment overaccumulation (Harvey, 1982).[35]

Technical change must be figured into such a model. Investment and technology are the two blades of the scissors of industrial growth, representing the demand and supply for new productive capacity. First, new technologies may be embodied in new products, which increase the rate of growth of demand (that is only possible because they also add new workers and incomes into the system to help absorb the additional output). Second, other new technologies will be embodied in more productive fixed capital, raising the rate of exploitation and hence the rate of profit.[36] Thus the tendencies to overproduction and falling profits in the first model will be delayed by the beneficial effects of technical change. Investment unleashes technical change (although not in direct proportion), and hence new investment can contravene the tendency to overinvestment for a period of time.[37]

Nonetheless, overaccumulation of capital will occur, regardless of the rate of technical change. That is, overinvestment can show up even where the forces of production are not stagnating. This has been visibly the case, for instance, in the extreme swings (of about 5 years duration) in the electronics sector over its brief history (Sturgeon & Walker, 1991). For the whole U.S. economy in the post-1965 period, this kind of overaccumulation shows up principally as a fall in the rate of profit despite a steady (if unspectacular) rise in the rate of labor and total factor productivity (Brenner & Glick, 1991). The same kind of long-term falling rate of profit is apparent in the 1880s and 1910s-1920s, as well, inscribed in the downside of the last two long waves of accumulation (Duménil & Lévy, 1989b; see also Mandel, 1975).[38] Concomitantly, overaccumulation showed up in all these downturns as excess competition (too many new firms offering substitute products) and excess debt (too many banks making unrecoverable loans).[39]

The other missing component of the stagnationist model is uneven development. It is common in crisis theory to consider intersectoral imbalances between capital goods and wage goods, using two-sector models (Harris, 1985). Aglietta (1979) and Lipietz (1986) use this sort of model. The consumer goods sector is chasing final demand but creates a secondary demand for capital goods. If both sectors are subject to the effects of business swings, then the capital goods sector will be whipsawed more sharply than consumer goods, and the whole economy will be less stable as a result.

Real economies are more complex, of course: they demonstrate persistent unevenness in rates of growth and accumulation among many different industrial sectors (Walker, 1988a).[40] This rests, in turn, largely on differences in rates of technical change—also on different rates of exploitation and growth in demand. In other words, as technology evolves, new sectors open up with rapid growth rates, some older sectors gain a new lease on life, and other sectors decline; in short, some sectors are always stagnating relative to others, but there is no general tendency to stagnation. There is only a process of uneven development.

Moreover, uneven development applies to the places in which differentially expanding sectors grow up, as we have previously argued. It is geographical-industrial uneven development. And it need not be confined to individual industries but can embrace groups of related industries and territorial aggregations, such as whole nation-states.

Uneven development has several pertinent effects for the model of investment and overinvestment, growth, and accumulation crisis. First, it worsens the tendency to overinvestment, because new sectors and places competing with established ones will be eager to expand as fast as possible, and all sorts of regional and national interests kick in to promote this. Korean state planners were by no means simply responding to net global demand growth or capital markets in pursuing their policy of hothouse industrialization (Amsden, 1989). Second, it puts an added edge on overcompetition, given the uneven distribution of competencies: Those most feeling the bite of competition are laggards in the duel to improve technology. Hence the truly appalling spiral of decline in the U.S. steel industry in the 1980s, for example. Moreover new competitors usually combine innovative products or production methods with cheaper, less militant labor, in a truly deadly package, as did the capitalists of Japan, Los Angeles, and Korea (Storper & Walker, 1989).[41]

Third, multiple sectors growing at different rates makes for a very complex pattern of interrelated business cycles, in which the leading sectors struggle to keep the aggregate economy afloat, while laggard sectors drag it down—and the whole is pulled this way and that. Silicon Valley was out of synch with the rest of the U.S. economy throughout the last decade, for instance. Finally, uneven development worsens problems of overaccumulation in declining sectors and places, or what Harvey (1985) calls the problem of "switching" capital from areas of relative stagnation to fast-growing sectors and places. Hence the massive plant closures (and unemployment) that swept the northeastern United States in the early 1980s.

The inclusion of overinvestment and uneven development solves three outstanding difficulties besetting the simple industrial revolution model of capitalist history, as presented earlier:

- Industrial development (technical change) is more or less continuous, particularly in the sense in which innovations are actually implemented through investment in new activities and equipment. It does not require any "wave of innovation" to propel accumulation, only waves of investment.

- Industrial epochs, or regimes of accumulation, rise and fall on the basis of long waves of investment, in tandem with unfolding technologies. Accumulation crisis will come about despite continual innovation—although it will, of course, come quicker if there is significant stagnation across many sectors.[42]
- The seeds of the new era are already planted in the old (an old Marxist principle that appears to have been forgotten by the Regulation School). This jibes with the evidence that long before the crisis of Fordism set in, many of the important innovations of the present epoch, such as microelectronics and just-in-time assembly, had already put in their appearance.[43] (This is even more clearly the case if the long wave is dated from circa 1940 through the mid-1980s, not the early 1970s, as is often done) (cf. Gordon, 1988).

In addition, uneven development makes it clear that accumulation crisis can be global at the same time as it hits different countries and regions differentially. Japan can be rising in the 1970s and 1980s even as the global economy suffers through relatively poor growth and greater instability; indeed, Japan's meteoric rise is part and parcel of the overcompetition, overinvestment, and instability problems besetting the system. The same could be said of a leading sector, such as microelectronics.

The above model of overaccumulation and uneven development contains all the essentials of growth and crisis in the postwar era. The question for the Regulation School at this point is: what does the theory of Regulation add to this classical explanation? Lipietz (1986, p. 27) ends his careful treatment of the falling rate of profit with a disclaimer against "a Talmudic harking back to a general Marxian theory of crisis," but this is pure window dressing. The fact remains that the mode of regulation does not add a jot to the explanatory power of his model.[44] To be sure, there is a breakdown of the four main sites of balanced growth or points of regulation: competitive undermining of oligopolies by new firms, competitive undermining of high wage rates/unionization by new labor forces, undermining of the hegemony of U.S. capital by international competition, and the bloating of the credit-system to finance such investments.[45] But these are all easily comprehended as elaborations of the basic model, not as something apart; and the important point is that the grinding of economic gears is still what shatters the carefully built-up institutional apparatus of regulation.[46]

In short, the Regulationist argument rests too much on the coherence and stability of regimes of accumulation and not enough on the essential role of contradiction and unevenness in the dynamics of capitalist development. It is fundamentally derived from the French traditions of organic theories of society, in the manner of Durkheim, and structuralism, in the manner of Levy-Strauss and Althusser (e.g., Aglietta & Brender, 1984; Lipietz, 1988).[47] As such, it contrasts with the vision of Marx and Schumpeter as to the tumult of modernism, marked by "creative destruction" and the way "all that is solid melts into air" (Faucher & DeBresson, 1990; Harvey, 1989).

The Flexible Specialization School is largely bereft of any explanatory theory of crisis by which the Golden Age of postwar mass production was undone. The key term in Piore and Sabel's (1984) account is *the breakup of mass markets* (see also, e.g., Scott & Storper, 1990). This breakup means that rigid Fordist production methods cannot respond as effectively as flexible production systems. They sometimes seem to attribute the breakup of mass consumption to changing tastes, but fashion can only be a minor contributor to the problem. A more plausible reason for the breakup of markets is the end of the postwar labor accord, with corresponding loss of disposable income among the middle ranks of the working class (this is simply the breakdown of the mode of regulation by another name (cf. Pollert, 1988). Certainly, redistribution could have had effects on the composition of demand, with a diminishing portion of mass-produced items suitable for the working class. But the upward redistribution that occurred in the 1970s and 1980s came after the crisis of profitability had already set in (Brenner & Glick, 1991). It was the crisis in accumulation that led capitalists to attack the working class's share of national income, helping precipitate a falling wage rate and breakdown of the labor accord in the 1970s and 1980s (Harrison & Bluestone, 1988).[48] In other words, the crisis of Keynesianism is an effect as much as a cause of the end of the postwar boom (Lipietz, 1986).[49]

Most plausibly, the breakup of mass markets can be attributed to excessive competition, as many writers put it. Growing competition—seen especially as international competition in the United States and Britain—is by far the most important cause of the breakup (Feldman, 1989). But overcompetition is due to overaccumulation.

Attributing increased competition to internationalization of markets, as Schoenberger (1988) does, only evades the connection between competition and accumulation; internationalization is due to the growth of effective competitors abroad—that is, worldwide capital accumulation—as well as more effective foreign competitors—that is, technological progress in an unevenly developing world. (As for competition from U.S. or European branch plants, they are also the result of investment of accumulated profits in the core looking for new outlets.)

Here, too, the timing of the crisis is closely related to uneven development in a way that Flex Spec theory cannot comprehend, given its "totalizing discourse" of mass production versus flexible specialization.[50] The Flex Spec camp sees flexibility as almost entirely a response to the crisis of the last 20 years, rather than as a development nurtured within the bosom of Fordism.[51]

CONCLUSION

The failure of Regulation theory and Flex Spec theory to explain growth and accumulation crisis are not surprising in light of the lack of true dynamics in their models of Fordism and flexibility. They lack the dynamism of both investment/accumulation and of technical change/advancing forces of production, as well as the unexpected turmoil induced by uneven development. In fact, the inability of these schools of thought to see the further evolution of the labor process across a wide swath of industrial activities is the principal cause of the strategic shifts they make in historical explanation. In the case of Regulation theory, Fordism bursts forth in the 20th century, creates fundamental problems of stabilization, and ultimately stagnates. In response to this simplistic account, the causal weight of the model is transferred to the institutional superstructure, or mode of regulation, and the result can hardly be called dynamic or historical at all. In the case of Flex Spec, demand shifts take us across the industrial divide from craft to mass production and back again (regardless of whether their origin is tastes, distribution, or state support). History circles back on itself, or shifts to and fro aimlessly, rather than moving forward with industrialization and capitalist development.

In contrast to the two prevailing schools, I have argued for a more dynamic, historical view of the past and the present, in which the evolving forces of production, driven by the classic laws of the capitalist mode of production, play a critically important role in economic development and in changes in the capitalist system over time and space. Those forces are necessary (if not sufficient) to any satisfactory understanding of growth, crisis, the character of production regimes, and uneven development. In so arguing, I am bucking much of the tradition on the Left, which woefully neglects the technological basis of development and modern life, as well as the current fashion to deny large historical structures and forces such as capitalist property relations. I am not opting for modernization theory or industrial society as the basic category of analysis. Yet I am aware that Marxists and their challengers often have a hard time answering the gut appeal of the theory of modernization because it refers in such large part directly to the experience of the productive (and disruptive) powers of industrialization (e.g., Berman, 1982). To recover the full significance of the term *labor*—the interaction with nature and the physical foundations of social life (Smith, 1984)—without losing sight of the powers of capital—that curious form of modern property—is simply to live up to the spirit of historical-geographical materialism.

Let me be clear that by this I do not mean that the relations of production follow along passively, adapting to the developing forces of production, as in the historical materialism of Cohen (1979). What I mean is that the shifting foundation of production—the amazing process of industrialization—has repeatedly knocked the props out from under established social arrangements and posed new puzzles for humanity to solve. How this unwinds is very much an open, experimental process, even though the contours of the prevailing social relations of production channel the movement in certain ways. The dialectic of forces and relations is an ongoing negotiation within a predominantly capitalist order, which, at this juncture, is not likely to give way to some kind of socialism through a millenarian rupture. None of this can be taken to diminish the role of politics and social struggle, unless it is unacceptable to make politics anything less than everything. Rather, it is to argue that the forces of production people develop and employ some basic terms for the world they live in, mold to their ends, and cry over.

NOTES

1. It is amazing to me that Regulation and Flexible Specialization theories have gained so much attention in the 1980s, while the ambitious synthesis of Marx and Schumpeter by Mandel (1975) is nearly forgotten. For all his flaws, Mandel attempted a coherent treatment of technology, accumulation, class relations, and historical epochs. For a useful comparison of the three models, see Webber (1990).

2. I shall try to differentiate clearly between Regulation theory and Flexible Specialization, even though there has lately been a great deal of cross-fertilization between the two (e.g., Leborgne & Lipietz, 1990; Scott & Storper, 1990).

3. The main advocates of Regulation theory are Aglietta (1976, 1979, 1982), Lipietz (1982, 1987), Boyer (1986b), Coriat (1979) and Mistral (Boyer & Mistral, 1978).

4. Owing much to the Annales School of history, American institutionalist economists, and Althusser's revolt against Stalinist orthodoxy in French communist thought. These methodological precepts resonate with ideas on the Anglo-American left, such as the English philosophical movement called Realism (and to a lesser extent Structuration theory) in the attempt to deal with open and complex systems in a nonreductionist way while still having recourse to the explanatory power of underlying structure and mechanisms (Sayer, 1984).

5. Early efforts, principally by Piore and Sabel (1984) and Becattini (1987), to put a shining face on flexible specialization by underplaying the exploitation of labor and overplaying the craft control of the process have generally been abandoned in the face of withering criticism (e.g., Boyer, 1988a; Pollert, 1988). But the more circumspect adherents never saw new methods of production as more than contingently connected to conditions of employment (e.g., Christopherson & Storper, 1988; Scott, 1988a).

6. Fordism sometimes refers to a production system, sometimes to the idea of paying high wages to absorb mass output. However, the story about Henry Ford paying $5 per day to sell his cars—that was picked up by Gramsci and through him Aglietta—is purely apocryphal: Henry did it to retain workers when his turnover rate on the new assembly line hit 200% per year.

7. More broadly, Regulation theory is a two-stage history of capitalism, with the 19th century seen as extensive growth of production, lack of mass market and competitive regulation and the 20th century as intensive production, mass consumption, and monopoly-state regulation. However, its treatment of the 19th century is quite weak (see below). My only difference with the critique by Brenner and Glick is that they slight industrial development before 1860.

8. What is more, the periods are most unlikely to be the same in the United States and Europe, as is usually implied (this after all the to-do about respecting the specificities of time and place!). Schumpeter (1939), by contrast, is very careful about the frequent nonconvergence of business cycles in different countries.

9. I can hardly agree with Leborgne and Lipietz (1990), therefore, that Flex Spec is a form of technical determinism. Technology hardly enters the picture at all. The whole problem with both schools is the almost complete indeterminacy of their models, in which history stops dead in its tracks.

10. A term that slights agriculture and urbanization if not used with care (Page & Walker, 1991).

11. This does not mean I am fully in accord with all the contemporary versions of long wave history (e.g., Berry, 1991; Bowles, Gordon, & Weisskopf, 1983; Hall & Preston,

1988). Schumpeter also provides an account for economic, technical, and institutional changes at the level of short swings, which virtually all other accounts ignore.

12. This is not to say that a fully satisfactory economic theory of technical change exists, and some kind of combination of evolutionary economics (e.g., Nelson & Winter, 1982) and Marxism seems to be the best we have (Storper & Walker, 1989; Webber, Sheppard, & Rigby, 1990).

13. Accumulation and class struggle are not the only things propelling industrialization; human ingenuity and natural systems have logics, as well (Mowery & Rosenberg, 1976; Sahal, 1981).

14. Labor valuation runs up against the heterogeneity of skills (quality of labor) and wages (costs of reproduction), a problem solved, I believe, by Itoh (1987). Capital valuation runs up against the problem that the price of capital goods implicitly includes their future income streams, assessed at the current interest rate (Harcourt, 1972). However, the question of measurement can quickly take us into the morass of value theory and capital theory, into which we shall not plunge in this chapter (see Walker, 1988a).

15. On the limits of a demand-led theory of technical change, see Mowery and Rosenberg (1976).

16. The central ideas of the Flex Spec thesis are three. First, capitalist firms are learning to respond more flexibly to more fragmented and unstable demands as mass markets break down, by producing a wider and more variable set of commodities and innovating new products more quickly. Second, they accomplish this end by means of more creative use of skilled labor, by more flexible relations among firms, and with the aid of new programmable machines. Third, this approach develops most forcefully where production becomes more flexibly organized; this occurs chiefly in vertically disintegrated networks of firms and the industrial districts in which they tend to cluster, but not without the help of regional systems of cooperation and governance and imitation by large firms and their subcontractor networks.

17. Also, firms are not all crowding into specialty niche markets using flexible methods for product diversification. Rather product expansion (not just diversification) has always been a basic strategy for expanding the realm of accumulation (although too much neglected in Marxist analysis in favor of cost reductions). This does not imply a new attention to flexibility so much as an increased awareness of the possibilities for sales inherent in opening up new fields of demand. The same is true of improvements in preproduction design, simulation, and market-testing phases of production: This systematizes the generation of new products and assures better realization of their value. But it is no more a matter of flexibility than the armies of sales workers developed throughout the last century.

18. In short, Regulation theory attributes to the Fordist epoch alone what has been a long-standing pattern of industrial capitalism, which Marx attributed to capitalist property relations (Brenner & Glick, 1991).

19. Taylorist and Fordist actually apply to rather different batch and mass production systems (Coombs & Jones, 1989).

20. Indeed it can be argued that the Regulation School really has no theory of technical change at all (Faucher & DeBresson, 1990; cf. Boyer, 1988b). This is partly due to the strategic shift in its model from production to consumption as the driving force of capitalist development—a very Keynesian move that leaves them surprisingly close, in the end, to the Flex Spec School.

21. This sketch is based on Walker, 1985b and 1993.

22. Technical change does not consist only in making the same things more cheaply, but also in meeting new needs—a point that Marx neglected (Morgan & Sayer, 1988; Schumpeter, 1934). With capital goods, better products improve productivity and performance in other sectors (Rosenberg, 1976).

23. These have been gleaned from a wide literature, from which a selection follows: Adler, 1985; Aoki, 1990; Cohendet, 1988; DeBresson & Walker, 1991; Dosi, Freeman, Nelson, Silverberg, & Soete, 1988; Florida, 1991; Forester, 1987, 1989; Freeman, 1987, 1991; Gardner & Sheppard, 1989; Hakansson, 1989; Hoffman & Kaplinsky, 1988; Kenney and Florida, 1988; Lazonick, 1990; Martinez and Jaramillo, 1989; Monden, 1983; Morris-Suzuki, 1988; Perez, 1985; Sayer, 1986; Scott, 1988b; Storper, 1989; Williams et al., 1987; Wood, 1989; Zuboff, 1988.

24. But see Storper and Scott (1992) for a sense of the expanding definition of industrial change now admitted into the broad compass of the Regulation School and flexible production theory.

25. On this point I agree with Coombs and Jones (1989), but see far more than the three paradigms they indicate (neo-Taylorism, neo-Fordism, post-Fordism). Their discussion, like so many, is also based entirely on the mechanical industries.

26. Or what Morris-Suzuki (1988) calls "perpetual innovation."

27. Kenney and Florida (1988) link the just-in-time to continuous innovation in defining a total Japanese production package that they see as far ahead of all competitors (see also Florida, 1991; Florida & Kenney, 1990).

28. See also the valuable amendments by Schoenberger (1988) on Fordism and Mistral (1986) on regulation at the international level.

29. To respond to Flex Spec, as if it were an obvious heresy from a known truth, by wheeling out the weary catechisms of globalization will not do (e.g., Amin, 1989).

30. Japan has been sorely misunderstood. It is distinctive both for its particular production achievements in automobiles, consumer electronics, shipbuilding, steel, and so on and for its force as a national economy. Gordon's (1988, p. 60) statement that, "The Japanese story is, by and large, one of corporatist collaboration between large corporations and the state," slights the productive base. At the latter level, arguments about whether Japanese production methods are neo-Fordist or flexible specialization are beside the point, since the national economy of Japan has a coherence that matters decisively in the struggle for hegemony. It is rather disingenuous, in light of Japan's weight in the world economy, for Sabel (1989) to argue that the new production regime is diffusing from Italy to Japan. Then, too, Anderson's (1987) comment that Japan is "the last great classically national economy" seems to me way off the mark; it is, rather, more a sign of British malaise to think that world hegemony is old hat.

31. Although aggregate figures on rates of profit do not quickly or simply translate into enterprise rates of profit to which capitalists respond directly (Walker, 1988a).

32. A similar and quite convincing list of shortcomings of Fordist production methods has been developed by many writers on the Anglo-American Left (see, e.g., Florida & Kenney, 1990; Knights, Wilmott, & Colinson, 1985; Littler, 1982; Wood, 1989).

33. And the valuable debate between Duménil et al. (1987) and Devine (in press). The Regulationists' views on this matter are almost completely a rehash of the Keynesian Alvin Hansen and the Marxian-Keynesian Paul Sweezy (1942), writing in the 1940s. Brenner and Glick (1991) discuss the underconsumptionist aspect of Regulation theory at great length, whereas I prefer to emphasize the problems in their treatment of production.

34. However, there is a remarkable and as yet unexplained rise in the productivity of capital in World War II (Duménil & Lévy, 1989a). This may mark an industrial

revolution spurred on by the war, which is completely absent in the history told by the Regulationists; but it is as yet unexplained.

35. Such a model generates disequilibrium owing to differential rates of change between demand and supply, behind which lie imbalances in fixed and circulating capital, that is, fixed capital cannot be adjusted quickly enough to avoid overinvestment and overproduction. One cannot simply invoke long-term adjustment to overcome such short-term imbalances; in neoclassical fashion, the process of adjustment is sufficiently imperfect that it generates patterns of instability (oscillations) in growth. It does not, except rarely, produce the kind of radical short-term rupture and stagnation depicted in Keynesian theory (Duménil & Lévy, 1989b, 1990).

36. It is a good idea to include compensating reductions in constant capital due to cheapening of capital goods, more efficient use of materials, and additions of labor-intensive activities owing to a widening division of labor and product innovation.

37. I beg the question here of the existence of swings and industrial epochs of varying lengths and overlapping occurrence.

38. The role of the productivity of capital (i.e., nonlabor inputs) in the postwar falling rate of profit is very much in doubt. U.S. total factor productivity appears to have wavered with shorter business cycles in the 1950s to 1970s, without any clear long-term decline (Brenner, 1991). At the same time, Duménil and Lévy (1989a) show a falling productivity of capital throughout the 20th century, except for the rise during World War II. This sort of long, long-term fall in the productivity of capital does not alter the model of long waves or shorter business cycles based on investment outrunning productivity to produce a falling rate of profit. (If there were a real break in capital productivity during the war, it would only help explain the extraordinary vigor of the postwar expansion period.)

39. Although I am not discussing the Social Structure of Accumulation School in this chapter, a couple of words are in order about their theory of crisis, which is driven principally by rising worker militancy and wages (Bowles et al., 1983). Although the latter may have worsened the rate of profit in the mid-1960s, there is no evidence that wages outran accumulation for the preceding period and considerable evidence that wages have fallen in the 1970s and 1980s without yet putting accumulation back on its feet (Brenner & Glick, 1991). In the model of overaccumulation, worsening income distribution would not shrink aggregate demand but rather shift its composition. In particular, capitalist class profits and savings would be higher, leading to a more rapid rate of investment (and credit creation, as the savings flow through banks into new investment), which would worsen the process of overaccumulation. This would have been particularly apparent in the United States during the 1920s when this country was the leading area of capitalist expansion; today much of the new investment is shifted elsewhere.

40. I do not agree with Glick's portrait of profit equalization (Brenner & Glick, 1991; Glick & Ehrbar, 1990). I don't think that high capital mobility is incompatible with permanent disequilibrium growth, nor that such an assumption is necessary, either for crisis theory or the critique of monopoly theory.

41. Competition is not just a matter of spatial diffusion of Fordist technology to peripheral areas generating low-wage competition for the core (cf. Gramsci, 1971, p. 311). Fordism had long been expanding globally into lower-wage areas (Europe and Japan), where it helped raise wages and sustain the long postwar boom (Schoenberger, 1988); why did this end? Why did low-wage competitors in Asia who were once laughed at for their shoddy goods ultimately become threats to American and European capital?

42. In other words, the model does not ride on the outcome of the debate over stagnating Fordist methods in key sectors such as automobiles, in key places such as the United States and France; it works in any case. Mandel (1975) was correct to embed technological revolutions in a matrix of long waves of investment and business activity but still clung too closely to Schumpeter's idea of clusters of innovations.

43. Just as the new Fordist methods (among other things) were being installed rapidly in the 1920s. On the unevenness of sectoral development at that time (defined somewhat differently) and its import for crisis theory, see Devine (in press).

44. Note the way Bertrand (1986), in discussing postwar growth in France in a much more institutionalist manner, skips around the issue of why the mode of regulation broke down. The explanatory failure of regulation theory for the crisis of the 1920s and 1930s is even worse, of course. According to the theory, there is no effective mode of regulation at the time—so how then is any balance achieved at all?

45. Regulation theorists have made a concerted exploration of financial matters and state intervention, which I skip by here at some risk (see, e.g., Aglietta, 1979; Lipietz, 1979, 1983).

46. For an excellent explication of the various explicit or implicit economic models of crisis adhered to by Aglietta, Lipietz, Boyer, and Bertrand, see Duménil and Lévy (1990).

47. See also the critique by Peet (1989) and Faucher and DeBresson (1990).

48. The sequence of events is this: Profits fell all through the long postwar upswing (by some accounts) or by 1966 (by others), but the edifice was not seriously breached until 1970-1975. The wage accord then began to come apart, with hyperinflation in the 1970s and deflation in the early 1980s. This may have allowed the rate of profit to rise from perhaps the mid-1970s and certainly in the 1980s, even though capitalists continued to be beset by volatile conditions and intensified competition.

49. One can add the state into this account, as the Flex Spec School usually does; its theorists have a strong interest in state regulation of production and consumption, which I do not treat here (Piore & Sabel, 1984; Sabel, 1989; Scott & Storper, 1990). But the same caveats hold about the timing of the right-wing attack on government and the end of the welfare state, which occurs almost entirely after 1978 (Harrison & Bluestone, 1988).

50. I use the bracketed term ironically in response to Flex Spec advocate Michael Storper's (1987) wrongheaded postmodernist critique of Marxism.

51. As an aside, Flex Spec theorists have very little to say about money and finance. This is, I surmise, related to their greater distance from the theory of value and capital that animates the Regulation School via Marxism.

REFERENCES

Abernathy, W., Clark, D., & Kantrow, E. (1983). *Industrial renaissance: Producing a competitive future for America.* New York: Basic Books.

Adler, P. (1985). Technology and us. *Socialist Review, 85,* 67-98.

Aglietta, M. (1976). *Régulation et crises du capitalisme.* Paris: Calmann-Lévy.

Aglietta, M. (1979). *A theory of capitalist regulation.* London. New Left Books. (Original work published 1974)

Aglietta, M. (1982). World capitalism in the eighties. *New Left Review, 136,* 3-41.
Aglietta, M., & Brender, A. (1984). *Les metamorphoses de la societe salariale: la France en projet.* Paris: Calmann-Lévy.
Amin, A. (1989). Flexible specialisation and small firms in Italy: Myths and realities. *Antipode, 21*(1), 13-34.
Amsden, A. (1989) *Asia's next giant: South Korea and late industrialization.* New York: Cambridge University Press.
Anderson, P. (1987). The figures of descent. *New Left Review, 161,* 20-77.
Aoki, M. (1990). A new paradigm of work organization and coordination? Lessons from the Japanese experience. In S. Marglin & J. Schor (Eds.), *The golden age of capitalism: Reinterpreting the postwar experience* (pp. 267-293). New York: Oxford University Press.
Baran, P., & Sweezy, P. (1966). *Monopoly capital.* New York: Monthly Review Press.
Becattini, G. (Ed.). (1987). *Mercato e forze locali: Il distretto industriale.* Bologna: Il Mulino.
Berman, M. (1982). *All that is solid melts into air.* New York: Simon & Schuster.
Berry, B. (1991). *Long-wave rhythms in economic development and political behavior.* Baltimore, MD: The Johns Hopkins University Press.
Bertrand, H. (1986). France: modernisations et piétinements. In R. Boyer (Ed.), *Capitalismes fin de Siècle* (pp. 67-105). Paris: Presses Universitaires de France.
Bowles, S., Gordon, D., & Weisskopf, T. (1983). *Beyond the waste land: A democratic alternative to economic decline.* Garden City, NY: Anchor.
Boyer, R. (Ed.). (1986a). *Capitalismes fin de siecle.* Paris: Presses Universitaires de France.
Boyer, R. (1986b). *La théorie de la régulation: Une analyse critique.* Paris: Éditions La Découverte.
Boyer, R. (Ed.). (1988a). *The search for labor market flexibility.* Oxford, UK: Clarendon.
Boyer, R. (1988b). Technical change and the theory of regulation. In G. Dosi, C. Freeman, R. Nelson, G. Silverberg, & L. Soete (Eds.), *Technical change and economic theory* (pp. 67-94). New York: Pinter.
Boyer, R., & Mistral, J. (1978). *Accumulation, inflation, crises.* Paris: Presses Universitaires de France.
Braverman, H. (1974). *Labor and monopoly capital.* New York: Monthly Review Press.
Brenner, R. (1977). The origins of capitalist development: A critique of neo-Smithian Marxism. *New Left Review, 104,* 25-92.
Brenner, R. (1991). *International crisis and U.S. decline.* Unpublished manuscript, Center for Social Theory and Comparative History, University of California, Los Angeles.
Brenner, R., & Glick, M. (1991). The regulation approach: Theory and history. *New Left Review, 188,* 45-120.
Brusco, S., & Sabel, C. (1983). Artisanal production and economic growth. In F. Wilkinson (Ed.), *The dynamics of labor market segmentation* (pp. 99-113). London: Academic Press.
Chandler, A. (1977). *The visible hand.* Cambridge, MA: Harvard University Press.
Cherry, R., D'Onofrio, C., Kurdas, C., Michl, T., Moseley, F., & Naples, M. (Eds.). (1988). *The imperiled economy* (2 vols.) New York: Union for Radical Political Economics.
Christopherson, S. (1988). *Overworked and underemployed: The redistribution of work in the U.S. economy.* Unpublished manuscript, Department of City and Regional Planning, Cornell University, Ithaca, NY.

Christopherson, S., & Storper, M. (1988). New forms of labor segmentation and production politics in flexibly specialized industries. *Industrial and Labor Relations Review, 42*(3), 331-347.

Clark, G. (1989). *Unions and communities under siege: American communities and the crisis of organized labor.* Cambridge, UK: Cambridge University Press.

Cohen, G. (1979). *Karl Marx's theory of history: A defence.* Princeton, NJ: Princeton University Press.

Cohendet, P. (1988). *New advanced materials: Economic dynamics and European strategy.* Berlin/New York: Springer-Verlag.

Coombs, R., & Jones, B. (1989). Alternative successors to Fordism. In H. Ernste & C. Jaeger (Eds.), *Information society and spatial structure* (pp. 107-116). New York: Belhaven Press.

Coriat, B. (1979). *L'atelier et le chronometre.* Paris: Christian Bourgois.

Coriat, B. (1983). *La robotique.* Paris: La Decouverte/Maspero.

Cusumano, M. (1985). *The Japanese automobile industry.* Cambridge, MA: Harvard University Press.

DeBresson, C., & Walker, R. (Eds.). (1991). Networks of innovators [Special Issue]. *Research Policy, 20*(5), 363-512.

Devine, J. (1983). Underconsumption, overinvestment and the origins of the great depression. *Review of Radical Political Economy, 15*(2), 1-28.

Devine, J. (Ed.). (1986). Empirical work in Marxian crisis theory [Special Issue]. *Review of Radical Political Economics, 18*(1&2), 1-260.

Devine, J. (in press). Falling profit rates and the causes of the 1929-33 collapse: Toward a synthesis. *Research in Radical Political Economy.*

Dohse, K., Jurgens, U., & Malsch, T. (1985). From Fordism to Toyotism? The social organisation of the labour process in the Japanese automobile industry. *Politics and Society, 14*(2), 115-146.

Donaghu, M., & Barff, R. (1991). Nike just did it: International subcontracting and flexibility in athletic footwear production. *Regional Studies, 24,* 537-552.

Dosi, G., Freeman, C., Nelson, R., Silverberg, G., & Soete, L. (Eds.). (1988). *Technical change and economic theory.* New York: Pinter.

Duménil, G., Glick, M., & Rangel, J. (1987). Theories of the great depression: Why did profitability matter? *Review of Radical Political Economics, 19*(2), 16-42.

Duménil, G., & Lévy, D. (1989a). Micro adjustment behavior and macro stability. *Seoul Journal of Economics, 2*(1), 1-37.

Duménil, G., & Lévy, D. (1989b). *The regulation school in light of one century of the U.S. economy* (Working Paper). Paris: CREPREMAP.

Duménil, G., & Lévy, D. (1990). *Les régulationnistes pouvaient-ils apprendre d'avantage des classiques?* (Working Paper). Paris: CEPREMAP.

Faucher, P., & DeBresson, C. (1990). *L'école de la régulation on technological change.* Unpublished manuscript, CREDIT, Université de Québec à Montréal.

Feldman, M. (1989). *The flexibility thesis and vertical disintegration.* (Working Paper BV89-2, University of Rhode Island Graduate Program in Community Planning and Area Development).

Fitzsimmons, M. (1986). The new industrial agriculture: The regional integration of specialty crop production. *Economic Geography, 62*(4), 334-353.

Florida, R. (1991). *The new industrial revolution.* (Working Paper No. 91-07, Carnegie Mellon University, School of Urban and Public Affairs).

Florida, R., & Kenney, M. (1990). *The breakthrough economy.* New York: Basic Books.

Forester, T. (Ed.). (1987). *The information technology revolution*. Cambridge, MA: MIT Press.

Forester, T. (Ed.). (1989). *The materials revolution*. Cambridge: MIT Press.

Forty, A. (1986). *Objects of desire: Design and society, 1750-1980*. London: Thames and Hudson/Cameron.

Fraser, S., & Gerstle, G. (Eds.). (1989). *The rise and fall of the New Deal order*. Princeton, NJ: Princeton University Press.

Freeman, C. (1982). *The economics of industrial innovation* (2nd ed.). London: Frances Pinter.

Freeman, C. (1987). *Technology policy and economic performance: Lessons from Japan*. London: Frances Pinter.

Freeman, C. (1991). Networks of innovators: A synthesis of research issues. *Research Policy, 20*(5), 499-514.

Freeman, C., Clark, J., & Soete, L. (1982). *Unemployment and technical innovation*. Westport, CT: Greenwood Press.

Friedman, D. (1988). *The misunderstood miracle: Politics and economic decentralization in Japan*. Ithaca, NY: Cornell University Press.

Gardner, C., & Sheppard, J. (1989). *Consuming passion: The rise of retail culture*. London: Unwin Hyman.

Gertler, M. (1988). The limits to flexibility: Comments on the post-Fordist vision of production and its geography. *Transactions of the Institute of British Geographers, 13*(4), 19-32.

Glick, M., & Ehrbar, H. (1990). Long-run equilbirium in the empirical study of monopoly and competition. *Economic Inquiry, 28*, 151-162.

Gordon, D. (1988). The global economy: New edifice or crumbling foundation? *New Left Review, 168*, 24-65.

Gordon, R. (1991). Innovation, industrial networks, and high technology regions. In R. Camagni (Ed.), *Innovation networks: Spatial perspectives* (pp. 174-195). London: Belhaven.

Gramsci, A. (1971). *Prison notebooks*. New York: International.

Hakansson, H. (1989). *Corporate technological behavior: Cooperation and networks*. London: Routledge.

Hall, P., & Preston, P. (1988). *The carrier wave: New information technology and the geography of innovation, 1846-2003*. Boston: Unwin Hyman.

Harcourt, G. (1972). *Some Cambridge controversies in the theory of capital*. Cambridge, UK: Cambridge University Press.

Harris, D. (1985). The theory of economic growth: From steady states to uneven development. In G. Feiwel (Ed.), *Issues in contemporary macroeconomics and distribution* (pp. 378-394). London: Macmillan.

Harris, N. (1986). *The end of the third world*. London: Tauris/Penguin.

Harrison, B., & Bluestone, B. (1988). *The great U-turn: Corporate restructuring, laissez faire and the rise of inequality in America*. New York: Basic Books.

Harvey, D. (1982). *The limits to capital*. Oxford, UK: Basil Blackwell.

Harvey, D. (1985). *The urbanization of capital*. Baltimore: The Johns Hopkins University Press.

Harvey, D. (1989). *The condition of post-modernity*. Oxford, UK: Basil Blackwell.

Hirschhorn, L. (1984). *Beyond mechanization*. Cambridge: MIT Press.

Hoffman, K., & Kaplinsky, R. (1988). *Driving force: The global restructuring of technology, labor and investment in the automobile and components industries*. Boulder, CO: Westview.

Hounshell, D. (1984). *From the American system to mass production, 1800-1932*. Baltimore: The Johns Hopkins University Press.

Itoh, M. (1987). Skilled labour in value theory. *Capital and Class, 31*, 39-58.

Jenkins, R. (1987). *Transnational corporations and uneven development*. New York: Methuen.

Johanson, J. (1989). Business relationships and industrial networks. In *Perpectives on the economics of organization* (Crafoord Lectures 1, Institute of Economic Research, pp. 65-78). Lund, Sweden: Lund University Press.

Katzenstein, P. (Ed.). (1989). *Industry and politics in West Germany*. Ithaca, NY: Cornell University Press.

Kenney, M., & Florida, R. (1988). Beyond mass production: Production and the labor process in Japan. *Politics and Society, 16*(1), 121-158.

Kern, H., & Schumann, M. (1987). Limits of the division of labour: New production and employment concepts in West German industry. *Economic and Industrial Democracy, 8*(2), 151-170.

Knights, D., Wilmott, H., & Colinson, D. (Eds.). (1985). *Job redesign*. Aldershot, UK: Gower.

Lazonick, W. (1990). *Competitive advantage on the shopfloor*. Cambridge, MA: Harvard University Press.

Leborgne, D., & Lipietz, A. (1988). New technologies, new modes of regulation: Some spatial implications. *Society and Space, 6*(3), 263-280.

Leborgne, D., & Lipietz, A. (1990). *Fallacies and open issues about post-Fordism* (Working Paper No. 9009). Paris: CEPREMAP.

Lipietz, A. (1979). *Crise et inflation. Pourquoi?* Paris: Maspero.

Lipietz, A. (1982). Toward global Fordism? *New Left Review, 132*, 33-47.

Lipietz, A. (1983). *Le monde enchante*. Paris: Maspero/La Decouverte.

Lipietz, A. (1986). Behind the crisis: The exhaustion of a regime of accumulation. *Review of Radical Political Economics, 18*(1&2), 13-32.

Lipietz, A. (1987). *Mirages and miracles*. London: Verso.

Lipietz, A. (1988). *De L'Althusserisme et la théorie de la régulation* (Working Paper No. 8920). Paris: CEPREMAP.

Littler, C. (1982). *The development of the labour process in capitalist societies*. London: Heinemann Educational.

Mair, A., Florida, R., & Kenney, M. (1988). The new geography of automobile production: Japanese transplants in North America. *Economic Geography, 64*(4), 352-373.

Mandel, E. (1975). *Late capitalism*. London: New Left Books.

Marglin, S., & Schor, J. (Eds.). (1989). *The golden age of capitalism: Reinterpreting the postwar experience*. New York: Oxford University Press.

Markusen, A., Hall, P., Deitrich, S., & Campbell, S. (1991). *The rise of the gun belt*. New York: Oxford University Press.

Marshall, M. (1987). *Long waves of regional development*. London: Macmillan.

Martinez, J., & Jaramillo, C. (1989). The evolution of research on coordination mechanisms in multinational corporations. *Journal of International Business Studies*, Fall, 489-514.

Marx, K. (1967). *Capital* (Vol. 1). New York: International. (Original work published 1863)

Mensch, G. (1979). *Stalemate in technology*. Cambridge, MA: Ballinger.

Mistral, J. (1986). Régime international et trajectories nationales. In R. Boyer (Ed.), *Capitalismes fin de siècle* (pp. 167-202). Paris: Presses Universitaires de France.

Monden, Y. (1983). *Toyota production system: A practical approach to production management*. Atlanta: Industrial Engineering and Management Press.

Moore, B. (1966). *The social origins of dictatorship and democracy.* Boston: Beacon.

Morgan, K., & Sayer, A. (1988). *Microcircuits of capital.* Oxford, UK: Polity.

Morris-Suzuki, T. (1988). *Beyond Computopia: Information, automation and democracy in Japan.* London: Kegan Paul.

Mowery, D., & Rosenberg, N. (1976). The influence of market demand upon innovations: A critical review of some reent empirical studies. *Research Policy, 8*(2), 102-153.

Nelson, R., & Winter, S. (1982). *An evolutionary theory of economic change.* Cambridge, MA: Harvard University Press.

Page, B., & Walker, R. (1991). From settlement to Fordism: The agro-industrialization of the Midwest. *Economic Geography, 67*(4), 281-315.

Peet, R. (1989). Conceptual problems in neo-Marxist industrial geography. *Antipode, 21*(1), 35-50.

Perez, C. (1985). Microelectronics, long waves and world structural change. *World Development, 13*, 441-463.

Perlo, V. (1982). The false claims of declining productivity and its political use. *Science and Society, 46*(3), 284-327.

Piore, M., & Sabel, C. (1984). *The second industrial divide.* New York: Basic Books.

Pollert, A. (1988). Dismantling flexibility. *Capital and Class, 34*, 42-75.

Porter, G., & Livesay, H. (1971). *Merchants and manufacturers.* Baltimore: The Johns Hopkins University Press.

Rosenberg, N. (1972). *Technology and American economic growth.* New York: Harper Torchbooks.

Rosenberg, N. (1976). Technological change in the machine tool industry, 1840-1910. In *Perspectives on technology* (pp. 9-31). Cambridge, UK: Cambridge University Press.

Sabel, C. (1982). *Work and politics.* New York: Cambridge University Press.

Sabel, C. (1989). Flexible specialization and the reemergence of regional economies. In P. Hirst & J. Zeitlin (Eds.), *Reversing industrial decline?* (pp. 17-70). New York: St. Martin's.

Sabel, C., Heerigel, G., Kazis, R., & Deeg, R. (1987). How to keep mature industries innovative. *Technology Review, 90*(3), 26-35.

Sabel, C., & Zeitlin, J. (1985). Historical alternatives to mass production: Politics, markets and technology in nineteenth century industrialization. *Past and Present, 108*, 133-176.

Sahal, D. (1981). *Patterns of technological innovation.* Reading, MA: Addison-Wesley.

Sassen, S. (1988). *The mobility of labor and capital.* New York: Cambridge University Press.

Saxenian, A. (1991). The origins and dynamics of production networks in Silicon Valley. *Research Policy, 20*(5), 423-438.

Sayer, A. (1984). *Method in social science: A realist approach.* London: Hutchinson.

Sayer, A. (1986). New developments in manufacturing: The just-in-time system. *Capital and Class, 30*, 43-72.

Sayer, A. (1988). Post-Fordism in question. *International Journal of Urban and Regional Research, 13*(4), 666-693.

Schoenberger, E. (1988). From Fordism to flexible accumulation: Technology, competitive strategies and international location. *Society and Space, 6*(3), 245-262.

Schoenberger, E. (1990). Some dilemmas of automation. *Economic Geography, 66*, 232-247.

Schumpeter, J. (1934). *The theory of economic development.* Cambridge, MA: Harvard University Press.

Schumpeter, J. (1939). *Business cycles.* New York: McGraw-Hill.

Scott, A. (1988a). *Metropolis: From the division of labor to urban form.* Berkeley: University of California Press.

Scott, A. (1988b). *New industrial spaces.* London: Pion.

Scott, A., & Storper, M. (1990). *Regional development reconsidered* (Working Paper No. 1). Los Angeles: UCLA, Lewis Center for Regional Policy Studies.

Shaikh, A. (1987). The falling rate of profit and economic crisis in the United States. In R. Cherry (Ed.), *The imperiled economy* (Vol. 1, pp. 115-126). New York: Union for Radical Political Economy.

Smith, N. (1984). *Uneven development.* Oxford, UK: Basil Blackwell.

Soja, E. (1989). *Post-modern geographies.* London: Verso.

Standing, G. (1992). Alternative routes to labour flexibility. In M. Storper & A. Scott (Eds.), *Pathways to industrial and regional development.* London: Routledge.

Storper, M. (1987). The post-enlightenment challenge to Marxist urban studies. *Society and Space, 5*(4), 418-426.

Storper, M. (1989). The transition to flexible specialisation in the U.S. film industry: External economies, the division of labour, and the crossing of industrial divides. *Cambridge Journal of Economics, 13,* 273-305.

Storper, M., & Scott, A. (1988). The geographical foundations and social regulation of flexible production complexes. In J. Wolch & M. Dear (Eds.), *The power of geography* (pp. 21-40). Boston: Allen & Unwin.

Storper, M., & Scott, A. (Eds.) (1992). *Pathways to industrialization and regional development.* London: Routledge.

Storper, M., & Walker, R. (1989). *The capitalist imperative: Territory, technology and industrial growth.* Oxford, UK: Basil Blackwell.

Sturgeon, T., & Walker, R. (1991). *Speculative urbanization in Silicon Valley: The building boom of the 1980s.* Unpublished manuscript, Department of Geography, University of California, Berkeley.

Sweezy, P. (1942). *The theory of capitalist development.* New York: Monthly Review.

Tedlow, R. (1990). *New and improved: The story of mass marketing in America.* New York: Basic Books.

Van Duijn, J. (1983). *The long wave in economic life.* London: Allen & Unwin.

Walker, R. (1977). *The suburban solution: Capitalism and the construction of urban space in the United States.* Unpublished doctoral dissertation, Department of Geography and Environmental Engineering, The Johns Hopkins University, Baltimore.

Walker, R. (1985a). Is there a service economy? The changing capitalist division of labor. *Science and Society, 49,* 42-83.

Walker, R. (1985b). Technological determination and determinism: Industrial growth and location. In M. Castells (Ed.), *High technology, space, and society* (pp. 226-264). Beverly Hills, CA: Sage.

Walker, R. (1988a). The dynamics of value, price and profit. *Capital and Class, 35,* 147-181.

Walker, R. (1988b). The geographical organization of production systems. *Society and Space, 7,* 377-408.

Walker, R. (1989a). Machinery, labour and location. In S. Wood (Ed.), *The transformation of work?* (pp. 59-90). London: Unwin Hyman.

Walker, R. (1989b). A requiem for corporate geography: New directions in industrial organization, the production of place and uneven development. *Geografisker Annaler, 71B*(1), 43-68.

Walker, R. (1989c). What's left to do? Theses on a flyer back. *Antipode, 21*(2), 133-165.

Walker, R. (1993). The hidden dimension of industrialization: An expanding division of labor. *Futures, 25*(6), 673-693.

Webber, M. (1990, April 23). *Fordism, post-Fordism, flexibility and all that.* Paper presented to the Association of American Geographers, Toronto.

Webber, M., & Rigby, D. (1986). The rate of profit in Canadian manufacturing. *Review of Radical Political Economics, 18*, 33-35.

Webber, M., Sheppard, E., & Rigby, D. (1990). *Technical change.* Unpublished manuscript, Department of Geography, University of Melbourne.

Williams, K., Cutler, T., Williams, J., & Haslam, C. (1987). The end of mass production? *Economy and Society, 16*(3), 405-439.

Williamson, H. (Ed.). (1951). *The growth of the American economy.* New York: Prentice Hall.

Wood, S. (Ed.) (1989). *The transformation of work?* London: Unwin Hyman.

Zuboff, S. (1988). *In the age of the smart machine.* New York: Basic Books.

8

Making Space

Planning as a Mode of Thought

DAVID C. PERRY

On the 110th floor [of the World Trade Center in New York City] . . . a poster, sphinx-like, addresses an enigmatic message to the pedestrian who is for an instant transformed into a visionary: It's hard to be down when you're up. (Michel de Certeau, 1984, p. 92)

To decipher discourse through the use of spatial, strategic metaphors enables one to grasp precisely the points at which discourses are transformed in, through and on the basis of relations of power. (Michel Foucault, 1980, p. 70)

AUTHOR'S NOTE: This chapter benefits greatly from the intellectual contributions found in the work of Robert Beauregard, Derek Gregory, and Neil Smith. However, my current interest in the spatiality of planning began, as does this chapter, with Michel de Certeau, Michel Foucault, and Henri Lefebvre. The critical and substantive support of Gilbert Chin and especially Helen Liggett has been very important, as was the institutional support I received while visiting Cleveland State University as the Albert A. Levin Chair of Urban Studies and Public Service.

The history of the evolution of planning roles can be understood as a global conversation between the planning profession and its situation. (Donald Schön, 1983, p. 205)

A SPATIAL APPROACH TO PLANNING

In his essay, "Walking in the City," Michel de Certeau recounts his visit to the top of the World Trade Center. From the top he describes the spectacular view one has of all other buildings, the streets, and the geographic boundaries and topographic faultlines, both natural and man-made, that compose the New York landscape. From this vantage point we join him in looking over the landscape, our eyes moving from one tall building down to a lower one, looking up toward midtown and beyond to Harlem and turning back down to Wall Street and the waterfront. Standing there it becomes clear that although this is a truly extraordinary view of the city, we still can't see what is going on in the buildings below or next to us—in fact we have no idea what is going on in the floors immediately beneath our feet. As for the streets, if we can see them at all, the activities of those walking and riding in them are, from this vantage point, effectively invisible. No matter how grand and far-reaching the view, we don't see *everything* from the top of the World Trade Center.

We cannot depend upon this singularly lofty position to get a clear sense of what is going on elsewhere; we have to get back on the elevator and go down a few floors, or go to another building and then another and so on. But such travels are not enough because our understanding of the city remains far from complete. No matter how many buildings we visit and how good our vantage points are, the views from above remain, by themselves, no more than particularized representations—"the exaltation of the scopic" of "vision" that is at once refreshing (in the difference of its view of the city), clean, and clear (in its removal from the relative chaos of the mobility and endless labyrinths of the street) and yet blind (to the views to be had from the tops of other buildings) and unresponsive (to the infinite array of patterns of individuated everyday life).

The sign at the top of the World Trade Center sums all this up: "It's hard to be down when you're up." So it is for planners. It's hard to produce a plan that at once captures the conditions of the society, city, or policy area and also meets the demands of each of the citizens experiencing the problems society is mobilized to process. It's hard to be both scopic and comprehensive and immediate and individually responsive.[1]

Modern urban life is carried out in a planned society—planned both up and down. All of us are citizens of what Spiro Kostof (1991) has called "the planned, or designed or created city . . . *la ville crée*" (p. 43). The source of such a social logic is authoritative—constituted through a set of power relations that manifest themselves spatially in both material and immaterial ways (Lefebvre, 1991). These plans are made all the more clear when they are placed in relief against our practices of another kind of city—*la ville spontanée*—the "chance-grown" or "geo-morphic" (Kostof, 1991, p. 43), the "lived" or "everyday" (Lefebvre, 1991; de Certeau, 1984) urban space.[2] This latter space—the city of ir-regularity (Castagnoli, 1971, p. 124)—is both the object of planning and its anathema: planning mediates between the *freedom* of the city as ville spontanée and the orderly production of the city as ville crée. Together they are generative forces contributing to the far more complex "(social) production of space" (Lefebvre, 1991) as a whole.

In spite of this dialectical function of planning, there is still confusion over *how* to think about planning. Ironically it is planners themselves who appear to be the most confused about the role of planning as an agency/instrument of control enmeshed or embedded in the relations of power (see the conversation between Michel Foucault and Gilles Deleueze, 1977). At a time when there appears to be literally no end to the ways in which planning is being exercised in modern society, the planning profession itself is undergoing a crisis of professional identity. One observer laments that the profession is plagued by a seemingly limitless set of specialties and subspecialties, which has caused deep internal fractures among its members and so many different definitions that they are best captured in "mathematicians' notation . . . [suggesting that] there is really a Planning(1), Planning(2) . . . Planning(n)" (Levy, 1992, p. 81). All of this has produced a nearly endless stream of conferences, techniques, and approaches while at the same time the number of professional planning jobs is drying up in reaction to economic and political forces beyond the control of the profession.

In summary, planning seems to be at once ineffable and ubiquitous, causing more than a few planners to look a bit nervously back at Aaron Wildavsky's 1973 essay (see Beauregard, 1989; Brooks, 1990; Levy, 1992; Lucy, 1994; Schön, 1983). After cataloging the various approaches planners take to their trade, Wildavsky (1973) concluded that "If Planning Is Everything, Maybe It's Nothing." William Lucy (1994), for one, marshaled a review of the various approaches to planning and suggested that "If Planning Includes too Much, Maybe It Should Include More." What joins both authors, quite surprisingly, is not the apparent debate over the "expansiveness" (Lucy, 1994) of planning, but their concern over how successfully planning activities either maintain or challenge the social order (the dominant relations of power). Wildavsky finds that planning is so unsuccessful as a practice that it should be read more as an "act of faith" than as a legitimate practice of power. William Lucy subscribes to the notion that planning, if it is properly defined in its role of system mainte-nance,[3] can actually be expanded to include even more features of social/policy formation.

Put another way, the more legitimate the planning mandate, (that is, the more successfully the profession is embedded in the service of the dominant political economy), the more its activities can be expanded to successfully produce other relations of power. Lucy (1994), in his search for an acceptable (legitimating) definition, sug-gests that the core ingredient in an expansive planning practice is serving "healthy" people and places. Robert Beauregard (1990) calls for a synthetic "planning-as-development" theme of city building, targeting the real estate, industrial development, architecture, and investment nexus as the processal center of a "holistic" planning. Like-minded planning theorists and practitioners traverse between the two poles represented by Lucy and Wildavsky—in a conscious quest for a "common core" (Brooks, 1990, p. 212) within which to root planning's legitimacy. Without such a common core or defining concept, contemporary planning scholars argue, planning will con-tinue to be a profession with a "lost sense of identity, and purpose, as well as . . . influence and legitimacy in the arena of policy-making and development" (Brooks, 1990, p. 219). The problem is planners never seem to arrive at a collectively agreeable core of action, much less theory. And, in all likelihood, such a paradigmatic core will not materialize because planning is one of those professions that is of its context born. "The institutional context of planning practice is notoriously unstable and there are many contending views of the profession, each of which carries a different image of the planning role and a different picture of the body of useful knowledge" (Schön, 1983, p. 204). The result, as read by critics and planning advocates alike, is a consistent marginality of the formal *profession* of planning in the real world and a collective malaise inside the profession.[4] Even from within a perspective where the legitimacy of planning is unproblematic there are endless debates among proponents of alternative definitions of planning.

THINKING ABOUT THE HISTORY
OF PLANNING . . . SPATIALLY

Rather than set out on a similarly unsatisfactory quest for paradigmatic clarity and legitimacy, I will argue here that the search for the best definition of planning is better directed toward thinking differently: We should think about planning spatially. Instead of trying to come up with a politics and technology for planning that everyone can agree upon, I offer a spatial approach suggested by Foucault's work. Thinking spatially means seeing the various politics and technologies of planning—its various discourses—in their contextual place(s) in society. They become examples of particular relations of power that constitute the conditions of freedom and dominance in the socially produced urban space. Michael Dear and Allen Scott (1981) argue that planning, like urbanization, is a "social event," not a free-standing and independent moral and/or scientific occurrence. Planning is embedded in the dominant relations of social formation—deriving its spatial logic and historical meaning from "the general pattern of society as a whole" (Dear & Scott, 1981, p. 4). Therefore when we think of planning we should think of it as part of the production and reproduction of the social relations of power.

This approach ties the investigation of planning to its actual participation in the construction of social/physical space. Rather than insert the various types of planning into "abstract space" (or assertion of a singularly legitimate paradigm or politics)[5] in order to distance them from the "clutter of existing and competing ideas" (Smith, 1992, pp. 60-64), this approach seeks out that clutter as part of the space in which planning is generated. To leave planning in what Lefebvre calls abstract space is to render the very *idea* of planning less than complete. Planners do not so much climb up on the material abstraction of the tall building of comprehensive planning, for example, as they produce that space—that building—with all its vision and all its blindness. To think of planning spatially is to think of it not as the conceptualization of relations within the boundaries of abstract space but to see it as both the critical interrogation and affirmative intervention of such abstraction, as the "production of space."[6]

Against an approach that sees planning evolving through time into a singular planning profession, the history of planning can be viewed as sets of practices that have participated in the changes from mercantile to industrial and ultimately postindustrial urban forms. In the early years of the 20th century, planners were identified with the creation of comprehensive master plans, carried out by corporatist, boardlike commissions with central responsibilities for the overall, apolitical planning of the city: "The planner framed his role at the center of a system for which he planned, in relation to agencies that would implement his plans and clients who would benefit from this" (Schön, 1983, p. 205). The product of such a process (the plan) was informed by these corporate relations of production as well. Perhaps the most famous master plan was and remains the Regional Plan of New York. The first volume of the plan, published in 1927 by the Regional Plan Association (RPA), begins with a description of the city and the purposes to which the city and planning are to be put:

> The metropolis, in one of its aspects, is essentially a piece of productive machinery competing with other metropolitan machines. It will prosper or decline as compared with other metropolises in rough proportion to the relative efficiency with which it can do economic work . . . that is, produce goods [and] services. The area of New York and its environs may be likened to the floor space of a factory. Regional planning designates the best use of this floor space—"the proper adjustment of area to uses." (RPA, 1927, p. 18)

However, just as planning practices offered plans that replicated and legitimated the relations of power found in the capitalist city, they also served to challenge the excesses of capitalism. Planning embodies the contradictions of capitalism, both as a practice of corporatist industrialism and a response to the chaos of the "wild city" (Castells, 1976) such relations of production produce (Boyer, 1983). Frederick Howe (1926/1969), the legendary turn of the century reformer, lamented:

> The American City lags behind the work it should perform. It is negative in its function, rather than positive in its services. It has been stripped (by industrial capitalism) of power and responsibility. It is politically weak and lacks ideals of its possibilities. It has little concern for its people and they in turn have little concern for it. We have failed to differentiate between those activities that are private and those that are public. We have failed too to provide protection to the individual from inequalities of power and position, and have left him prey to forces as dangerous to his life and comfort as those against which the police are employed to protect. Further than this, we have failed to shift to society the burdens of industry that the coming of the city has created. We have permitted the sacrifice of low wages, irregular employment, and disease to be borne by the individual rather than the community. (p. v)

This is the city of "les classes dangereux"—who were at once the source of fear and paranoia and the object of righteous indignation over their conditions of oppression (Wilson, 1991, p. 7). They lived in a city where land uses, vehicles, races and ethnicities, men, women, and children were, in Howe's words, "inadequately planned." The very disorder, pain and chaos of the urban evoked an ideal alternative: the "rational city" (Boyer, 1983). "With the exception of Washington," Howe (1926/1969) opined, "there was no realization of the permanence of the city, of the importance of streets and open spaces, of building regulations, transportation, waterfronts and the physical foundations which underlie the city's life" (p. 194). In a very real sense, planning was also "a response to the turmoil of modernization" (Beauregard, 1989)—both as a responsive model of corporate capitalism and a challenge to the worst excesses of the very forces of privatism (Warner, 1974).

From the beginning, therefore, there was *no* clear or single definition of planning. Planning is a hard profession in the spirit of the poster at the top of the World Trade Center: both comprehensive and visionary (RPA) and at the same time critical and immediate. It is far more realistic to conceive of planning spatially—as a dialectically determined synchrony of public interventions generated by and in response to the order and chaos of the industrial city. Planning is seen then as less a product of clear mandate and agreeable paradigm of comprehensiveness than as a mixed dialectical response to the contradictions of the capitalist city. As Alan Altsuhler (1965), writing a half a century later, observed, planning "is usually a contradiction and ambivalence" (p. 1).

From a spatial practice viewpoint, planning is not so much a response to the institutional contradictions of social formation as it is the embodiment of such conditions of contradiction and ambivalence (Perry, 1994). The planning literature on the roots of modern planning serves as de facto evidence of this point: Rather than think of planning spatially and synchronically, most practitioners and scholars search determinedly for *the* appropriate definition, *the* holistic paradigm of politics, practice, and technical expertise. Although many scholars argue that planning was really a movement toward comprehensiveness (Beauregard, 1989, 1990; Fainstein, 1991) and master planning, others are just as willing to suggest that planning was really a product of social reform and the desire for safe and healthy streets (Felbinger, 1995), homes, and workplaces (Howe, 1926/1969). Still others have suggested that planning was either an aesthetic impulse (Beard, 1926) or the product of a utopian movement captured in early visionary models such as Ebenezer Howard's "garden cities" and Tony Gariner's *cite industrielle* and continuing to Le Corbusier's mid-1920's Voison Plan for Paris or Clarence Stein's "sunshine village" (Barnett, 1986; Relph, 1987). In short, for all the boilerplate associated with the notion that planning in the first instance was a visionary exercise in comprehensive planning, there is equally strong evidence that planning was/is the product of strong street-level nostrums of social reform, revisionist utopian politics, applied scientific technologies of health and safety, and architectonic and landscape aesthetics. If we think of planning, from the outset, as essentially comprehensive—or as utopian or reformist or rational or aesthetic—then we miss the fact that these various discourses were (and still are) *all* planning and together composed the spatiality of early 20th-century American planning as a social agency of legitimation and critique of the industrial city. They are all (in various discourses of consort, opposition, and internal contradiction) legitimating parts of and/or critical responses to the massive geographic and demographic changes (Fairfield, 1993), the emerging dominating logic of corporate and industrial capital, and the unhealthy and chaotic socioeconomic circumstances of human distress and poverty that were relational conditions of the late 19th century "private city" (Warner, 1974).

Charles Beard (1926) summarized the municipal planning movement as an aesthetic and scientific impulse to achieve that Holy Grail of industrial technologists, economic efficiency, and, in the process, to point out "enough waste and follies in any existing system of urban economy to arouse . . . advocates of urban planning . . . in the field of public health, the housing reformers and some social philosophers" (pp. 275-276). Robert Fogelsong (1990) observes that planning quickly transformed from a political movement to a managerial one, where comprehensive plans became less efficacious, planners became managers and regulators, and the distinction between planner and administrator became exceedingly small. The management/planning of the city was grounded in the regulation of land use (Boyer, 1983): the public production of the legal logic of land employed as a factor of the capitalist mode of production. The economic use (Peterson, 1981) and the public definition of real property were joined. The proactive tools of land management became land use controls, plans, and zoning regulations. As a result John Levy (1992) concludes that even today, "the planner is part of the administrative apparatus of land development and a facilitator of community development" (p. 81). He adds that "for planning, this is an age when tactics are dominant and grand strategies and grand visions are much less prominent" (p. 81).

The transformation of early planning from highly visible vision and reform to relatively invisible and institutional tactics and regulation has been accompanied by parallel forays of other more centralizing tendencies to plan policies such as "urban renewal, urban and regional transportation, health services, public education, mental health and criminal justice" (Schön, 1983, p. 205). These forays, with their institutionalizing administrative structures, seem to specialize in plans designed to solve problems that either failed . . . or created problems worse than the problems they had been designed to solve. Some of the phenomena planners were most anxious to influence—poverty, crime, urban congestion and decay—seemed tenaciously resilient to intervention. (Schön, 1983, p. 205)

Planners seemed to be mistaken in the way they conceived of the problems, the plans, and the solutions. Their effectiveness at implementation of these plans was a failure at two levels: (a) the relative artificiality and inapplicability of the plans they offered and (b) the problematic position they held in the process of policy practice itself, due to their lack of direct expertise.

In the face of such deficiencies, a new planning practice joined the practices of master planning, management, regulation, and policy planning. Known variously as social planning, advocacy planning, or equity planning, this new form added an important and directly critical voice to planning—one that did not simply represent a critique of the social condition of the city and the political economy but a critique of planning itself. Here scholars as diverse as Donald Schön, Herbert Gans, Jane Jacobs, Frances Fox Piven, Norman Krumholz, Lisa Peattie, and John Friedmann set out to show how planners themselves were practitioners of the very relations of power that produced the social contradictions and economic inequities that composed much of the planning agenda. "Planners," wrote Donald Schön, "acting ostensibly in the public interest actually served the interests of real estate developers and large corporations by displacing the poor and ethnic minorities" (p. 208). What is important here is not the notion that somehow social planning replaced policy planning, but that planning, in its various manifestations of the production of space, now *included* a formally articulated critical position. Nor is it necessary to debate whether policy planning *displaced* land use planning or whether land use planning *replaced* comprehensive planning. What is significant is that the general discourse of planning—the overall spatiality of planning—*contains* all of these various planning(s). None of these notions of planning are whole or inclusive; they are all partial and constitutive of what planning was/is becoming. Again, to return to Foucault (in Foucault & Deleueze, 1977), each represents a different way in which planning facilitates (or confronts) and/or embodies the relations of power that produce the city/society.

A SPATIAL APPROACH TO CURRENT PLANNING PRACTICE

Most recently the paradigmatic metaphor used most by practitioners and scholars to describe the planning profession has been development—in particular economic development. The economic development notion of planning has emerged, like progressive planning, out of the chaos of the city. Again changes in the capitalist mode of production in the city and globally have had profound effects on planning. Susan Fainstein (1991), in a recent issue of the Journal of the American Planning Association, put it bluntly:

> The foremost impetus driving new modes of planning has been the restructuring of the urban economy. In response to deindustrialization and the simultaneous expansion of the service sector, local governments have actively sought to attract new industries to their jurisdictions by offering packages of land and financing. Second, conservative national administrations have stressed market-based solutions to allocative questions and have promoted growth over redistribution. Third is a more proactive stance toward planning. (p. 22)[7]

This current definition of planning, born of this new economic era, has complex ramifications for some of the old conundrums of planning. Gone is stimulating reference to the contradictions of capitalism that triggered reformists like Frederick Howe and equity planners like Norman Krumholz. Even the tactics of traditional land use physical planners and public infrastructure planners, who were inclined to mystify—through regulations, bureaucracy and engineering and design technologies—the conflictual relationship they had with capital accumulation and the negative and inequitable impacts of such accumulation on the community, are minimized. The connection between the economic structure and planning legitimacy is now straightforwardly claimed, and the tactics developed to stimulate economic growth are frankly enumerated (Fainstein, 1991). Ideology—that is, democratic ideology—is no longer evoked to situate the planner's role: rather the contradiction between planning and capital is eliminated through a new mystification of the role of planner as developer—one who lives by the abstract code in which private advantage is equated with public benefit. Today, Fainstein (1991) observes, this planning merges in a context where "if the argument that what is good for business is good for everyone is not wholly accepted, neither is it opposed by a widely held alternative formulation" (p. 23). There is no longer a tension between accumulation and redistribution: It is assumed that accumulation will ultimately generate redistribution.

There is no illusion left as to where the "real" planners of the restructuring urban world are: They are not making abstract comprehensive plans that function in the public interest, they are "figuring out the local power structure and . . . [assuming] a role compatible with it" (Fainstein, 1991, p. 25). This role, if it is to be proactive, will be decidedly favorable to investment capital. The notion of planner as public advocate has been directly joined by the highly visible affirmation of planner as a facilitator, negotiator, and deal-maker—no longer to be found in the neutral "back room" of technological services and land use regulations, but in a highly entrepreneurial function serving the needs of investment capital, industrial and service sector firms, and labor. In some ways Fainstein is right, at least if you review the recent history of cities in the United States. In almost every city there can now be found a full range of new development specialists—in industrial development agencies and community development agencies, in Chambers of Commerce and a whole host of new not-for-profit private foundations and business groups, in public authorities and special district governments of all varieties.[8] The notion of planning as part and parcel of the development of the local, regional, and global economy has now captured almost every segment of institutional relations and has blurred boundaries of what used to be called the public and private sectors.

Yet just as the practice of planning as development has become more and more ubiquitous, crossing sectors of society as well as various agencies and levels of government, the notion that planning can be narrowed and defined within the confines of the development metaphor produces its own set of contradictions. As the politics of development and the planning of cities and their edges proceeds within this new restructuring logic of capital accumulation, new forms of the "wild city" materialize as well. These include heightened conditions of hopelessness, new forms of underemployment and unemployment, increased physical spaces of decline, and psychological as well as physical "zones of fear" (Davis, 1992). In addition increased informalization of the economy and new migrations of people into and out of cities constitute a full array of issues that demand recurring perspectives of land use, management, comprehensive planning, reformist advocacy, and other practices of planning that challenge the dominant relations of production and social reproduction as much as they maintain them.

The splintering of urban space (McLean & Perry, 1994)—into "figured" (Boyer, 1995) spaces of tightly concentrated central city business districts, edge-city shopping mall, and mixed-use industrial and office parks; and "disfigured" (Boyer, 1995) spaces of declining social services, increasing hopelessness, uneven patterns of real estate, migration, unemployment, service delivery, poverty and unemployment—is both produced and reproduced in new global networks of capital, labor, and information (Casella, 1993). The notion that we can or should achieve a stable, inclusive profession or definition of planning in such an environment of splintered cities and rapidly changing, globalizing "spaces of flows" (Thrift, 1993) is more in question than ever before. If planning is born of its context, this fragmenting future should produce forms of planning that are even more spatially differentiated than the planning(s) of the past. In this non-Euclidian world (Friedmann, 1993), which Casella (1993) calls "quantum," people now link

> knowledge to action, emphasize real time, and encourage appreciation of regional and local variety. In a quantum world there is also heightened concern over the long-term future, precisely because the future seems to be in danger of getting out of control. Planning must cope with the dislocations of rapid change and address the future too. (Casella, 1993, p. 485)

As a result planners like Casella and Stuart Meck (1990) argue for a form of planning that seems less connected to a centrally defined profession and more tied to accomplishing politically achievable results within the immediate context in which the planner is found. The tools of a planner's trade, Casella suggests, are increasingly technological, multidisciplinary, and intellectually free, meaning that planners will be even less likely to conceive of their profession through a discrete array of technologies; their disciplinary reach will be greater than ever before, given the rapid shifts in the splintering urban context; and given the swift and complex shifts of economic and social formation, they will be intellectually less tied to any preordained outcome.

All of this, contends Casella (personal interview, July 10, 1994), will be practiced increasingly by planners located outside bureaucracies altogether.[9] He estimates that the fastest-growing sector of planning activity is the individual consultant category, where planners are connected by computer, rather than bureaucratic position or proprietary function, to the (social) production of (urban) space. The agential place of planning, to say nothing of its metaphoric or paradigmatic space of function, is shifting rapidly. The dynamics, indeed the "cyber-spatiality" of planning is changing/still becoming.

Seen spatially, planning is quite different from the postcard tourism that takes a visitor to the top of the World Trade Center, or at least it requires a different form of urban travel.[10] It is not impelled by a voyeuristic interest in "seeing all" of the city; it is the political mobilization of knowledge in the service of social order, where order is experienced differently and found to be different in the different spaces of the city. To think of planning as simply a scopic exercise of scale limits it to a single politico-technological snapshot of society, which invites criticism or rejection based on, among other things, alternative views or core definitions of planning representing other techniques or scalar appropriations of the social order.[11] Planning is not so much any one of these various approaches as *it is the diversely configured space of all of them—all the planning discourses of social formation—as they exemplify what Foucault (1980, p. 70) described as those "points where discourses are transformed in, through and on the basis of power."* From this perspective the history of the approaches to planning can be viewed synchronically as well as critically. Planning is not so much a linear progression of practices—one displacing another—as it is an emerging *spatial practice* joining one new approach to another in the evolving production and reproduction of the relations of capital and the urban society attendant to it.

MAKING SPACE: WHAT PLANNERS DO

Spatial theory provides a useful approach to the question: What do planners, as instrumental practitioners of the social relations of power, do? Answering this question requires a consideration of planning as a *mode of thought*—a thinking that engenders/incorporates action. This requires a process different from the conventional characterizations of planning discussed previously, ones where planning is "rethought" in terms of new paradigms (of comprehensiveness or equity or social policy) or agencies of "societal guidance" (Beauregard, 1990, p. 210). To borrow from Immanuel Wallerstein (1991),[12] a bit of "unthinking" is in order here. The argument extends beyond a contribution to the critical thought that sees planning as part of the abstractions that produce relations of dominance. To consider planning as a *spatial practice* intent on the (social) production of space implies breaking down the mode of thinking that continues to separate the abstract spaces of social formation from the lived or everyday. In short the process of rethinking planning has traditionally allowed planners to think of what they do as essentially that of "making plans": the master plans, policies, or some other form of tool or agency of change. To think of planning, instead, as a spatial practice suggests that what planners do is *not* simply make plans but rather "make space."

The first part of this chapter considered the spatiality of planning: That is, planning should be thought of spatially as a changing and increasingly complex feature of the (social) relations of power, producing and reproducing the state and market, at both the institutional and the lived or everyday levels. If this review of American planning tells us anything, it is that planning is always remaking itself as it is embedded in and responds to a world that itself is always in the process of being remade. That is, the various ways of planning are not so much displacements as they are transformative additions to planning in the face of urban change. As such the space of planning is best represented as a gerund—a verb-noun—both fixed in the social and physical relations (space) of the moment and changing in relation to both the past and the future (time). This means that planning is always more than one thing—it is both the planned and the unplanned, engaging the future (direction or goals) and the present, the distant and visionary, and the proximate and labyrinthine. Therefore planning infers not fixedness, but openness—this openness offering not a pluralism of positions or approaches, but the necessary, "gerundic" state of a pluralized practice in the face of the time(s)/space(s) of contemporary social formation(s). In this sense planning is more than a conceptual practice or intellectual technology whereby the lived and perceived experiences of society are joined. This version of planning is an example of what some critics call the production of an "abstract space"—a space scientifically or technologically grounded in a political-intellectual exercise of inclusiveness[13]—in which the various experiences of the city are rationally captured and attended to. As suggested above, such representations of urban space, grounded in the legitimating nostrums of the dominant political economy, are always only partial. The limits of such conceptualization are uncovered in the face of "a world that is constantly remaking itself" (Grossberg, 1993, p. 1).

The practices of everyday life—those "street corners" of the urban scene that one can never see from the top of the World Trade Center—are aspects of planning most easily ignored, no matter how clear the day or finely tuned the technology of viewing. But to conceive of planning as a mode of thought is not only to consider its technology, rationality, ideology, and process but also to understand that the space planners make includes that which their technology excludes, their professional distancing misses, and their processes actually confound. The notion of planning as a spatial practice—a dialectic of constant remaking in response to a world that is constantly being remade—grounds planning in everyday experience. This includes places or sites of spatial production—at all scales, the body, the family, the home, the workplace, the neighborhood, the city, the region, the world. Planning is always more or less comprehensive, developmental, equity-oriented, regulatory—a shifting, recursive spatiality that is characterized not only by the intellectual positions of planning, but also by the places or sites of intervention and the way in which such intervention travels. Planning then is a spatial practice that ensures continuity and some form of cohesion but, because of its dialectical and contradictory nature, not coherence.

Certain considerations are key to planning as a spatial practice: context, travel, connection, and scale. Planning, as suggested earlier, is of its *context* born—a social event, as Dear and Scott (1981) put it, that is both the product of and the producer of (social) space. Planning is a *lived* practice that is at once the genesis and the object of its *abstract practice* of design, strategy, policy, and regulation. And planning is also the practice of visible, geometric, physical, and ultimately *abstract relations* of social order (power) that "pass from the 'lived' to the abstract in order to project that abstraction onto the level of the lived" (Lefebvre, 1970, p. 241). The source of critical planning, advocacy, and equity rests most often in the everyday or lived complex and labyrinthine features of social phenomena, whose real significance (for a planning grounded in such phenomena) rests in their "fluidity and malleability" (Wallerstein, 1991, p. 71)[14]

The visit of de Certeau to the top of the World Trade Center is not only a helpful way to consider the spatiality of planning; it is also a heuristic of planning as a spatial practice. If the goal is to get beyond the boundaries of a planning defined as a professional, efficient, and technical "spatial science" (Gregory, 1994, p. 400) producing abstract representations of space (Lefebvre, 1991) or "facsimiles" of the city (de Certeau, 1984) and to include the city as lived at different scalar levels (Smith, 1992), then the practice of planning must be considered a dialectic one, always *traveling* between the lived space and the abstract space of society. It is this travel that is at once most bothersome to planners and critics and the most important feature of practice.

Most scholars and theorists treat planners like the tourist who gets to the top of the World Trade Center and takes a picture of "the city," producing a product, a fixed facsimile of the urban—a technical, scientific, professionally produced replication and obvious abstraction of the lived experiences below. But, as practitioners will attest, planning is not a single tour to a fixed site—it is a traveling to many sites; not a visit *to* a place—it is the *making* of space. This making is a dynamic practice of traveling the distance between the abstract and the lived. Making (social) space for planners includes not only what is seen but what is unseen—what the plans include, theoretically, and what they exclude, what they abstractly represent through scientific logic and bureaucratic rationality and what is lived yet unrepresented. Understood this way, planning is at once a facsimile of power and an act of exclusion and domination that, if critically practiced, can also include the "other," which these acts tend to exclude. Planning, to repeat the words of the poster (de Certeau, 1984, p. 92), is "hard"—it is the practice of being "down when you are up." The irony of planning is that it at once promises such distance and is victimized by it: providing a distant vision of a better future and often excluding from the vision those who do not fit "productively" into the functions of the dominant political economy.

The notion of making space also implies *scale*.

> The continual production and reproduction of scale expresses the social as much as geographical contest to establish boundaries between different places, locations, and sites of experience. The making of place implies the production of scale insofar as places are made different from each other; scale is a criterion of difference not between places so much as between different kinds of places. (Smith, 1992, p. 64)

Scale implies the territorialization of power across geographies of production and reproduction, such as the nation-state, the region, and global economic, informational, and financial networks. Scale also includes spaces of social activity; from the individual to the home and the neighborhood, these spaces are the grounded sites of both the material and metaphorical relations that represent social and cultural processes.

The ways in which the policies and practices of the nation-state and the city are connected to the social processes and relations of the individual are part and parcel of the critical spatial practices of planning. Making space implies scalar interconnectedness—a traveling between sites, a professional "jumping" of scales (Smith, 1992) in both the illumination of and the engagement with the contradictions planning intervention can produce and which such a traveling practice attempts to resolve.

The goal of planning today is to make/remake space in all its complexity. This includes the physical and relational sites of individual and collective experience: the home, work, neighborhood, city or region, nation, or globe. This is not to argue that the goal of the spatial practice of planning should be to produce "the nation" or "the home," for example. Rather than make products like housing plans, a planning practice that makes space links the policy to the everyday user of the housing unit and makes not the policy but a workable and working space—at once lived (in) and well-designed, built, financed, and regulated.

The process is a reflexive one that necessarily includes a wide range of relationships. For example, in the (social) production of (public) housing, this would include the dialectic among a number of components, including the contestation between users, local housing authority officials, and fiscal levels of government.

Planning, so conceived, is a recursive process. Whereas we can think of the urban designer as producing a physical design of the built geographic site and the architect as producing the design of the housing unit, planning is that gerundic process concerned with the ongoing making of the unit, the design of the housing project, the building of the unit, the actual inhabitants of the unit, the transformation of these units from projects to homes, the maintenance and rehabilitation of the units, the repopulation of the units with new tenants, the decline and destruction of the units, and so on. Contrary to the more narrow professional interventions of almost all others at the site or scale of the production of space, the planner's work is never done; it is, to repeat, a recursive spatial practice—meant to include both the design and building of physical infrastructure and the satisfactory use of the built space and the contested politics of what constitutes the public realm at the scale or site of the home. In sum, planners do not work on a different scale than the other design professionals so much as they make a different *kind* of space, informed as much by the experiences of the lived space of the users of the home or unit as by the institutional politics of budgets, regulations, and bureaucratic mandates.

PLANNING AND THE PRODUCTION OF SCALE

Two examples of planning as the practice of making space are the scalar venues of home and region. The space of home is usually excluded from planning because it is too small and not easily represented in the abstract political relations of professional planning. The space of region is often excluded from economic planning in favor of the economistic notion of development, because it too has no effective proprietary or electoral territory of abstract political-economic representation.

Home

A typical approach to public housing is to work at the scale of housing policy, wherein the conditions of housing needs are defined, a plan devised, and the policy implemented. An alternative is to practice housing planning at the scale of the home, where the meaning of housing to individual householders is represented by planners first through the mediums of shared daily experience and then translated or traveled to the scale of housing policy produced by a public housing authority or other agency of the state. Jacqueline Leavitt and Susan Saegert (1988, 1989) report on a version of this planning practice, which they call the "community-household model." Grounded in the domestic work of the home, as practiced most often by women, this model integrates the lived experiences of everyday home life into housing and social service plans and programs. Housing planners using this model are required to travel between the lived experience of householders and the abstract institutional representations of housing authorities, master plans, and building and zoning regulations. The planners are oriented toward making better homes—their spatial practice becomes one of jumping scales as they undertake the hard process of carrying out the dialectics of comprehensive housing services that produce homes for individual families.

In a study of landlord-abandoned buildings in New York City conducted in the mid-1980s, Saegert and Leavitt (1988) found that the city was managing over 26,000 residential units in 4,000 abandoned buildings. They discovered that "such wholesale abandonment jeopardized the shelter security of the largely black and Latino, often female, low income tenants who inhabited the buildings" (p. 489). Through extensive interviews with the tenants of some of these buildings and with planners in the city housing agencies, they began to uncover a spatial practice of housing planning that was firmly embedded in both the lived conditions of the tenants and what they called the more abstract planning tools of community and government support. Their study

shows that a combination of existing social networks, extensive technical involvement with technical assistance groups and political advocates, and programs that legitimate and provide resources for indigenous leaders' efforts while reinforcing tenant participation have led to successful, direct control by tenants of [these abandoned buildings]. (Leavitt & Saegert, 1988, p. 495)

What started out, for housing professionals, as an apparently impossible situation of economic abandonment, social deprivation, and inflexible governmental programs was transformed significantly by an approach that defined planning as a long-term recursive process. This process incorporated the strategies poor people used to cope with landlord abandonment and devised successful tenant management and ownership programs. Leavitt and Seagert have schematized this hard process of being up and down into a five-stage community household model: Planning homes entails:

1. The mobilization of everyday domestic skills of coping/reacting to crisis
2. The recognition of block or building-level networks of communication, goods sharing, and leadership development
3. Community-level identification with the place of residence through the reinforcement of shared stories and memories of "place" or community
4. Community-level identification with the neighborhoods and buildings where the tenants live through organizations such as churches, stores, clubs, gangs
5. City-level response to the community-household representation of the housing or other social issue through putting plans and agencies in the direct service of these de facto community household-produced programs. (Leavitt & Saegert, 1988, p. 497)

Another example of planning as a spatial practice at the scale of the home is the long-term planning housing studio headed by Jacqueline Leavitt at UCLA. In 1989, Leavitt and her students entered into an agreement with the Resident Management Corporation (tenants' council) of the Nickerson Gardens housing project in Watts, a neighborhood of South Central Los Angeles, to conduct a pilot survey of tot-lots and laundry services in the project. Nickerson Gardens is, according to Leavitt (1993, p. 55), the largest public housing complex west of the Mississippi River, with 1,066 units housing 4,900 people, over 40% of whom are children. The majority of the families are African American, although there are now over 600 Latino families in Nickerson. An estimated 10% of the units are abandoned due to poor physical condition, and many of the remaining units are in various states of mechanical disrepair. The complex is plagued with poor maintenance, including overhead outside lights that have not been repaired in 14 years (Leavitt, 1992, p. 119), plumbing that shuts down all running water for long periods of time, broken recreational equipment, streets filled with potholes, and tot-lots, which, by day, were filled with glass, infected sand, and broken equipment and by night became "adult hangouts where raucous drinking was punctutated by drug deals" (Leavitt, 1992, p. 122).

Of all these issues, the ones that commanded the attention of the residents and convinced them to contract with professional planners to somehow help them bridge the gap between the policy-making administrators, architects, and planners of the Housing Authority of Los Angeles and themselves were tot-lots and laundromats. The studio was asked, on the basis of a survey, to prepare a report, financial proposals ,and physical designs for both services: to reha-bilitate the tot-lots and prepare designs for laundry facilities. The tot-lots were to be redesigned in line with the perceived needs of parents and children. The models for laundromats were to provide the residents and the Housing Authority with information on two different approaches: (a) decentralized laundries located throughout the housing complex and (b) a large free-standing, off-site facility that would serve Nickerson and the surrounding neighborhood, thereby acting as both a laundry and a training and revenue-development project for the RMC.

The initial experience of Leavitt and her students, as they tried to provide data for such revised plans, was quite frustrating. The cul-tural and experiential distance between the planners and the resi-dents was quite wide. To reduce the distance and "travel," from the space of planner to tenant householder required that both Leavitt and her students spend long periods of time in Nickerson, in the lived space of the housing units.[15] Second, rather than use traditional survey methods of planning to abstractly represent the conditions of the housing units, they began, over weeks, to meet with the residents in their homes, in kitchens around potluck meals and door prizes, to discuss what it was like to live in the Gardens and what it would take to live better. Through such meetings they learned what should be included in the survey and then, rather than conduct the surveys themselves, they accompanied the leaders of the residential council to the units and acted as scribes (Leavitt, 1992, p. 123) while the residents conducted the surveys. The task of the planners then was to turn this information into technically useful physical designs and fiscally acceptible funding proposals that would fit into the plans of the Housing Authority and its architects, thereby creating a legitimate discourse between the residents and the planners over what sort of homes the units of Nickerson were and could be. In a community filled with the most powerful gangs, the highest rates of poverty, and dramatic differences between races and ethnicities, the physical condition of the housing units, while important, was less significant than the (social) production of a safe and comfortable home (space). Planning, as it was articulated here, had become a spatial practice: one of home making.

Over a period of years, rather than the originally projected 3-month graduate planning studio, the planning studio helped to facilitate a shift in the way housing policy would at a minimum be debated—the issues for the Housing Authority when considering the condition of Nickerson Gardens now included a full-scale consideration of tot-lots as an extended, safe, and accessible part of the home—where parents and children could visit and play, day and night. By 1992, two lots had been built with Housing Authority monies, and the residents and planners were developing proposals for others. Leavitt and the student planners had also designed proposals for the laundromats—both in the housing buildings and the larger commercial project. The residents were considering

> a variety of ideas for their laundry facility: a radio, television, vending machines, and a bathroom. More importantly, they have ideas for additional service that would be available while washing their clothes: having a baby-sitter, a playground for the children, a day care center, sewing workshops, . . . books and a telephone. (Leavitt, 1993, p. 56)

In short the plans included making the space even more a home.

The community-household model treats the planning process as a recursive process that becomes part of the lived experience of householders, legitimates the demands of home making, uses technical designs of the professional planners, and informs and updates the master plans of the Los Angeles Housing Authority.

Region

Another way to look at planning is to consider it as part of the
production of region. This is region in a broad sense, not only as a
physical area but also a territorialization of politics and economics.
The City of Buffalo and its surrounding region of Western New York
(WNY) offer a case in point.

By the late 1970s, Buffalo was the clear victim of long-term deindustrialization. Unemployment in the region had reached double
digits, the population had declined precipitously, per capita income
was one fifth below that of comparable regions of the state, and the
jobs provided by the manufacturing sectors of the economy had
dropped from almost one half to barely one fifth of overall employment, as steel, machine, auto, and heavy metals production firms shut
down or left the region (Perry, 1987; Stanback & Noyelle, 1982).
Although many of the job losses were replaced by growth in the
service sector, the rate of growth in these sectors remained uncom-
petitively below national rates (Kraushaar & Perry, 1990). What
further complicated the state of the regional economy was the increased pattern of dependency that accompanied these changes—
60% of all local firms and 95% of all manufacturing firms employing
over 100 employees were outside-owned, and almost all recent agree-
ments in the transfer of ownership of firms benefited larger global
and national outside capital. The fastest-growing parts of the economy were in the public sector, and the dependency of the region on
increased social services, welfare, and other government mandated
transfers to supplant the shaky regional wage was more pronounced
than in any other region in the state. Last, all major capital investments in new firm startups or in expansions in excess of $750,000
included some form of governmental subsidy, such as loans and tax
incentives.

The combined patterns of economic decline, rising social disparities, and distress were both served and exacerbated by increased
economic dependency on outside ownership of the region's economy
and increased subsidies from the public sector. The region's industrial economy was closing down, unable to function without the input
of investment from outside capital and with almost complete dependence on public sector subsidies to retain, much less stimulate, firm-

level activity. Taken together these relations of production and reproduction made for a region of powerlessness—a space of deindustrialization and dependency that embodied the contradictions and
disparities of advanced industrial capitalism (Bluestone & Harrison,
1982; McLean & Perry, 1994; Perry, 1987; Smith & Feagin, 1987;
Stanback & Noyelle, 1982).

Regional economic development planning in WNY was anything
but regional. Instead it was a fragmented plethora of programs and
organizations mobilized to meet the needs of capital on a firm-by-firm
basis or the goals of local governments on a jurisdictionally competitive deal-by-deal or tax-abatement by tax-abatement basis. "The situation resembled an . . . [intra-regional] 'entrepreneurial economy' but
with the public sector agencies playing the role of the entrepreneur . . . competing to 'cut the best deal' with private firms" (Perry,
Kraushaar, Lines, & Parker, 1985, p. 28). As one economic development professional put it: "Our policy is the 'first firm through the
door'" gets the public support" (Perry et al., 1985, p. 29). In this
environment there was no strategic analysis of the regional economy
or interest in a more (globally) interactive and regional supportive
economy. In fact, it had become quite the opposite: In the desperate
days of structural economic change in this Rust Belt region, regional
economic development was a form of "get your own as fast as you
can"—cut a deal and cut out the competition whether it is overseas
or over in the next county.

These policies had become the practice in many of the nearly 80
public and quasi-public agencies assigned to promote the economic
development of the counties, towns, cities, and villages of WNY.
Chambers of commerce, local development corporations, industrial
development agencies, job training and assistance groups, and municipal development offices all had their own jurisdictions and their
own separate mandates. In addition there were at least 26 different
state departments and agencies administering economic development plans and programs. This intergovernmental profusion of agencies, incentives, and deals could require as many as 30 different state,
federal, and local ports of call for a firm looking for help (Perry et al.,
1985). In sum, the economic development process in the region could
be as quick as a one-stop shop at the local industrial development agency
(IDA) or an intergovernmental nightmare. Either way, the notion of

regional economic development—where the firms, workers, and citizens of the WNY area could be spatially represented as a region of shared individually and collectively experienced economic decline and dependency— was lost.

In the early years of his administration, Governor Mario Cuomo, confronted with both statewide and regional variations of this economic decline, initiated the process of creating a statewide economic development plan. We, at the SUNY/Buffalo Department of Planning, were assigned the task of producing a draft of the section of the plan for distressed regions. Using Buffalo as an example, we defined the assignment as one of building/rebuilding the region, rather than establishing planning strategies to accomplish development. In addition to designing more traditional incentive and retention packages, our goal therefore was to define a process (a) embedded in networks of structural and global interdependence rather than dependency and (b) characterized by independent regional political power and internal clarity of communication rather than powerlessness and fragmentation. In short our plan was not organized around a series of developmental "end states"; instead we hoped to establish a recursive agential process that would make/remake the economy in a region being made/remade (Grossberg, 1993) during an era of economic restructuring.

We suggested the creation of a Regional Economic Development Corporation (REDC), a regional public authority serving the multi-county WNY area most identified with economic decline and social distress, political dependency, and fragmentation. The public authority model was chosen because of its independence. The clear fiscal and political independence of a public authority would go a long way toward turning around the externally perceived notion of regional political-economic powerlessness and would serve as a centralizing feature of the fragmented economic development efforts within the region. The REDC would be a legally independent agency under the state's public benefit corporation law, with its own bonding (both general and revenue) power, a board of directors with members appointed by the governor from the various levels of government, and agencies of development. As a public authority it would be able to hire its own technically skilled staff in finance, development, and human capital. It would have the ability to negotiate the sale of its own bonds, which in the tradition of many statewide authorities, would be tax exempt and secured by both state guarantees and a revenue-generating reserve fund. Finally, it would maintain institutional and fiscal ties to the larger statewide development authorities, such as the Urban Development Corporation (UDC) and the Job Development Authority.

The result, it was argued, would be the creation of a state policy that formally established regional economic development as a clear objective of statewide economic renewal. The "arm of the State" would be regional, not tied to bureaucratically cumbersome state agencies or to the myriad of locally circumscribed agencies, but responsive to the space of the region itself—a space defined by the contradictions of economic restructuring and growing political-economic dependency in the context of wider networks of politics and economics. The institutional power of an on-site, permanent, independent, and regionally circumscribed public authority, with the political legitimacy of state law and gubernatorial appointments to its board and the fiscal power that comes with dual access to state appropriations and the private bond markets, would give this regional authority the potential to travel the hard distance between up and down, between the powerful dependencies the region had in its relations with outside ownership and capital and the daily lived experienced of economic restructuring in the firms and workplaces of Buffalo and the rest of WNY.

This proposal to serve the region as a space of political and economic relations was shelved. Although the logic of placing a primary emphasis on the region had its proponents at the local level, the political leadership at the state level was not willing to take seriously the creation of a structure designed to put the political economy of a region, no matter how distressed, in a direct and priviledged relationship with state resoruces and the bond markets. In the place of a REDC, WNY was left the newly formed Western New York Economic Development Corporation (WNYEDC). The only ostensibly regional public authority in New York, WNYEDC was maintained as a wholly owned subsidiary of the powerful statewide UDC. Although WNYEDC had some of the characteristics of the regional political economic process suggested in the REDC model, it had been created more for internal political reasons than as an agency of planning reform. Therefore, as a subsidiary of the UDC, WNYEDC was effectively a branch office of big government, rather than the bastion of regional planning independence we had suggested (Perry et al., 1985).

Even so, over the years WNYDEC has been the only agency actually engaged in the service and production of the economy as a region and has emerged as a center of communication and coordination—working to define political-economic relations between labor, capital, and the state in ways that are responsive to, but decidedly independent of, the proprietary relations of a particular firm or the politics of a particular jurisdiction. The authority's privileged, albeit dependent, subsidary status within UDC has produced almost a decade of record receipts in terms of the traditional measures of jobs (90,000) and state loans, grants, and incentives (tens of millions of dollars annually) (Madore, 1994); the authority has also been able to marshal resources and staff to facilitate not plans but new networks/relations (or regions) of industry—a spatial discourse (in the most pragmatic sense) among producers, suppliers, labor, research, training, and education in such activities as food processing (WNYEDC, 1994), medical equipment (Liberante, 1994; WNYEDC, 1994), automobiles (Luria, 1992, WNYEDC, 1992), and wood products (WNYEDC, 1990).[16] "The goal," suggests WNYEDC President Judith Kossy (personal communication, August, 24 1994) "is to nurture and integrate these factors into new sectors [i.e., regions] of production." In a region where jobs and productivity have declined, the goal has been first and foremost to rebuild regional capacity. Therefore, the objective of the agency has been to establish/reestablish the *relations*, not only the product lines, of the actors in a particular economic activity. "Once the region becomes aware of the importance of the industry (as a geo-economic sector), we can help companies here become aware of each other with regard to product development, sales and research and development," said one official of the authority (Liberante, 1994).[17] From the work station to the classroom, to the investment bank, to the suppliers and retailers—the goal of the agency is to produce the recursive space, once more, of a *region* of economic activity. This region or space of material production is ultimately grounded in WNY—from down on the factory floor on up to the level of a new sector of production.[18] In this sense the agency, on a daily basis, embodies the very regional contradictions it seeks to confront; the relations of power and the issues of redefinition of the space(s) of dependency in the region.

Ironically what serves the WNYEDC well in this regard is its undemocratic independence from subregional electoral or local oversight. Its political independence from local control and its fiscal independence through its own state lines of finance serve to provide the region with a representative spatial practice.

CONCLUSION

The thread that winds its way through this chapter is that if we think of planning spatially, then planning is best practiced as making space. In this chapter I have attempted to provide a framework for such an analysis. I have tried to illustrate the spatiality of planning historically, and I have concluded with a brief discussion of some current examples of how to apply this approach to the conditions and conflicting forces of the planning context.

Instead of thinking of planning as a scopic practice of one or another certain science or knowledge of the urban (one tall building or another), it is far better to consider planning as a spatial, strategic discourse capable of representing its practice(s) or different discourses, like the city, as coming from different perspectives related to different scales of the urban. Applying such a notion of spatiality to the way we think about planning helps, I have suggested, situate planning as a mode of thought—as a spatial practice characterized neither by the "grand view" of a fixed or paradigmatic pinnacle nor the immediate fluidity of everyday life. The spatial practice of planning is the gerundic making of space—traveling the dialectic distance between abstract and concrete space. The spaces of home making and regionalism are not presented as the answer to what planning should be but as examples of what planning is.

NOTES

1. See, among others, Brooks (1990), Lucy (1994), and Levy (1992), who would all profess the need to establish some common core for planning.

2. There is a rich transdisciplinary literature on la ville spontanée. Recently much has been made of the work of Charles Baudelaire, especially the essays in the 1964 *The*

Painter of Modern Life and Other Essays. Walter Benjamin has also studied the flaneur and the city—encouraging a whole range of scholars on the lived city—the city of everyday life (de Certeau, 1984) or the city as a labyrinth (Wilson, 1991).

All of this leads to a similarly oriented literature in the social sciences on "politics at the street level" and the "figured/disfigured city." See also the work found in a collection of essays organized by Margaret Rosler (1991).

3. Lucy suggests that rather than carving planning up into particularly circumscribed professional and intellectual domains, that planning can actually be represented in the opposite way: in a "more expansive view" of the field. This expansiveness can only occur, Lucy suggests, if planning has a central principle from which to guide it. This principle for Lucy (1994) is "that healthy places nurture healthy people, and that public policies should aim at sustaining both healthy people and healthy places, not one or the other" (p. 305). In this way Lucy returns us to the metaphor of health—a broader more expansive version of the original reform goal of healthy people and places that first blended social reformers and engineers—or political change and technology in the planning of the chaotic political, economic, and social environment of the early industrial city.

4. The literature on planning may not have a collective identity but does seem to share a growing collective sense of what Brooks calls malaise over its identity, purpose, and legitimacy. See, among others, Peter Ambrose (1986), Thomas and Healey (1991), Boyer (1983), Perry (1994), Reade (1987), Altshuler (1965), Wildavsky (1973), Lucy (1994), and Levy (1992).

5. See Friedmann (1987) and Beauregard (1990) for a discussion of the morality of planning—its goals of social justice and redistribution and the fact that this morality should be grounded in an agreeable practice of intervention.

6. This is an important caveat because it allows for a different notion of how we (spatially) think about planning. To invoke the notion of the "production of space," writes Neil Smith (1992), is "to problematize the universal assumption of absolute space . . . also [rendering] problematic the whole range of spatial metaphors grounded in the assumption of absolute space" (p. 64).

7. Here Fainstein uses the notion of entrepreneurship developed by Peter Eisinger (1988).

8. See the collection of essays in Judd and Parkinson (1990). Also see the myriad reports and studies put out by the Council on Urban Economic Development, including CUED's journal, *Economic Development Commentary,* the *Economic Development Quarterly,* and the new studies of public and private not-for-profits and foundations put out by the Frey Foundation.

9. More than one half of the almost 30,000 members of the American Planning Association are not employed in the public sector, and this number is growing.

10. For a discussion of the notion of travel as an intellectual activity—one of theory and practice, see Edward Said's (1984) essay "Traveling Theory," pp. 226-247 in his collection *The World, the Text and the Critic,* and the wonderful discussion of the topic in the first chapter of Derek Gregory's (1994) book, especially pp. 9-14.

11. These other approaches to planning being examples of other visions or centers of what Foucault (1980) calls knowledge/power.

12. See Immanuel Wallerstein (1991) for a discussion of this notion of unthinking as compared to rethinking.

13. Wildavsky (1973) suggested that such an exercise was really one of "faith" rather than rationality, whereas Friedmann (1987) and Beauregard (1990) argue for planning

as a responsive moral force and Brooks (1990) suggests a combination of political pragmatism and technology. Meck (1990) argues for an end to utopian comprehensiveness and a new hard-boiled pragmatism that comes from serving the interests at hand and therefore being "inclusive."

14. See Derek Gregory (1994, p. 9) for a wonderful introduction to contemporary spatial theory; also see James Clifford (1986, p. 22).

15. This section of the chapter is derived from a report on this project delivered in the form of a seminar conducted by Jacqueline Leavitt at SUNY at Buffalo as part of the Clarkson Chair week seminar on planning, Spring 1991, and an interview with Leavitt conducted on August 23, 1994.

16. It is impossible in the space here to describe, in any detail, the actual examples of this process including a new Medical Products Network of producers and suppliers, an automobile forum that links Detroit with producers and suppliers in a discourse on auto parts production activity in WNY, and an industrial effectiveness program that takes government and basic research to the site of production in new models and relationships of government, industry and university research. Further, WNYEDC is serving as a new space for coordinating overall planning activities for the regional and state planning agencies, as well as serving as the linkage between various sites of training and education and labor and industrial sector needs in a variety of areas.

17. Liberante, Carrie. (1994, July 16). NY growth industry: Medical projects. *The Buffalo News*, pp. B1-B9. Reprinted with permission.

18. An example is the emergence of the Center for Industrial Effectiveness at SUNY, Buffalo, where research and expertise are actually taken to the factory floor in an attempt to include management, workers, and new research on efficencies of production in sites of economic production.

REFERENCES

Altshuler, A. A. (1965). *The city planning process: A political analysis*. Ithaca, NY: Cornell University Press.

Ambrose, P. (1986). *Whatever happened to planning?* London: Methuen.

Barnett, J. (1986). *The elusive city: Five centuries of design, ambition and miscalculation*. New York: Harper & Row.

Baudelaire, C. (1964). *The painter of modern life and other essays*. New York: De Capo Press.

Bluestone, B., & Harrison, B. (1982). *The deindustrialization of America: Plant closing, community abandonment, and the dismantling of basic industries*. New York: Basic Books.

Beard, C. (1926). Some aspects of regional planning. *American Political Science Review, 20*, 273-283.

Beauregard, R. A. (1989). Between modernity and postmodernity: The ambiguous position of U.S. planning. *Society and Space, 7*, 381-395.

Beauregard, R. A. (1990). Bringing the city back in. *The Journal of the American Planning Association, 56*(2), 210-215.

Boyer, M. C. (1983). *Dreaming the rational city: The myth of American city planning*. Cambridge: MIT Press.

Boyer, M. C. (1995). The great frame-up: Fantastic appearances in contemporary spatial politics. In H. Liggett & D. C. Perry (Eds.), *Spatial practices: New theories of social process* (pp. 81-109). Thousand Oaks, CA: Sage.

Brooks, M. P. (1990). The city may be back in, but where is the planner? *The Journal of the American Planning Association, 56*(2), 218-220.

Casella, S. (1993). A quantum response to non-Euclidian planning. *Journal of the American Planning Association, 59*(4), 485.

Castagnoli, F. (1971). *Orthogonal town-planning in antiquity.* Cambridge: MIT Press.

Castells, M. (1976). The wild city. *Kapitalistate, 4-5,* 2-30.

Clifford, J. (1986). Introduction: Partial truths. In J. Clifford & G. Marcus (Eds.), *Writing culture: The poetics and politics of ethnography* (pp. 1-26). Berkeley: University of California Press.

Davis, M. (1992). *The city of quartz.* New York: Vintage.

Dear, M., & Scott, A. J. (1981). *Urbanization & urban planning in capitalist society.* London: Methuen.

de Certeau, M. (1984). *The practice of everyday life* (S. Rendall, Trans.). Berkeley: University of California Press.

Eisinger, P. (1988). *The rise of the entrepreneurial state.* Madison: University of Wisconsin Press.

Fainstein, S. S. (1991). Promoting economic development: Urban planning in the United States and Great Britain. *Journal of the American Planning Association, 57*(1), 22-33.

Fairfield, J. D. (1993). *The mysteries of the great city: The politics of urban design, 1877-1937.* Columbus: Ohio State University Press.

Felbinger, C. (1995). Conditions of confusion and conflict: Rethinking the infrastructure-economic development linkage. In D. C. Perry (Ed.), *Building the public city: The politics, governance and finance of public infrastructure* (pp. 103-137). Thousand Oaks, CA: Sage.

Fogelsong, R. E. (1990). Planning for social democracy. *The Journal of the American Planning Association, 56*(2), 215-216.

Foucault, M. (1980). *Power/knowledge: Selected interviews and other writings 1972-1977* (C. Gordon, Trans.). New York: Pantheon.

Foucault, M., & Deleueze, G. (1977). Intellectuals & power. In D. F. Bouchard (Ed.), *Language, counter-memory, practice: Selected essays and interviews* (pp. 205-217). Ithaca, NY: Cornell University Press.

Friedmann, J. (1987). *Planning in the public domain.* Princeton, NJ: Princeton University Press.

Friedmann, J. (1993). Toward a non-Euclidian mode of planning. *The Journal of the American Planning Association, 59*(4), 482-485.

Gregory, D. (1994). *Geographical imaginations.* Cambridge, UK: Basil Backwell.

Grossberg, L. (1993). Cultural studies and/in new worlds. *Cultural Studies in Mass Communication, 10,* 1-22.

Howe, F. (1969). *The modern city and its problems.* College Park, MD: McGrath. (Original work published 1926)

Judd, D., & Parkinson, M. (Eds.). (1990). Leadership and urban regeneration. *Urban Affairs Annual Reviews, 37.*

Kostof, S. (1991). *The city shaped: Urban patterns and meanings through history.* Boston: Little, Brown.

Kraushaar, R., & Perry, D. (1990). Buffalo, New York: Region of no illusions. In R. D. Bingham & R. W. Eberts (Eds.), *Economic restructuring of the American Midwest*. Norwell, MA: Klwuer Academic.

Leavitt, J. (1992). Women made fire: Public housing criticism in Los Angeles. *Frontiers, 13*(2), 109-130.

Leavitt, J. (1993). Shifting loads: From hand power to machine power to economic power. *Intersight, 2*, 53-57.

Leavitt, J., & Saegert, S. (1988). The community-household: Responding to housing abandonment in New York City. *The Journal of the American Planning Association, 55*, 489-500.

Leavitt, J., & Saegert, S. (1989). *From abandonment to hope: The making of community-households in Harlem*. New York: Columbia University Press.

Lefebvre, H. (1970). *La révolution urbaine*. Paris: Gallimand.

Lefebvre, H. (1991). *The production of space*. Oxford, UK: Basil Blackwell.

Levy, J. M. (1992). What has happened to planning? *The Journal of the American Planning Association, 59*(1), 81-84.

Liberante, C. A. (1994, August 21.) WNY growth industry: Medical products. *The Buffalo News*, pp. B1, B19.

Lucy, W. H. (1994). If planning includes too much, maybe it should include more. *The Journal of the American Planning Association, 60*(3), 305-318.

Luria, D. (1992). *Auto forum*. Buffalo, NY: WNYEDC.

Madore, J. T. (1994, July 16). WNY gets record economic aid from state. *The Buffalo News*, pp. B1, B9.

McLean, B., & Perry, D. C. (1994). *The splintering metropolis: New divisions of gender, race and economics in the northeastern production cities* (Policy Working Paper Series). Buffalo: State University of New York at Buffalo.

Meck, S. (1990). From high-minded reformism to hard-broiled pragmatism: American city planning faces the next century. *The Planner, 76*(6), 11-15.

Perry, D. C. (1987). The politics of dependency in deindustrializing America: The case of Buffalo, New York. In J. Feagin & M. Peter (Eds.), *The capitalist city: Global restructuring and community politics* (pp. 113-137). Oxford, UK: Basil Blackwell.

Perry, D. C. (1994). Planning and the city: The turbulent practice. *Planning Theory, 10/11*, 23-42.

Perry, D. C., Kraushaar, R., Lines, J., & Parker, E. (1985). *Ending regional economic dependency: Economic development policy for distressed regions* (Studies in Planning and Design). Buffalo: Center for Regional Studies at State University of New York, Buffalo.

Peterson, P. E. (1981). *City limits*. Chicago: University of Chicago Press.

Reade, E. (1987). *British town and country planning*. Philadelphia: Open University Press.

Regional Plan Association (RPA). (1927). *Major economic factors in metropolitan growth and arrangement*. New York: Regional Plan of New York.

Relph, E. (1987). *The modern urban landscape*. Baltimore: The Johns Hopkins University Press.

Rosler, M. (1991). *If you lived here: The city in art, theory and social activism*. Seattle, WA: Bay Press.

Said, E. (1984). *The world, the text and the critic*. Cambridge, MA: Harvard University Press.

Schön, D. A. (1983). *The reflective practitioner: How professionals think in action*. New York: Basic Books.

Smith, M. P., & Feagin, J. R. (1987). *The capitalist city: Global restructuring and community politics*. Oxford, UK: Basil Blackwell.

Smith, N. (1992). Contours of a spatialized politics: Homeless vehicles and the production of geographical space. *Social Text, 33*, 55-81.

Stanback, T., & Noyelle, T. (1982). *Cities in transition*. Totowa, NJ: Allanheld, Osmun.

Thomas, H., & Healey, P. (Eds.). (1991). *Dilemmas of planning practice: Ethics, legitimacy and the validation of knowledge*. Aldershot, UK: Avebury Technical.

Thrift, N. (1993). An urban impasse? *Theory, Culture & Society, 10*, 229-238.

Wallerstein, I. (1991). *Unthinking social science: The limits of nineteenth-century paradigms*. London: Polity.

Warner, S. B. (1974). *The private city: Philadelphia in three periods of its growth*. Philadephia: University of Pennsylvania Press.

Wildavsky, A. (1973). If planning is everything, maybe it's nothing. *Policy Sciences, 4*, 127-153.

Wilson, E. (1991). *The sphinx in the city: Urban life, the control of disorder, and women*. London: Virago.

WNYEDC. (1990). *Year-end report, 1989-1990*. Buffalo, NY: Author.

WNYEDC. (1992). *Year-end report, 1991-1992*. Buffalo, NY: Author.

WNYEDC. (1994). *Year-end report, 1993-1994*. Buffalo, NY: Author.

9

◉

City Sights/Sites of Memories and Dreams

◉

HELEN LIGGETT

IMAGES AND SPACE

Many urbanists are familiar with William Whyte's (1988) work, *City.* In it he reports the findings of several overlapping projects covering a time span of nearly 2 decades, all centered around the accumulation of visual evidence: videotapes and photography. His sponsors in the activity of capturing the spatial habits of New Yorkers have been the City of New York and various private and public foundations, including the National Geographic Society.

Whyte's "evidence" is used in a social science mode: that is, to provide support for this or that assertion or question about the city. For example, Whyte can tell you how people gather in front of department stores and that people will sit outside on warm sunny days, almost no matter how architecturally difficult it is made for them to do so. Because Whyte is rather assertive about his preferences for life at the center, it is easy to forget how completely he operates within the logic of discovery. There is no difference, in other words, in his work, between good numbers and good pictures.[1]

Much earlier another famous chronicler of city life, Fredrick Engels, spent 20 months wandering around Manchester recording what he saw. "He wanted above all 'more than a mere *abstract* knowledge of my subject'" (quoted in Marcus, 1973, p. 257). To that end he literally walked the streets. Here is one of his most often repeated observations, taken from "The Great Towns," in *The Condition of the Working Class in England in 1844:*

> The town itself is peculiarly built, so that someone can live in it for years and travel into it and out of it daily without ever coming into contact with a working class quarter or even with workers—so long, that is to say, as one confines himself to his business affairs or to strolling about for pleasure. (quoted in Marcus, 1973, p. 258)

Engels further notes that the well-to-do can travel from their homes

> to their places of business in the center of town by the shortest routes, which run right through all the working class districts, without even noticing how close they are to the most squalid misery which lies immediately about them on both sides of the road. This is because the main streets which run from the Exchange in all directions out of the city are occupied almost uninterruptedly on both sides by shops, which are kept by members of the middle and lower-middle classes. . . . These serve the purpose of hiding from the eyes of wealthy gentlemen and ladies with strong stomachs and weak nerves the misery and squalor that form the completing counterpart, the indivisible complement, of their riches and luxury. (quoted in Marcus, 1973, p. 259)

As Steven Marcus (1973) points out, Engels's mode of analysis has great depth on at least two accounts. First, instead of using his observations as evidence in the social science research sense of hypothesis testing or to illustrate previous analysis, Engels produces an analysis of the structure of the industrial city. Second, Engels shows how the spatial separations that define the city also mask the extent to which the classes are bound to each other in mutually constitutive relations. Thus Engels shows the spatial practices he

Figure 9.1. City Sights/Sites: Public Square, Cleveland, Ohio

analyzes to be active components in the exploitive relations of the industrial capitalism he so abhors.

Whyte and Engels introduce two themes that are brought to bear on each other in this chapter: (a) spatial theory in which space is seen as a generative component of social life and (b) the use of images to interpret spatial conventions (see Figure 9.1).

SPATIAL ANALYSIS AND IMAGINARY GEOGRAPHIES

In *The Production of Space*, Henri Lefebvre (1991) writes in a vein that has more in common with Engels than with Whyte, looking at space as an active component of constructing, maintaining, and challenging social order. Lefebvre is interested in developing a unitary theory of space that also defines space as process. By unitary he means applicable to all levels, from classrooms, to buildings, to neighborhoods, cities, regions, and the globe. By process, he means to see space as continually being produced. In Lefebvre's thinking formulating space involves both social space, in the sense of domains or realms of *understanding*, and physical space, the *material* of group life.

After a lengthy and careful review of the notion of space in Western thought, Lefebvre (1991) rejects "empty container" and "abstract category" notions of space and insists instead that we think of the production of space as an ontological process. Lefebvre does not say that the notion that space is empty, waiting to be used, is outdated. In fact, he is concerned that it continues to have valence in academic disciplines and in the policy sciences, where it blinds these professions to both preexisting and emergent spatial practices that articulate meaning in spaces and for those who use them. For example, when Lefebvre writes: "Talk of city planning refers to nothing at all" (p. 389), he is pointing to how institutionalized notions of space have obtained iconographic status. However, they are not only internally referential. What disturbs Lefebvre is that such systems are imposed and actualized in the production of urban space.

Lefebvre's spatial theory is rooted in a long tradition of materialist thought, committed to bringing the abstract and material to bear on each other. Just as Marx points out that commodities can be thought of as "concrete abstractions" (material embodiments of labor power) Lefebvre sees space embodying social order. Whereas Marxist thought ties the abstract and material to relations of exchange, Lefebvre (1991) privileges relations of assemblage and sees modes of bringing together that produce space as modes of constituting value. Actions, relations producing space, are what space is. In the current era, complex "entities and peculiarities, relatively fixed points, movements, and flows and waves—some interpenetrating, others in conflict, and so on" (Lefebvre, 1991, p. 88) constitute social/physical space. From this perspective, even the most "natural" forms of space, such as designated wilderness areas in the American experience, are cultural processes. That is, nature is nature to a culture, grounded and designated within a way of life.

Rather than focusing on the description of particular places, as Whyte does, or on analyzing the dynamics of a specific way of life as Engels does, Lefebvre's reach is methodological in the broad sense of the word.[2] Spatiology as a mode of inquiry makes possible spatial analysis, which combines the social and the physical in an interrogation of spatial production as ongoing relations that are not just reflections of a way of life but instead are its projections. Just as Engels's perspective complicates Whyte's by adding an analytic component, so Lefebvre complicates the notion of space by adding action and context.

A familiar example from American historical geography illustrates this move from simple analysis of spatial designations to complex readings of spatial practices. Bringing the riches of the West closer to Eastern markets and financial centers with the transcontinental railroad is a process of assembly familiar to us from grade school textbooks. But we probably learned a version of this story told from the perspective of geographic literalism. From the viewpoint of active spatial theory, the implications of the railroad are more complex than pointing out that it made it possible to go across the country in fewer days. What the transcontinental railroad did was to contribute to the assembly of a new *kind* of space and new forms of spatial enactment. It transformed notions of hinterlands and participated in the reorganization of control of the American landscape. The famous *New Yorker* map showing New York and the West Coast, with something vast and undifferentiated in between that may be called Utah or Colorado, is a playful child of this new form. This is saying more than it is easier to get places now than it used to be. It is to suggest that the production of space is inseparable from the operation of culture and the functioning of a social order.

Contemporary spatial theory has refined this notion of imaginary geography[3] in the politically revealing observation that the command centers of global cities are closer to each other than the centers of each are to the depressed areas within them.[4] Engels's work is precursory, but he did not expand his analysis into a general theory of the production of space because his concern was, as the title of his study announces, the condition of the working class.

Lefebvre develops a three-part model for research into the relations of assembly that produce space: representations of space, spatial practices, and representational spaces. Each includes the relation between physical and social space in the constitution of imaginary geographies that are also real.

Representations of space are codified and often institutionalized ways of knowing space. This category is the direct descendent of traditional notions of space as an abstract category, notions that Lefebvre impunes. Representations of space form self-referential worlds, or detached ideologies that then can be used instrumentally to create certain kinds of space. Urban planning with its tools such as zoning, concepts such as "highest and best use," and projects such as "coastal zone management," is one of his examples. In general Lefebvre (1991) identifies representations of space as "the space of scientists, . . . urbanists, technocratic subdividers and social engineers, as of a certain type of artist with a scientific bent" (p. 38). His critique of representations of space is based on the tendency of this mode to *impose* a reality in the construction of it. In his words, "identifying what is lived and what is perceived with what is conceived" (p. 38).

The fact that planning is more powerful and highly developed in the European context does not limit the applicability of this form of spatial assembly. American examples of the force of representations of space abound. For example, after the Civil War, when photography was still relatively new, the U.S. government sponsored survey expositions to the West that included photographers.[5] The survey information, including the visual images, were constructed with an eye toward assessing the value of western space for the East. Value was construed in terms of the existence of raw materials that would be valuable to the newly industrialized nation. The photographs from this era have since been used to argue for the preservation of western lands, but to the careful viewer they still bear the marks of their original purpose, for example, in the placement of figures to provide a sense of scale, and in their concentration on various kinds of rock formations that indicate the potential presence of valuable minerals.[6] To the extent that land not holding potential for agricultural production or resource extraction is judged to be worthless, representations of space similar to those organizing the surveyors' view prevail. They conceive of the West as potential space for the production of material wealth by the means of industrial capital. The West, as a living functional aspect of American culture or as perceived and transversed by those inhabiting it, is canceled out or figured in only as such experiences support dominant modes of representation.

Spatial practices have to do with the everyday social/spatial patterns of people in particular places. This is what Lefebvre calls "life
as perceived." Engels suggests that the spatial practices of the residents of Manchester are limited and that the customary limits differ
according to class.[7] Members of the working class were unlikely to
drift out to the residential suburbs of the managerial class on their
free day, if they had one. Similarly, contemporary citizens move in
limited patterns, and so our spatial practices create the space of a
partial city, with our familiar work, home, school, shopping routines
at the center. Of course, this varies, as did the patterns reported by
Engels, according to class and other life circumstances. The cultural
organization of these variations in spatial practices would be a rich
source for research into how social distinction operates in the sense
that Bourdieu (1984) has studied it. More centrally to this chapter,
spatial practices and representations of space can have any number
of variations of conjunction and disjunction. As in black and white
photography, where an image is not actually produced in black and
white, but rather in relations among grays, the most powerful use of
spatial categories is to ask how they produce conventional spatial
forms relationally.

To say this in a different way, the spatial patterns of everyday life
are markedly different from the Automobile Association of America
(AAA) map everybody gets when they first move to a place. That
difference is lodged in the supreme selectivity of daily spatial practices as opposed to the universal neutrality assumed by cartographic
representation of space. Lefebvre is at pains to point out that spatial
practices reach beyond cartography in the way the meaning is embedded in them. The AAA map does not pretend to tell you if you
want to live there.

Nor, as a matter of fact, will many planning documents. Map 4,
"Potential Housing Development Sites," which is included in Volume
2 of the *Cleveland Civic Vision 2000 Citywide Plan* (1991, p. 33) is a
good example (see Figure 9.2). Using the terminology of spatial
analysis, the Cleveland housing site map is a paradigmatic example
of institutionalized representations of space.[8] As such it is not informative about spatial practices.

Yet neither the AAA map nor Map 4 stands alone in opposition to
the spatial practices of everyday life. They both work, or make sense,

250

Figure 9.2. Map 4, Potential Housing Development Sites, *Cleveland Civic Vision*

in terms of shared, if not exactly singularly agreed-upon, cultural codes and expectations. The working out of the different articulations of these gradations in the sense of which shall dominate or hold and that shall be vacuous or be challenged are part of the "processes of assembly" Lefebvre calls the production of space. To understand the processes at work in these particular examples, we have to include Lefebvre's third category, representational space.

Representational space is heavily loaded, deeply symbolic, and embedded culturally, not necessarily entailing conscious awareness. It calls on shared experiences and interpretations at a profound level. In Lefebvre's (1991) words, it is

> space as directly *lived* through its associated images and symbols, and hence the space of "inhabitants" and "users," but also of some artists and perhaps of those, such as a few writers and philosophers, who *describe* and aspire to do no more than describe. (p. 39; italics in original)

To use language from another lexicon, representational spaces are the loci of meaning in a culture. Representational space is central for Lefebvre, ironically, not because it is rare, which his initial definition makes it appear to be, but because it is integral, yet unacknowledged (-able) in most systems of meaning with which we conventionally construct space. Thus from Lefebvre's perspective there appears to be a dearth of profound examples in contemporary life and the crowding out by appropriative forms to such an extent that it becomes difficult even to express a sense of loss.

It is helpful to begin with widely differing examples of profound and appropriative space to get a sense of representational space, "life as lived," as distinct from representations of space and spatial practices. One of the best examples of almost universally recognized profound representational space is the Vietnam War Memorial.[9] As the churches and temples have, in effect, emptied out, it stands as one of the few representational spaces in America that most Americans acknowledge in terms central to our national identity.

On the other hand, as examples of appropriative representational space, we are surrounded by the cascading fountains, tropical plantings, and classical references culturally coded as indicators of the exotic, of leisure, or of elegance at shopping malls.[10] The paraphernalia of marketing cities offer further examples. Cleveland, for instance, as the "Comeback City," is marketed in terms of the lifestyle identified in popular culture with the kind of economic base city promoters aspire to. The magic or dream of a fantasy postindustrial city is part of the apparatus of trying to reconfigure past-industrial cities. Images of representational space have been presented in conjunction with implications about spatial practices in a simple brochure advertising the cultural advantages of Cleveland and the grace of the nearby residential suburbs. The logic of marketing includes the hope that this will play a role in constructing a future Cleveland moving toward destinations based in representations of space framed by the economic development discourse.[11]

Representational space is crucial to developing spatiology as a mode of analysis because this dimension is woven into productive processes. To say this is to bring to forth the dynamics of social life that a straightforward observational mode such as Whyte employs may observe, but not interpret; and a generative model based in political economics such as Engels employs tends to deemphasize. Relations among different modes of assembly are the key to interpreting the production of space at particular sites.

That is to say processes of assembly are dialectical, not discreet and oppositional. For instance, the housing map discussed above (see Figure 9.2), from Volume 2 of *Cleveland Civic Vision* (1991, p. 33), can be subject to a more detailed analysis by examining the context in which it appears. The cover of Volume 2 is dominated by a handsome color photograph of single-family residential units in an older neighborhood. The Central Business District (CBD) and Lake Erie and a beautiful blue sky form the background of the picture. In this setting, of course, the houses are not being represented as single-family dwellings, but rather as well-kept homes in an older neighborhood—that is, as an urban community.

The community is a representational space that encompasses the memory of a time and place, a fulfilling way of life and also a dream for the future. The responsibility for making up the difference between this community of the mind and "available housing sites" represented in Map 4 is bridged by the reader. The existence or nonexistence of the spatial practices that would close the gap between the two is lost because of how the notion of community informs each. The memory of the imagined community (the cover) is projected onto the figure of a potential future (the map). In case the reader doesn't know, the cover fairly shouts it out: Here is the attitude one is expected to bring to this plan.

This is an example of how the different modes of spatial assembly that Lefebvre proposes are not only not discreet but also work in relation to each other to present a meaning. If citizens, as readers of the plan, believe community is a thing—and automatically link it to potential housing sites—then the quality of actual housing (or lack of it) can be more easily influenced by moves not accessible to them, while Cleveland neighborhoods are at the same time assessed in terms not dictated by them, yet to which they will be held accountable, to themselves, among others. Thus, *Civic Vision* is aided as a tool of spatial production by the memory of community, of how the nostalgic neighborhood exists as a representational space in the industrial heartland of America.

Another example of the mixing of modes in plans to produce space is found in *Investing in the Future: Cleveland Tomorrow's Strategic Picture for the '90's* (1993)—the document used to spell out how Cleveland's largest corporations have planned to guide the region's economic development. The organization formed to construct this plan is Cleveland Tomorrow.[12] Its mission is to help "co-ordinate the private sector's response to the structural economic transformation of the region" (p. 1) The economic transformation is defined as the need to produce jobs through a putatively renewed commitment to manufacturing, but the focus, in *Investing in the Future*, is on tourism: "The visitor industry is the most promising sector for substantial job creation" (p. 9). On the surface this appears to be a straightforward representation of space: hard instrumental reason talking.

Yet tourism is about fantasy: It makes the myth of a place real enough to ensure that tourists score a travel experience worth the time and effort. Sometimes the tamed exotic tourist experience is based on residents of an area themselves, for example, in Australia and the Pacific Islands. This doesn't seem likely for the Great Lakes region. Sometimes the tourist attraction is a harnessed natural wonder, such as Niagara Falls (Shields, 1991). This is easiest to pull off when you begin with a readily recognizable environmental asset. Another option is to heavily endow a site with meaning that ennobles the visitor. Pearl Harbor is an example. A preexisting code about national security and heroism constructs the tourist experience of the Arizona Memorial (Turnbull, 1993). Another approach is to create a tourist destination point. The list of Cleveland's assets in *Investing in the Future* (Wittgenstein, 1993, p. 18) suggests this route: the Cleveland Aquarium, Gateway Stadium and Arena, Great Lakes Museum of Science, Environment and Technology, Inventure Place, Metropark's new Rain Forest, NASA's Lewis Visitor Center, The National Heritage Corridor of the Cuyahoga Valley National Recreation Area, and of course, the Rock and Roll Hall of Fame. On the level of spatial planning Cleveland Tomorrow suggests:

> Create an amenities master plan. To gain a stronger regional identity as a visitor destination, we will need to be attentive to the things that weld the region together: new rail connections, bike paths, clear signage, attractive streetscapes that define important destinations. To achieve all this, we need a good amenities master plan. (1993, p. 19)

A recently enacted Cleveland city ordinance rises to the occasion, as it were, by tying response to signage proposals from neighborhoods to whether or not communities are considered to be potential tourist destination sites.

Here again rather than the discovery of Lefebvre's categories of processes of assembly, we see the need for ongoing interpretation of dialectic relations that enable their articulation. Symbolically loaded or representational space is used to define the rational in a constitutive way. Not only do the modes appear together, they work together, often in surprising ways. In the example above the relative importance of representations of space and representational space is reversed from what we would expect of policy discourse.

Volume 1 of *Cleveland Civic Vision* (1991) offers a final example of how instrumental reason (representations of space) consorts with representational space in dialectical processes of assembly. Volume 1 is devoted to economic planning and development in the CBD. Instead of a photo that looks backward to an idealized memory, such as the cover of Volume 2, the cover of Volume 1 is a photograph of an architect's model of a fully developed CBD. This looks forward.

But as a realist of the old school might point out, it is not real. It is a dream.

To summarize, Lefebvre's categories are the most powerful when they are used as tools of analysis, not applied as mutually exclusive categories to be sought out and observed. To ask questions such as, "Is this a representation of space or a spatial practice?" or "Where are the representational spaces here?" is to reduce their potential for the project of interpreting processes of assembly at work in the social/physical space. Instead, and this is Lefebvre's real gift to urbanists, the three categories are a beginning from which to analyze space as an activity and to ask questions about the dialectical relations in terms of which space is formulated and functions.

IMAGINARY GEOGRAPHY AND THE CITY AS SIGNED

Lefebvre is a far from neutral observer of spatial conventions. Against the fragmentation of a number of disciplines that place space in the service of external agendas, Lefebvre wants to recall the conditions of production. This knowledge would, for him, "be expected to rediscover *time* (and in the first place the time of production) in and through space" (p. 91).

There are at least two ways to understand the notion of rediscovering time. One, the least promising, presupposes an underlying truth of the situation, which is masked, hidden, or otherwise removed from cultural consciousness using a number of devices, of which representations of space are one. This approach leads to thinking in terms of restoring truth and also grounds the idealization of certain historical spatial patterns (Lefebvre, 1991, pp. 397-400). For example, for Lefebvre there is a certain centeredness and integrity to the medieval cathedral. Similarly, in Francoise Choay's (1986) early work she idealizes "pure" systems, of which non-Western or so called primitive societies are represented as the best examples. The Bororo village studied by Levi-Strauss is used as an example because the spatial practices and representational spaces within it are all of a piece: "In a word," Choay says, "it [the structure of the village] involves and determines the totality of behavior; the constructed system is saturated with meaning" (p. 163). In contrast to these contemporary cities are "mixed systems," their obsolescence held off by increasingly complex systems of supplementation, such as traffic codes and graphic signs.

What Choay (1986) has to say about signs and systems of supplementation is itself a wonderfully supple insight into the production of contemporary space. But an overly structuralist frame of pure versus mixed systems repeats the limited interpretation of Lefebvre "only" being concerned about destroying the dominance of abstraction (as if a material "really real" could then be expected to blossom forth). Both impede the application of spatial theory as a mode of analysis of ongoing spatial practices. Interpreting Lefebvre in modernist terms—that is, as interested in the restoration of truth—does honor one aspect of his work, but it devalues the way in which he challenges spatiology to develop appropriate theories to illuminate contemporary processes of assembly. Using time to recall and restore the congruences of a world in place represented by the medieval cathedral would be to reimpose the very categories of abstract philosophy that are the foundations of representations of space Lefebvre sees as constructing destructive contemporary space.

From a broader perspective the call to restore time does not mean *restore* as in "bring back," but rather to bring articulation processes to consciousness or awareness. "Recalling the conditions of production" is similar to what Foucault means by a history of the present. "To rediscover time . . . in and through space" is to incorporate time into the analytic process, in the sense of including the cultural context of production: of the space and of the analysis of the space—both. Thus the research, far from being invisible, is also recognized as located in time and space. Analysis that rediscovers time makes explicit representational space that appears to be lost to modern systems of spatial understanding.

The focus in Lefebvre and other spatial theorists on these "extra-conventional" aspects of space[13] is also recognized by Barthes (1986), who uses it as the basis for presenting an outline for an urban semiotics: "There exists . . . a conflict between signification and reason or, at least, between signification and the calculating reason which would have all the elements of a city uniformly assimilated by planning" (p. 91). Space means beyond the institutionalized practices we have devised to capture it. It escapes, in other words. In semiotics this habit of escape is thought to inhabit all meaning and if not captured is at least recognized by the notion of discourse (language in use). Thus Barthes asserts: "The City is a discourse" (p. 92). To move this statement from being merely metaphorical to being useful for analysis, he suggests conceptualizing the city in terms of signifying practices, the making and changing of meaning. Space then doesn't *stand* for anything, it is the development, play, and interchangeability of signification. The city depends on memories, it requires dreams; that is, aspects of life that representations of space exclude and some of what Lefebvre wishes to capture in his insistence on spatial practices and representational space are inseparable components of the dynamics of spatial production.

The semiological notion of infinite chains of signifers provides an analytic tool for writing about production of space as an ongoing process. Following poststructuralist thought in general, Barthes characterizes the relationship between signified and signifier as an unstable one. This is different from saying that there is no signified. Instead he says that a signified that may figure at the base of a signifier in a "simple" situation becomes folded into an ongoing process of signification. Many students are familiar with his early example from *Mythologies*, a magazine cover with a photograph of an African in a French uniform saluting a French flag (Barthes, 1972). The image, he points out, is of a French colonial soldier. Technically it is a sign composed of a signifier and a signified. As a whole it becomes a signifier for another sign, of French colonial might and legitimacy. This complete example, in turn, has become an example of how chains of signifiers work, repeated to graduate students the world over. This pedagogical example itself has now become a signifier of the era of the instructor's introduction to semiotics and also of French colonial history. Still the French soldier remains, saluting that French flag, someplace in the African desert. The simple example continues to be used to generate signification, according to the context in which it is interpreted. Barthes is applying a similar approach to the city in the assertion, "The City is a discourse," quoted above. It supplies the key to an appropriate methodology for Lefebvre's project to use time to restore space. Each interpretative step is an assertion itself, which uses stilled or stopped time to articulate the signifying processes at work.

From this broader interpretation of Lefebvre's project, the medieval cathedral does not represent a definitive signified but rather a memory of harmonious relations in all realms of spatial production. It is not medieval life, per se, that we should return to or want to restore. Lefebvre's interpretation restores medieval life to itself in the terms that he finds illustrative of modes of assembly that are "true" in the sense that they are in concert with one another. From his perspective this is a condition productive not only of good physical space (the cathedral) but of also of a good social order.

Diane Agrest (1991) is similarly interested in planning good contemporary public space, and like Barthes she uses a semiotics approach "to rediscover time (the time of production)." What urban designers ought to focus on, she suggests, is on developing a theory of place as a social production of sense. "The object of study," she says, "may be reformulated as the production of signification in the built environment through the articulation of various cultural codes within a culture and a mode of production" (p. 17). Against a narrow view of communication theory used in planning by Richard Meier and Melvin Webber, she argues that there are no simple channels and senders or receivers. Instead all are embedded in context. If space is examined from a semiotic viewpoint, spatial theory can be put to work in analysis that foregrounds context by asking: How is meaning working, here, at this site? "Signification is not thought of as what the 'thing' communicates but as the readings that, within a given culture, may be produced out of it" (Agrest, 1991, p. 24). This is not a closed notion of semiotics as "merely" the interpretation of preexisting codes, but rather a call for an open system. Raymond Ladrut (1986) phrases it well:

> To the question: how does the city speak of this to us?, we have replied: as a work of art, which means as an object charged with meaning by the production and the use men make of it. The only way to learn what the city tells us is to examine the field of the urban experience, the "lived" city. To search for a code is vain. (p. 120)

Seen in this context, the importance of Choay's comment about the increasing use of signs and systems of supplementation in the city becomes clearer. The chains of signifers in contemporary urban space include signifieds that can themselves be (literally) signs.

THE PHOTO/TEXT AND SIGHTS/SITES
OF MEMORIES AND DREAMS

It is not yet clear how to implement the analysis that Lefebvre outlines and Barthes, Agrest, Ledrut, and Choay situate in semiotics. If semiotic analysis is used in a structuralist mode to discover codes behind the space, it cannot capture the conditions of movements-that-escape, the ongoing production, the continual articulation of space that spatial theory identifies. The symbiotic relation between representations of space and the logic of discovery suggest that conventional social science methods, even when cast in a semiotic frame, are not adequate to the task. "Life," Lefebvre (1991) says, "is lived as a project" (p. 249). As Barthes and the others insist, interpretations don't end up at a final destination, they are part of a project of enactment.

Researchers can only study that project of enactment by participating in it, or more precisely, by acknowledging and accounting for their inevitable participation. The material that I want to explore below as a means to bring time back to space, to honor the "surplus" of signification excluded by conventional modes of analysis, and to include the conscious participation of the researcher in the process of analysis, is an approach that revolves around the photographic image. The photograph can be used as a tool in this sort of anlysis if it is taken in a self-conscious context that includes cultural inquiry and ignorance but also literacy and is then presented or interpreted in the same way to make a "photo/text."

Both Susan Sontag and Martha Rosler emphasize the violence of photography. Sontag (1973/1993) begins by saying, "To photograph is to appropriate the thing photographed. It means putting oneself in a certain relation to the world that feels like knowledge—and therefore, like power" (p. 96). Rosler (1993) relates the story of David Burnett, whose photograph of a prisoner detained in Santiago de Chile during the putsch in 1973 helped win him the Overseas Press Club's Robert Capa Award "for exceptional courage and enterprise" (p. 315). She asks, "What happened to the man (actually, men) in the photo?" and then points out that the question is "inappropriate when the subject is photographs" (p. 315). Both Sontag and Rosler also take the Farm Security Adminstration photographers to task. Sontag criticizes them for taking dozens of frontal pictures of one of their sharecropper subjects until satisfied that they had gotten just the right look on film—the precise expression on the subject's face that supported their own notions about poverty, despair, exploitation, dignity, light, texture, and space. (p. 97)

This is a particularly nasty swipe by Sontag, combining as it does elements of the human condition with the rules of formal photography. For both Sontag and Rosler, the critique is that the nature of the photographer (and by implication the essence of photography) is to take without giving. Rosler pushes this notion further than Sontag and finally produces a show on the Bowery that does not contain any photographs of living subjects, only sites they inhabit and words used to describe them and their situation. Fair enough, she has moved to take responsibility for the frame by making it explicit. But she has also reached a kind of end state in her search for a politically acceptable photography.

I think this is as far as this project can go in the direction of political sensitivity only if one defines the medium in terms of the photographer-subject relation. And although Rosler (1993) engages the issue of how photography operates politically, the possibilities she offers are limited because of these strictures on the conceptualization of what photography is. If we enlarge that, then we can enlarge what can be done politically with the medium in the way of analyzing the production of space.

Barthes (1981) points out that the field of photography is larger if one includes the reading of the photograph and the thing photographed.[14] That reading is the key to analysis as much as is the thing photographed itself. The reading need not be according to photographic conventions, either the formal ones Sontag lists or the institutional one Rosler illustrates as so wanting. As a self-declared amateur, Barthes takes liberties and allows himself to create photographic readings that raise rather than suppress questions of cultural context and processes of signification.

In addition, Barthes (1981) insists, against all expectations of him, that the photograph is of something "that has been. The referent adheres" (p. 6). There is an inescapable materiality to them that marks a time. This distinguishes photography from film, which is always moving forward. Film works by constructing a self-contained event, whereas photography is about something (else) and demands interpretation both before and after the event. Thus photography does more than invite conscious reflection, it almost requires it.

In Barthes's (1981) unprofessional, highly personal reflections on photography, he notes certain details that, given his background, training, and analytic powers, produce illuminating text about the photographs themselves, about the processes of making meaning of them, and about photography in general. In the end it is a photograph of his mother as a young girl that is the basis for his most moving and delicate insights. He declines to include a reproduction of it, pointing out that to the reader it would be just another picture of a certain type from a certain era. There is no clearer way to acknowledge and honor the role of the interpreter *indivisible* from "that which has been" than to honor these passages.

In some ways photography is fleeting; the moment, as they say, is past. But Barthes (1981) lays the groundwork for approaching photography from the opposite direction, as prolonging that which has been. His insistence on recognizing a point of view based in that materiality allows the articulation of a point of view or way of seeing that other approaches to analysis deemphasize. Photography makes the time/space to produce a reading, that is to say, meaning that can be subject to the rigors of a collective response. Photographing city space means isolating instants of meaning that have the potential to be noticed but can remain largely unformulated and unfound from other perspectives. In that way photography is like a writing; it is a writing. The term in photography for a picture taken but not yet developed into an image is *latent image*. The photograph itself can also be seen as the latent image of a composite of photo and text, the photo/text that is informative about spatial production.

Alan Trachtenberg's (1989) history of American photography, particularly his treatment of Walker Evans's *American Photographs*, presents a framework for thinking about how meaning is generated in the text/image interplay. In *American Photographs* (which appeared both in book form and as a show at the Museum of Modern Art in New York)[15] photographs were presented one after another in ways that encouraged the viewer to see how images play off of each other, as the basis for articulating themes identifying the American experience. As Trachtenberg puts it, "This book is for seeing as *reading*"

(p. 264). "The layering of points of view as well as objects, faces, signs, and all the details that designate place and time challenges the reader to participate" (p. 258).

The implications of this are that meanings are never present in their entirety. This is true even if photographs cite previous images, even if they are constructed by the photographer for a certain purpose, even if the subjects are participants. Rather than finding sources of meaning solely in the image, the author, or the voice of the subject, we have open processes of producing meaning.

> In this *American Photographs* evokes for itself not only a tradition of photography but a larger cultural enterprise, an intellectual as much as a literary and graphic tradition, which has taken America less as a place and a creed than as a process of becoming. (Trachtenberg, 1989, p. 284)

This openness repeats a central theme in spatial theory in general.

The only versions of the truth of Evans's images in *American Photographs* that exist are those that will have been completed after participation by viewers. Evans's genius lay in devising juxtapositions that lured viewers into that position of strength. Trachtenberg's (1989) insight is to make this strategy explicit. Viewers as readers become one site for the mobilization and demobilization of interpretation. Trachtenberg's commentary also suggest an extension: that this is how meaning works in general. With this in mind, we can look at several contemporary examples of image/text production and ask how they work to produce meaning. Each involves a politics.

For John Berger (Berger & Mohr, 1982) the text combined with the photograph arrests the ongoing possibilities that the visual image represents: "All photographs are ambiguous. All photographs have been taken out of continuity. . . . Yet often this ambiguity is not obvious, for as soon as photographs are used with words, they produce an effect of certainty, even of dogmatic assertion" (p. 91). This is one possibility. Yet he also describes "the photographic narrative form" as one in which the reader fills in the narrative, the spaces between the photographs, in a way that "restores a living context," a "context of experience" (pp. 287-288). He does this in a photo essay of French Peasants (with Jean Mohr) that does not include text. This is reminiscent of the form used in *American*

Photographs, but ironically, in part because of limited experience with European peasant culture, this reader found that the sequence produces a more limited range of speculation than Evans's work. More central to the matter under consideration, it is possible to find forms of montage that do use text and engage the reader/viewer/writer in creating a context of experience in undogmatic ways. Text alone (or its absence) does not ensure or bar dogmatism.

Juxtapositions of text and photographs can open up rather than close the illumination of memory (history) and dreams (possibilities). From the powerful political montages of John Heartfield in the 1930s, devised to provoke reflection on the nature of Nazi Germany (Ades, 1986; Buck-Morss, 1989), to current attempts to make a space for political/personal meaning, quite a range of possibilities exist. All are understandable in the framework that Barthes (1981) suggests, enlarging the photographer/subject relation to include the photographer/reader/image/object-that-has-been relation.

Feminists of a certain generation came into awareness in a context that included Barbara Kruger's stark announcement "Your gaze hits the side of my face."[16] Like many of her pieces, this one works by playing against conventional modes of representation. Commercially produced text and images are juxtaposed in ways that upset and challenge the pious narratives from which at least one of them was drawn.[17]

Duane Michels combines staged photographs and handwritten text in a more personal mode. As one commentator says, "He took to photography not because it documents a reality—and therefore makes something known—but because it confirms the surfaces upon which his mind operates" (Michels & Kozloff, 1990). The play between image and text is more continuous than in Barbara Kruger's work. For example, he has a series on Christ coming back to the inner city in which text and image repeat each other. "Christ eats dog food with an old Ukrainian lady in Brooklyn" shows the Christ figure at the kitchen table with an elderly Slavic woman. His work is also more personal than Kruger's. "If one day I should meet myself at a party, I wonder if I would like me" is only one example of this sustained reflection on identity and desire. The viewer is welcome, but there is also a voyeuristic quality about the invitation. Michels uses pious narratives against themselves in both his social commentary and in a subjective search in which he is both trampled by and eludes mail-order expectations of self.

In *Rich and Poor*, Jim Goldberg (1986) asked the subjects of his photographs to write their own comments to his images. In his mode of juxapositioning image and text the subjects are incorporated in the generative process. The photographer chooses, the subjects themselves dispose, and the reader is trapped into noticing the political conventions these juxtapositions reveal. "My dream was to become a shool [sic] teacher. I am used to standing behind Ms. Stone" shows a well-to-do matron in her kitchen with a servant women behind her. "My wife is acceptable. Our relationship is satisfactory" is heightened by the wife's effusive commentary on the husband and the photograph that shows an elderly man of substance sitting down with his formally dressed wife gazing at him. Goldberg leads the reader down a pious pictorial road, almost. He then allows alternative voices to frame the presentation.

None of these examples of image and text are about discovery, truth, or reality. They are about framing that makes meaning. Trachtenberg's phrase—viewing as reading—suggests an active value-laden environment that permits *and requires* varying degrees of reflection.

TWO EXAMPLES, USING PHOTO/TEXT FOR SPATIAL ANALYSIS

For Foucault (1986), contemporary spatial patterns differ from both medieval hierarchical space and capitalist extensive space of exchange. Contemporary space is characterized by what he calls *site*. Think of it also as *sight*. What we see. "Our epoch," he says, "is one in which space takes for us the form of relations among sites" (p. 23). Or our epoch is one in which space takes for us the form of relations among sights (second spelling). What *do* we see?

Last spring I started photographing cigarette billboards. Newport ads are the most common in Cleveland, and they change with the season. They always show a toothsome couple touching or wearing seasonal icons (listening to a shell in the summer, balancing apples in the fall, etc.) and having an incredibly good time. These billboards come in three sizes: small, medium, and large. The many small versions

Figure 9.3. A Small Newport Billboard

have the interesting feature of having no mention of, or images depicting, cigarettes on them (see Figure 9.3). Ironically, to the stranger to our
culture, they could be public health ads announcing the dangers of
smoking because they all carry the surgeon general's warning.

As a bow to the Great Myth of the West (Bright, 1992), I also sighted
the Marboro man riding up above the commuter corridor in a billow-
ing white coat (range wear).

The space of these billboards is empty behind the White Aryan and
Black Aryan couples who are united in representing the Disney-
erotic. The ads are decontextualized in the sense that the promise of
what cigarettes can do for you is not connected to a sophisticated,
cosmopolitan urban scene, such as those accompanying the image of
cigarettes in previous eras. Nor do they relate to the urban sites
anyone driving by them might see that day. But beyond the simple
Pleasure Pairs selling wares on the basis of desirable lifestyle choices,
these billboards are instructive about processes of assembly that are
contemporary spatial practices. The operative dynamic is escape
(from the city).

The small Newport billboards depict African American couples
and appear at eye level from the perspective of a person walking by.
The medium and large billboards depict similar white couples and
appear up above the ground: on top of buildings, if they are medium-
size and in the city (35 miles an hour going in and out of town); on
tall poles, if they are large and on the way into the city (45 miles and
hour and above on the freeway entrances—just minutes away from
where you live and play) (see Figure 9.4).

Foucault (1986) discusses both utopias and heterotopias as contemporary spatial forms. Previously heterotopias were sites of life
crises; today they are connected with deviation (from the norm and
from normal). The examples he suggests are predictable: "rest homes
and psychiatric hospitals and of course prisons and one should
perhaps add retirement homes" (p. 35).

Looking at photographs of billboards in the contexts just described
suggests that one could also add the urban terra firma. The space of
consumption is a blank no-place of utopias, whereas the heterotopic
space of deviation may be what we are driving through: and trying to
clean up the brown fields of, and reclaiming as waterfronts, and
planting incubators in. The spatial and ethnic distribution of bill-

Figure 9.4. A Medium Newport Billboard

boards says all too clearly that this spatial politics incorporates, without wanting to lose out on a good customer when it sees some, the racialization of space (Cross & Keith, 1993).

As discussed above, Cleveland's civic-minded elite are interested in developing the city as a tourist destination. In my search for an image of this policy, I was delighted and surprised to find a billboard that announced it (see Figure 9.5). It appeared to be the perfect image for the pretensions, hopes, and limitations of tourism. I took photos of the individual public and private officials who are portrayed on the billboard as symbols of the breadth of involvement in "Team Cleveland." I cleverly noticed that the image of the representative of the Ohio Department of Human Services was less clear than the others, being reproduced from a half-tone image. This seemed appropriate because it is less clear how her clients would benefit from "selling our city." But the overall image was distorted because of the angle from which the photograph had to be shot.

My cleverness turned out to be totally beside the point when I developed a second image.

Figure 9.5. The Team Cleveland Billboard

It was straight: It was also behind barbed wire. The power of what this conveys trivialized my earlier commentary. As a colleague of mine said when he saw the image, "Cleveland is a very complex place." No further comment. No actual text needed. With the first image I had merely illustrated a point I had come to previously. Now I was confronted with an enactment of the complexities of the past-industrial city trying to redefine itself in terms dictated by the postindustrial political economy. The material of the city itself ("that which was," to recall Barthes) percipitated an analysis of its spatial dilemmas.

For some time I had been climbing under, around, and through, not to mention standing on, barriers to get "good" photographs. This was using pictorial conventions to frame my vision. However, in the city itself, the space is about separation. Fences are everywhere. Meaning, distinctions that matter, and the identity through location of desirable, laudable, liveable space versus undesirable, reprehensible, and unlivable space are produced and reproduced physically and made unavoidable to all but the conventionally blind. As Berger (1972) would say, "that which has been" becomes the basis for "another way of seeing."

Again, this perspective has relevance to understanding the politics of spatial processes. Last spring the rumor circulated in Cleveland that a 15-year-old who had killed himself purchased the suicide weapon in the rest room of an upscale downtown shopping mall. The rumor included the information that although this story was carried in initial news reports, the "owners" later suppressed the story. Whether or not the rumor is true, the initial report and the subsequent story of its deletion are believable, because of the acceptance and presumption of separation as a basic principle of assembly of urban space.

Another sequence of events, less believable, would be organized around a different kind of response. For example, imagine a statement by the owners and managers of the center expressing their sorrow and offering condolences and support to the family. One could also think in terms of a memorial service, a commemorative plaque, or a scholarship to Cleveland State University in the boy's name. These would be indicators of a public commitment to community; an identity with the whole city; and a politics of community in the form of standing with right-minded citizens in condemning the death. If prevention in the future meant surveillance equipment in the rest room, certainly the technology exists—in fact, it is is already in place in some malls—and the management may have been planning something like that already. This commitment to community would be a notable violation of the rules of separation that operate as unexamined principles of urban assembly.

The literature critiquing malls as limited places misses the active component of malls as places of cultural production not only of reduced public space, but of a surplus population defined by their inability to keep moving and keep buying. This is codified in rules of behavior that have moved from discreet locations to central postings in many malls.[18] The death of the young boy in a way that implicates spatial practices of the city highlights dynamics already operating. The separations that define urban space are inseparably social and physical. This implies that the urban identities are as much a part of spatial practices as the material forms through which they circulate.

There is nothing inherent in photography or the interpretation of images in general that allows the researcher to see beyond conventional representation of space. But it does offer certain advantages, linked, I think, to its marginal status as an analytic tool. As modes of analysis are forged that use forms different from the logic of discovery, "making an analysis" replaces "gathering the facts." In this context, the photo as a prelude to the photo/text can contribute to analysis by arresting time, grounding conceptualization in the material reality of space, and involving the interpreter in a reflective way in the assembly of sense. The two brief examples presented above are meant to introduce the form and to give a sense of what is possible in a more extensive visually oriented format. They also suggest that it is possible to develop approaches to spatial analysis that go beyond the limitations of conventional representations of space. One way to present the aspects of spatial practices and representational space that Lefebvre and his followers see as central to collective existence and yet elude such representations of space is to go out into the city adopting a perspective Wittgenstein (1958) suggested for addressing philosophers: "I don't know my way about" (p. 49).

To this end the photographer who moves me the most is Atget, "documenting," as he called it. He developed an active relationship with the city, generating meaning, and by extension producing an extended family of intelligent readers.

NOTES

1. For a summary of the history and prejudices of the use of photography and film in sociology and anthropology see Denzin (1989). From within the sociological perspective, even so-called "qualitative" research, photography and film are justified as scientific tools of inquiry, hence the preoccupation with such questions as objectivity, verifiability, and so on. This is not to say that the history of sociology and photography aren't linked in interesting ways. Denzin (p. 212) points out that early issues of the *American Journal of Sociology* often contained photographs along with calls for social reform.

2. One of the ambiguities in Lefebvre's work is the way in which he appears to conflate historical analysis with the presentation of an analytic model of the production of space. This discussion is beyond the scope of this chapter, but it has bearing on issues discussed here, because it helps explain why Lefebvre comes to idealize the Middle Ages, as have other theorists, the most famous American example being Lewis Mumford.

3. See, for example, Michael Sorokin's (1992) introduction to his edited collection, *Variations on a Theme Park*, as well as the component essays. Rob Shields (1991,

especially "Introduction") has a related notion of imaginary geography tying it to liminality and the carnivalesque. A Lacanian notion of imaginary as applied by semiologists such as Barthes and Ladrut has also influenced my usage here.

4. See Saskia Sassen (1991) for in-depth empirical analysis of this phenomenon.

5. In histories of photography that focus on America, the sequence is conventionally: vague beginnings tied to portraiture; Matthew Brady and the Civil War; O'Sullivan, Watkins, and the survey of the American West. The next stage is identified with Stieglitz and the establishment of photography as legitimate (modern, formal) art. See Alan Trachtenberg (1989), "Naming the View" (pp. 119-163) for an analysis of four government surveys beginning in 1867. Richard Bolton (1992) politicizes the conventional history. Deborah Bright (1992) discusses the politics of landscape photography in the context of this conventional history.

6. The Rephotographic Survey Project completed in 1977-1979 located many exact sites in the original survey photographs and rephotographed them to produce a series that remained firmly in the document/art genre of photography. That is to say, the representations of space presented by the photographs piously reconstructed the original survey and the most conventional aspects of photography as art. The technical details of the project and reproductions of the photographs appear in Klett, Manchester, Vergurg, Bushow, and Dingus (1984).

7. And gender, but less by gender than a simplistic view that identifies women with the domestic sphere suggests. Working class women worked. The option of staying home was closed to them.

8. See Raphaël Fischler's essay (Chapter 2 in this volume) for an in-depth analysis of the rhetorical force of both visual and textual aspects of an urban plan.

9. This is one of the few areas of cultural politics in which there is agreement from a wide range of political perspectives. See, for example, Griswold (1986), MacCannell (1992), and Sturken (1991).

10. The mall literature is too prodigious to summarize here. Margaret Crawford (1992) discusses the representational aspects of malls. Mark Gottdiener (1986) is very good on their interior spatial layout. For a view of the political implications of mall space see Dennis Judd's essay (Chapter 6 in this volume).

11. See Brian Holcomb (1993) for analysis of campaigns marketing Cleveland and Pittsburgh in the 1980s.

12. Cleveland Tomorrow is an organization of 50 CEOs from the region's largest companies. A majority of them are headquartered outside the immediate Cleveland metropolitan area.

13. The notion that "something is missing" and that contemporary spatial processes are lacking or unfulfilling is a common theme among spatial theorists. De Certeau (1984) writes in this tradition when he takes his famous look down from the World Trade Center ("Walking in the City," pp. 91-110) The view from the top, as de Certeau describes it, recalls an architectural model, devoid of life of the city. In contrast, he privileges "ways of operating" on the street level: a category that collapses and contains both spatial practices and representational spaces. Foucault's (1986) heterotopias are the sites of "crises of deviation" in the society, in other words those sites that escape normalization. Shields (1991) writes about the cultural play of the profane and subliminal.

14. See also his earlier essay on press photography (Barthes, 1977), which uses a more strictly semiotic frame to analyze the mechanisms by which photographs connote.

15. *American Photographs* is reproduced in its entirety in Mora and Hill (1993).

16. See *Love for Sale: The Words and Pictures of Barbara Kruger* (Kruger & Linker, 1990). The text by Kate Linker puts Kruger's work in the context of poststructuralism, particularly Michel Foucault's notions of surveillance and normalization.

17. Kenneth Burke (quoted in Shapiro, 1988) calls "pious" texts that reproduce and legitimate particular "forms of meaning and value while appearing to merely represent 'the real'" (p. 136).

18. Malls' rules have evolved from generic admonitions to wear proper clothes and not talk politics to lists of specific forbidden behaviors almost exclusively oriented towards youth. In the year I have been photographing mall rules in downtown and surburban Cleveland the presentation of these rules has been changing from out-of-the way notices to prominately posted signs.

REFERENCES

Ades, D. (1986). *Photomontage*. London: Thames & Hudson.

Agrest, D. (1991). *Architecture from without*. Cambridge: MIT Press.

Barthes, R. (1972). Myth today. In *Mythologies* (pp. 109-159). New York: Hill & Wang.

Barthes, R. (1977). The photographic message. *Image, music, text* (pp. 15-31). New York: Hill & Wang.

Barthes, R. (1981). *Camera lucida: Reflections on photography*. New York: Hill & Wang.

Barthes, R. (1986). Semiology and the urban. In M. Gottdiener & A. Ph. Lagopoulos (Eds.), *The city and the sign* (pp. 87-98). New York: Columbia University Press.

Berger, J. (1972). *Ways of seeing*. Harmondsworth, UK: Penguin.

Berger, J., & Mohr, J. (1982). *Another way of telling*. New York: Pantheon.

Bolton, R. (1992). Introduction: The contest of meaning: Critical histories of photography. In R. Bolton (Ed.), *The context of meaning: Critical histories of photography* (pp. ix-xix). Cambridge: MIT Press.

Bourdieu, P. (1984). *Distinction*. Cambridge, MA: Harvard University Press.

Bright, D. (1992). Of Mother Nature and Marlboro men: An inquiry into the cultural meanigs of landscape photography. In R. Bolton (Ed.), *The context of meaning: Critical histories of photography* (pp. 125-144). Cambridge: MIT Press.

Buck-Morss, S. (1989). Natural history: Fossel. In *The dialectics of seeing: Walter Benjamin and the Arcades Project* (pp. 58-77). Cambridge: MIT Press.

Choay, F. (1986). Urbanism and semiology. In M. Gottdiener & A. Ph. Lagopoulos (Eds.), *The city and the sign* (pp. 160-175). New York: Columbia University Press.

Cleveland civic vision. (Vols. 1-2). (1991). Cleveland: Cleveland City Planning Commission.

Crawford, M. (1992). The world in a shopping mall. In M. Sorokin (Ed.), *Variations on a theme park* (pp. 3-20). New York: Noonday Press.

Cross, M., & Keith, M. (Eds.) (1993). *Racism, the city and the state*. London: Routledge.

de Certeau, M. (1984). *The practice of everyday life*. Berkeley: University of California Press.

Denzin, N. (1989). Film, photography, and sociology. In *The research act: A theoretical introduction to sociological methods* (pp. 210-233). Englewood Cliffs, NJ: Prentice Hall.

Foucault, M. (1986). Texts/contexts: Of other spaces. *Diacritics, 16*, 22-27.

Goldberg, J. (1986). *Rich and poor.* New York: Random House.

Gottdiener, M. (1986). Recapturing the center: A semiotic analysis of shopping malls. In M. Gottdiener & A. Ph. Lagopolulos (Eds.) *The city and the sign* (pp. 288-302). New York: Columbia University Press.

Griswold, C. L. (1986). Vietnam Veterans Memorial and the Washington Wall: Philosophical thoughts on political iconography. *Critical Inquiry, 12,* 688-719.

Holcomb, B. (1993). Revisioning place: De- and re-constructing the image of the industrial city. In G. Kearns & C. Philo (Eds.), *Selling places: The city as cultural capital past and present* (pp. 133-145). Oxford, UK: Pergamon.

Investing in the future: Cleveland Tomorrow's strategic picture for the '90's. (1993).Cleveland: Cleveland Tomorrow.

Klett M., Manchester E., Verburg J., Bushow, G., & Dingus, R. (1984). *Second view: The rephotographic survey project.* Albuquerque: University of New Mexico Press.

Kruger, B., & Linker K. (1990). *Love for sale: The words and pictures of Barbara Kruger.* New York: Harry N. Abrams.

Ladrut, R. (1986). Speech and the silence of the city. In M. Gottdiener & A. Ph. Lagopolulos (Eds.) *The city and the sign* (pp. 114-134). New York: Columbia University Press.

Lefebvre, H. (1991). *The production of space.* London: Basil Blackwell.

MacCannell, D. (1992). The Vietnam Memorial in Washington D.C. In D. MacCannell, *Empty meeting grounds: The tourist papers* (pp. 280-283). London: Routledge.

Marcus, S. (1973). Reading the illegible. In H. J. Dyos & M. Wolff (Eds.) *The Victorian city: Images and realities* (Vol. 1, pp. 257-276). London: Routledge & Kegan Paul.

Michels, D., & Kozloff, M. (1990). *Now becoming then.* Altadena, CA: Twin Palms.

Mora, G., & Hill, J. T. (1993). *Walker Evans: The hungry eye.* New York: Harry N. Abrams.

Rosler, M. (1993). In, around, and afterthoughts (on documentary photography). In R. Bolton (Ed.), *The contest of meaning: Critical histories of photography* (pp. 287-302). Cambridge: MIT Press.

Sassen, S. (1991). *The global city: New York, London, Tokyo.* Princeton, NJ: Princeton University Press.

Shapiro, M. (1988). The political rhetoric of photography. In M. Shapiro, *The politics of representation* (pp. 124-178). Madison: University of Wisconsin Press.

Shields, R. (1991). *Places on the margin.* London: Routledge.

Sontag, S. (1993). On photography. In *Anthology: Selected essays from thirty years of the New York Review of Books.* New York: Rea S. Kederman. (Original work published 1973)

Sorokin, M. (1992). *Variations on a theme park.* New York: Noonday Press.

Sturken, M. (1991). The wall, the screen, and the image: The Vietnam Veterans Memorial. *Representations, 35,* 118-142.

Trachtenberg, A. (1989). *Reading American photographs.* New York: Noonday Press.

Turnbull, P. (1993). *Let's remember Pearl Harbor: The semiology of the Arizona Memorial.* Paper presented at the Annual Convention of the International Studies Association, Acapulco, Mexico.

Whyte, W. H. (1988). *City: Rediscovering the center.* New York: Doubleday.

Wittgenstein, L. (1958). *Philosophical investigations.* New York: Macmillan.

Index

About the Authors

Robert A. Beauregard is a Professor in the Graduate School of Public and International Affairs at the University of Pittsburgh. He is the author of *Voices of Decline: The Postwar Fate of U.S. Cities* (1993), a study of the representational dynamics of urban decline.

M. Christine Boyer is Professor of Urbanism at the School of Architecture, Princeton University. She is the author of *The City of Collective Memory* (1994) and *Manhattan Manners: Architecture and Style 1850-1890* (1985). In addition, she has written many articles and lectured widely on the topic of urbanism in the 20th century, the gap between architecture and city planning, and the future of the physical form of American cities. She is currently writing a series of essays titled *CyberCities: Urban Form in the 21st Century* and researching a book titled *The City Plans of Modernism*.

Stuart Alan Clarke is the Director of the Atlanta Outward Bound® Center in Atlanta. He has taught political science and American studies at Yale University, Wesleyan University, and Williams College. He writes about culture and the politics of racial representations.

Raphaël Fischler is Assistant Professor in the School of Urban Planning at McGill University in Montreal, Canada, where he teaches physical planning and urban design. His other interests are in the fields of planning history, theory, and education. He recently spent a year in Israel studying Israeli planning practice.

Dennis R. Judd is Professor of Political Science in the Department of Political Science, University of Missouri, St. Louis. He has published numerous articles and chapters on urban politics, urban economic development, national urban policy, and comparative urban politics. Among his 10 books are three recent titles: *City Politics: Public Policy and Private Power* (with Todd Swanstron), *The Democratic Facade* (with Dan Hellinger), and *The Development of American Public Policy* (with David B. Robertson). He currently is conducting research on urban tourism and on the environmental impacts of urban development.

Helen Liggett is an Associate Professor on the Faculty of the Levin College of Urban Affairs at Cleveland State University. She writes at the intersections of cultural theory and public issues. Recent works appear in *Planning Theory* and *Urban Affairs Quarterly*.

David C. Perry is Professor of Planning at the School of Planning and Architecture at State University of New York at Buffalo. His research and teaching interests include urban political economy, planning theory, and policies of infrastructure, economic development, and community change. His books include *Rise of the Sunbelt Cities* and the soon-to-be-published *Building the Public City: The Politics, Governance and Finance of Public Infrastructure* and *The Cleveland Metropolitan Reader*.

Richard A. Walker is Professor and Chair of Geography at the University of California, Berkeley. He received his Doctorate from The Johns Hopkins University, under the direction of David Harvey, in 1977. He has written on a diverse range of topics including urban history, environmental policy, philosophy, industrial location, and

California studies. He is co-author, with Michael Storper, of *The Capitalist Imperative: Territory, Technology and Industrial Growth* (1989) and, with Andrew Sayer, of *The New Social Economy: Reworking the Division of Labor* (1992). He is a longtime activist in public affairs with such groups as the Coalition to Stop the Peripheral Canal and the Faculty for Human Rights in El Salvador and Central America.

Lightning Source UK Ltd.
Milton Keynes UK
UKHW041905260319
339946UK00001B/55/P